'Gifts in wills have the potential to change th
supporters and the wider public in legacy cor
more crucial or more exciting. This book is a
fundraisers shape their legacy strategy, influe
the variety of ways in which they can raise awareness and inspire people
to include a gift in their will.'
Dominique Abranson Dip IDM, Legacy and In-Memory Manager, WaterAid, and
Chair of the Institute of Fundraising Legacy Marketing and In Memoriam Special
Interest Group

'This little gem of a book is a very easy read that will answer all your
questions and help you to build your legacy programme from start to
finish. You'll find yourself referring to it again and again, no matter what
level you are working at.'
Emma Deabill, Alumni Relations and Development Co-ordinator,
University of Portsmouth

'It's great to see an updated edition of this fantastic book, which offers
valuable insights from a number of different experts in the field. Irrespective
of the size of your organisation or the extent of your experience, you'll find
really practical takeaways that will enhance your fundraising practice.'
Craig Fordham, Director of Legacies, Macmillan Cancer Support

'I read *Legacy and In-Memory Fundraising* cover to cover: the fact that
the chapters are written by different contributors made it an interesting
read. An excellent overview into getting started and where legacies fit into
a charity's fundraising strategy – I would really recommend this book.'
Judith Howard, Trusts, Foundations and Legacies Co-ordinator,
Royal Ballet School

'Legacy income presents a huge opportunity for charities of all sizes, but
the challenge for everyone is knowing how to make the most of that
opportunity. Look no further. This excellent resource provides everything
you need to know about legacy fundraising in one slim volume. With
contributions from the legacy world's premier league, this book will
benefit your legacy programme whether it is already well established or
just beginning.'
Stuart Noble, Acting Director of Fundraising, Bible Society

'Producing innovative legacy campaigns and motivating your fundraising
team with new ideas are important for legacy managers. *Legacy and In-
Memory Fundraising* will help you do this by giving your team the
confidence to nurture donor relationships, ultimately resulting in lasting
legacies. From absolute beginners to more experienced legacy fundraisers,
this is a must-have for any charity aiming to meet its legacy income targets.'
Ian Roome MInstF, Head of Fundraising and Volunteering, Over and Above NHS
Charity, Northern Devon Healthcare NHS Trust

Fourth edition

Legacy and In-Memory Fundraising

Edited by

Claire Routley and Sebastian Wilberforce

dsc
directory of social change

In association with:

SUSTAINABLE
PHILANTHROPY
WITH
PLYMOUTH
UNIVERSITY

Institute of
Fundraising

Published by the Directory of Social Change (Registered Charity no. 800517 in England and Wales)

Head office: Resource for London, 352 Holloway Rd, London N7 6PA

Northern office: Suite 103, 1 Old Hall Street, Liverpool L3 9HG

Tel: 020 7697 4200

Visit www.dsc.org.uk to find out more about our books, subscription funding websites and training events. You can also sign up for e-newsletters so that you're always the first to hear about what's new.

The publisher welcomes suggestions and comments that will help to inform and improve future versions of this and all of our titles. Please give us your feedback by emailing publications@dsc.org.uk.

It should be understood that this publication is intended for guidance only and is not a substitute for professional advice. No responsibility for loss occasioned as a result of any person acting or refraining from acting can be accepted by the authors or publisher.

First edition published 1998 by the Charities Aid Foundation
Second edition 2001
Third edition 2010
Reprinted 2014
Fourth edition in both print and digital formats published 2018

ISBN 978 1 78482 030 5 (print edition)
ISBN 978 1 78482 031 2 (digital edition)

British Library Cataloguing in Publication Data
A catalogue record for this book is available from the British Library

Cover and text design by Kate Griffith
Typeset by Marlinzo Services, Frome
Print edition printed and bound in Great Britain by CPI Group, Croydon

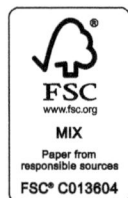

FSC
www.fsc.org
MIX
Paper from
responsible sources
FSC® C013604

This book is dedicated to
Phillippa Wilberforce
1961–2018

Her kindness, passion and genuine interest
in individuals would have made her a
good fundraiser, as those qualities made
her a hugely loved wife.

Contents

About the Fundraising Series

Despite paid fundraisers having existed in some form since the middle ages, fundraising as we know it today is still an emerging profession. The Institute of Fundraising has only been in existence for just over 30 years, and it is only relatively recently that academics have begun to pay attention to the science behind giving to others.

A vitally important element of any profession is its body of knowledge – this is what enables members of a profession to grow, learn and reflect. Immersing oneself in that knowledge is, arguably, what makes one a professional fundraiser.

This series is an important part of bringing together fundraising's body of knowledge. It combines the best of the practical knowledge of experienced fundraisers with, increasingly, the expanding body of academic knowledge around giving and asking.

The series seeks to address the full range of fundraising activity and techniques. Each volume addresses a key element in the spectrum of fundraising techniques. As fundraising techniques evolve and develop, new titles in the series are added and old ones revised. Each title seeks to explore a fundraising activity within its historical, ethical and theoretical context, and relate it to current fundraising practice as well as guide future strategy. The series offers something for anyone who is aspiring to be a professional, whatever the size or type of their organisation or the stage of their career.

The University of Plymouth Hartsook Centre for Sustainable Philanthropy is proud to partner with the Directory of Social Change in the series' production. Furthermore, the series would not be possible without the input of many dedicated professionals involved in its writing and production; we thank everyone who has contributed to its development.

Adrian Sargeant PhD, Professor of Fundraising and Director
Claire Routley PhD, Research Fellow
University of Plymouth Hartsook Centre for Sustainable Philanthropy

About the Directory of Social Change

The Directory of Social Change (DSC) has a vision of an independent voluntary sector at the heart of social change. We believe that the activities of independent charities, voluntary organisations and community groups are fundamental to achieve social change. We exist to support these organisations in achieving their goals.

We do this by:

• providing practical tools that organisations and activists need, including online and printed publications, training courses, and conferences on a huge range of topics;

• acting as a 'concerned citizen' in public policy debates, often on behalf of smaller charities, voluntary organisations and community groups;

• leading campaigns and stimulating debate on key policy issues that affect those groups;

• carrying out research and providing information to influence policy-makers, as well as offering bespoke research for the voluntary sector.

DSC is the leading provider of information and training for the voluntary sector and publishes an extensive range of guides and handbooks covering subjects such as fundraising, management, communication, finance and law. Our subscription-based websites contain a wealth of information on funding from grant-making charities, companies and government sources. We run more than 300 training courses each year, including bespoke in-house training provided at the client's location. DSC conferences and fairs, which take place throughout the year, also provide training on a wide range of topics and offer welcome opportunities for networking.

For details of all our activities, and to order publications and book courses, go to www.dsc.org.uk, call 020 7697 4200 or email cs@dsc.org.uk.

About the authors

Meg Abdy

Meg has been analysing the legacy market since 1994, when she co-ordinated the first ever legacy forecasting project, now known as Legacy Monitor. Legacy Monitor is the leading legacy benchmarking programme in the UK and has expanded internationally to include a programme in the Netherlands.

As a co-founder of Legacy Foresight, Meg has been involved in every aspect of the business from its inception – from forecasting to focus groups and from scenario-building to social media.

Today Meg is the Managing Director at Legacy Foresight, responsible for programme management and business development, with particular interests surrounding in-memory giving, international markets and donor research.

Sarah Bolt

Sarah is an associate in the Dispute Resolution Team at Stone King LLP specialising in acting for charities and individuals in legacy related disputes. Sarah has particular experience in dealing with probate and trust disputes.

She also works with charities to protect and defend their interests across a wide variety of disputes, such as governance issues, trustee and membership dispute and contract disputes.

Dan Carter

Dan is Global Legacy Director at the International Fund for Animal Welfare and was Head of Legacies from 2011 to 2016 at Marie Curie. He has worked in fundraising and marketing for thirteen years with the past nine focusing on legacies.

Dan has strong passion and experience in developing marketing strategies for legacies across organisations focusing on inspiration to motivate people to leave the greatest gift of all.

Jonathan Cook

With more than 17 years' experience in the charity and not-for-profit sector, Jonathan is an expert in organisational, fundraising and marketing strategy. He has worked with the likes of the Royal Horticultural Society, Diabetes UK, Voluntary Service Overseas, Parkinson's UK and Save the Children.

In 2012 he founded the fundraising agency Insight-ful, which combines insight, analysis and creativity to enable charities to develop innovative, inspirational and financially successful fundraising products.

Daniel Fluskey

Daniel is Head of Policy and Research at the Institute of Fundraising and leads its policy development and research work, which involves keeping up to date with member priorities, promoting innovation in fundraising and working with key stakeholders (including civil servants and politicians) to make sure fundraising and giving are key priorities for the current and future governments.

Daniel (Dan) Harris

Daniel is a partner and Head of International and Cross-Border with Stone King LLP. He advises UK and overseas private clients as well as charities and other solicitors on succession and taxation issues in all jurisdictions of the world. As a member of the charity legacy team he acts for some of the UK's largest charities, providing advice on complex cross-border legacies, as well as providing training on cross border charity legacy administration and marketing.

He is a full member of the Society of Trusts and Estates Practitioners (STEP) and the Franco British Lawyers Society and a member of the Law Society of England and Wales Cross Border Special Interest group.

Stephen George

Stephen is the founder of Good Leaders, a fundraising and leadership coaching consultancy that specialises in helping charity leaders be better leaders and raise more money. He has over 30 years' fundraising experience at all levels in the UK and internationally, with organisations such as NSPCC, UNICEF, RNIB, Action on Hearing Loss, Maggie's Centres and Scope. Stephen is also an international speaker, writer and podcaster. He has worked on global legacies strategies for international NGOs, was Development Director for Legacies at the NSPCC and was Chair of Remember a Charity, a UK consortium that promotes gifts in wills.

Eifron Hopper

Eifron is Legacy Income Manager for the RNLI. He has worked in the voluntary sector since 1993, prior to which he practised as a solicitor. He has worked for a number of charities including The Children's Society, Trinity Hospice, RNIB and Lighthouse in Poole. As a legacy and community fundraising specialist, he was involved with setting up Remember a Charity and has sat on many fundraising boards and taskforces over the years. He writes and speaks regularly on legacy matters.

Russell James

Russell has been Professor and Chair of Personal Financial Planning with the CH Foundation at Texas Tech University since 2013, and before that he was Assistant Professor at the University of Georgia. During his career he has headed up a fundraising department as Director of Planned Giving and has practised law specialising in estate and gift planning, and charity law.

He lectures in charitable planning and behavioural economics and his research interests are in charitable giving, charitable estate planning, and behavioural and neuro-economics. He is published regularly in the American academic press.

Kate Jenkinson

Kate is Head of In-Memory Consultancy at Legacy Foresight. She spent over ten years working in charities as a direct marketing, legacy and in-memory fundraising manager before joining the not-for-profit agency Whitewater in 2007 as Strategic Planner. There, she worked on legacy strategy for the NSPCC, RNLI and RSPCA among others, immersing herself in primary research. She was also a key member of the Our Lasting Tribute team. Kate has been instrumental in helping to shape the work of In-Memory Insight, the trail-blazing, cross-sector consortium on in-memory giving.

Nigel Magson

Nigel has 30 years' experience in the data services industry, developing innovative approaches to systems, data management and insight thinking. His work in the not-for-profit sector led him to co-found the Insight Special Interest Group in 2006, which champions and develops insight skills and application in the sector.

In 2014, Nigel was recognised through the Outstanding Contribution Award (awarded at the Institute of Fundraising's Insight in Fundraising

Awards) for his role in developing the Insight Special Interest Group and raising the professional use of insight and analytics in the sector. He has authored many papers on analysis topics, including several on loan to value, the use of data in legacy fundraising, and segmentation approaches. He has also spoken in many sector conferences. In 2012 Nigel co-founded Adroit Data & Insight, which works worldwide with many not-for-profits to benchmark and analyse data. Adroit is at the forefront of developing analytics solutions (including artificial intelligence) for organisations and increasing their fundraising income.

Chris Millward

Chris has over ten years' experience in managing charity legacy fundraising and administration. He has worked for both Macmillan Cancer Support and Save the Children. He was chair of Will Aid for three years and a member of the Institute of Fundraising's Special Interest Group for Legacies and In-Memory Committee, as well as Remember a Charity's Campaign Council. Chris is CEO at the Institute of Legacy Management, the professional body for charity legacy administrators in the UK.

Stephen Pidgeon

As a platform speaker, teacher and consultant, Stephen speaks and teaches throughout the world. Twenty years after setting up and running the UK's largest fundraising agency, Brightsource/Tangible, he now works with charities in the UK, Ireland, Norway, Canada and the USA. He has a special interest in stewardship and legacy marketing, as well as an interest (from a critical point of view) in looking at the way charities mistreat their supporters.

He is a visiting professor at the University of Plymouth Hartsook Centre for Sustainable Philanthropy, a trustee of the development agency Voluntary Service Overseas (VSO) and Chair of VSO Ireland. Stephen writes regularly and critically in the sector press and was given the Institute of Fundraising's Lifetime Contribution Award in 2015. His first book, *How to Love Your Donors... to Death*, was published in the same year.

Richard Radcliffe

For the past 30 years, Richard has specialised in legacies in positions such as Executive Chair of Smee & Ford, where he started the UK's first dedicated legacy consultancy. He sold Smee & Ford ten years ago and has since run his own consultancy.

Richard has met around 28,000 supporters and service users for over 500 charities to gain their perceptions of the charities they support. He has researched will-making and legacy-giving traditions in over 30 countries, helping to develop strategies for large and small charities in the UK and internationally. He has been Chair of the International Fundraising Congress and Institute of Fundraising Convention for four years. He has conducted extensive research on donor happiness and how older generations make decisions about financial issues.

Fiona Riley

Fiona is Head of Legacy Marketing at the British Heart Foundation and has worked in fundraising for over 12 years. She has worked for charities ranging from national causes, including Scope and Marie Curie, to international organisations such as Save the Children (in the UK) and Animals Asia (in Hong Kong). Fiona has spoken on legacies at practitioner conferences. During her career, she has also been the chair of Will Aid and served on committees for Remember a Charity's Campaign Council and for the Institute of Fundraising's Legacy and In-Memory Giving Special Interest Group.

Claire Routley

Claire has worked in fundraising for 15 years, specialising in legacy fundraising for over a decade. In 2011, she completed a PhD looking into why people choose to leave legacies to charity. Having worked for a number of different charities, she is now a consultant specialising in legacy and in-memory fundraising, a research fellow at the University of Plymouth Hartsook Centre for Sustainable Philanthropy and a tutor for the Institute of Fundraising's qualification courses.

Ashley Rowthorn

Ashley Rowthorn is Managing Director of the Legacy Group, which includes Legacy Link (a legacy administration consultancy) and Legacy Voice (a legacy marketing agency). He is a highly knowledgeable legacy fundraising specialist with over ten years' experience in the sector. He has led the Legacy Marketing teams at Alzheimer's Society and Royal Voluntary Service, and is a regular speaker at Institute of Fundraising conferences and events. Ashley is a current member of the Remember a Charity Campaign Council.

Rod Smith

Rod joined Stone King LLP in January 2013 as a partner in the Trusts and Estates team in London. He specialises in advising on, and drafting, complex wills and trusts, powers of attorney, applications for deputyship and the administration of trusts and estates.

Rod is a member of the Society of Trust and Estate Practitioners (STEP) and sits on the Law Society's Wills and Equity Committee and the Law Society's Money Laundering Task Force.

Paul Sutton

Paul is a partner and Head of the Dispute Resolution Team at Stone King LLP. He undertakes a broad range of work including breach of trust and general commercial and contractual disputes and has particular expertise in charity-related claims. Paul also has extensive experience of contentious probate and legacy dispute cases including Inheritance and acts on behalf of both private clients and charities in connection with such claims.

He is a member of the Association of Contentious Trust and Probate Specialists and of the Professional Negligence Lawyer's Association.

Sebastian Wilberforce

Sebastian is a process analyst working as a consultant in the not-for-profit sector in New Zealand. With the aim of helping to improve outputs, he works across governance and management systems, including fundraising. Sebastian has been an editor of this book since its first edition 20 years ago. At that time he was a legacy fundraiser for one of Britain's biggest charities, RNIB, having previously worked as a solicitor specialising in trust and charity law. Since then he has been a legacy fundraising consultant to many not-for-profit organisations in New Zealand and also brings experience from the commercial sector, having co-owned a multi-channel, consumer-focused business for eight years.

Justine Williams

Justine is a fundraising and marketing consultant and is undertaking a long-term contract as Director of Fundraising and Communications at Katharine House Hospice, Oxfordshire. Justine has held similar interim leadership positions at Practical Action, Riders for Health and the People's Dispensary for Sick Animals. Before moving into consultancy, she was Director of Income Generation at Garden Organic and spent 20 years working in other senior fundraising roles. Justine has also been Chair of the Institute of Fundraising's working group for the code of practice on legacy fundraising and has previously been a chair of Will Aid.

Katy Williamson

Having started a career in finance after graduating from the University of St Andrews, Katy quickly realised an altruistic life was much more appealing. In 2006 she began working in fundraising for the MS Society Scotland, where her knowledge grew thanks to a hugely supportive team. She went on to present a session on stewardship at the Institute of Fundraising conference before moving on to specialise in legacy fundraising at the British Red Cross in 2010. After six years there, Katy began to work in legacy fundraising with Cancer Research UK. After losing her father to cancer and seeing her mother saved by Cancer Research UK's research, this is something of a personal crusade.

Acknowledgements

We, the editors and publisher, would like to thank all the charities, companies and individuals who have given their time and experience to this book.

We are grateful to the following people and organisations in particular for their permission to use case studies featuring their organisation and/or to reproduce their material(s) to enrich the value of this book to readers:

- Chapter 5: WaterAid

- Chapter 9: Smee & Ford

- Chapter 12: Ros Fry, Regional Legacy Manager, South West, at Cancer Research UK

- Chapter 13: Tenovus Cancer Care and the NSPCC

- Chapter 14: Marie Curie and Louise Pavoni, Digital Communications Manager, Remember a Charity

The authors noted would like to thank the following people and organisations:

- Meg Abdy: Legacy Monitor clients for continuing to share key insights with the sector

- Stephen George: Allan Freeman at Freestyle Marketing

- Eifron Hopper: Colleagues at Clear (www.clear-software.co.uk) for their assistance in putting together his chapter

- Kate Jenkinson: The NSPCC

- Nigel Magson: Age UK, The Children's Society, Capacity Marketing and Adroit Data & Insight

- Stephen Pidgeon: Cancer Research UK

- Fiona Riley: Remember a Charity

- Katy Williamson: The British Red Cross and Cancer Research UK

Sebastian Wilberforce's wife, Phillippa, died of breast cancer during the production of this book. He would like to thank his co-editor, Claire Routley, and the team at DSC for their understanding and support while he cared for Phillippa and was unable to focus on this project.

Foreword

The UK is a generous nation, but there is still so much opportunity: 35% of people surveyed in the UK say they would be happy to leave a gift in their will, compared with the 6.3% who currently do it.[1]

The reality is that legacies aren't really about death at all, but an opportunity to shape the world beyond our lifetime. This is a hugely powerful, inspirational concept and one that forms the basis of the best legacy fundraising campaigns.

We have now begun to really understand the science behind *why* people give, thanks to leading academics such as Dr Claire Routley and Professor Russell James. Their insights in chapter 2 are a perfect introduction to this book.

But great legacy and in-memory fundraising is also about great leadership: about championing legacies at the very top of every organisation – which Stephen George (chapter 5) and Richard Radcliffe (chapter 10) advocate for superbly. And this is where this new edition of *Legacy and In-Memory Fundraising* comes into its own, successfully blending the rigour of research with the pragmatism of experience through the various perspectives of its contributors.

This book reads like a 'who's who' of some of the greatest legacy and in-memory fundraisers over the past decade. From crafting your case for support to creating conversations and from legacy forecasting to legal pitfalls – this book has it all.

I am also delighted to see that chapters on two new subjects have been added to this fourth edition, reflecting a changing market and an increasing confidence in encouraging legacy giving. Dan Carter (chapter 14) gives his tips on digital media, which has become an increasingly important channel (unheard of just a few years ago) for creating conversation, and Kate Jenkinson (chapter 16) gives her reflections on in-memory-motivated giving and fundraising, which is becoming increasingly important to many good causes.

But, beyond this practical advice for all fundraisers, this book offers something else – the chance to connect donors with the causes that they really care about. Ultimately, this means that the voluntary sector must not shy away from such conversations but instead shine a light on the

---

[1] *Legacy Trends: Discovering potential thorough data* [PDF], Smee & Ford, 2017, https://smeeandford.com/whitepaper, p. 2, accessed 30 December 2017. While legacy conversations need to be handled sensitively, we certainly shouldn't be afraid of them. Nor should we allow our fears to limit supporters' opportunities to choose to give through their will.

impact of legacy and in-memory income. My congratulations to all of the contributors in this book and to all those who successfully apply these insights to help charities' work live on.

Rob Cope, Director, Remember a Charity, and Director of Development, Institute of Fundraising

CHAPTER ONE
Legacy giving in context

Meg Abdy

Introduction

Legacy Foresight, of which I am a director, has been analysing the UK legacy sector for over two decades, and the topic never ceases to fascinate and often move my colleagues and me. On the one hand, legacy incomes represent the accumulated decisions of thousands of individuals about the world they want to leave behind them. On the other, they reflect some of the greatest economic, political and social themes of our age. Understanding what drives legacy giving overall can help you to stimulate, manage and plan your own legacy fundraising.

Gifts in wills are a very important source of income for UK charities. In 2016, UK legacy giving was worth a total of £2.8 billion.[1] According to NCVO (National Council for Voluntary Organisations), legacies represent 14% of the fundraised income received by UK charities and 5% of all incoming resources.[2] For larger organisations it's more important still: across the 1,000 largest charities ranked by legacy income, gifts in wills account for 27% of fundraised income and 12% of total income.[3]

Of course, gifts in wills are not only financially important to charities but also emotionally significant. For many donors, a legacy is their largest and most heartfelt gift: a reflection of a deep-rooted, sometimes lifelong connection to a cause and a sign of their desire to leave the world a better place. That's why legacies *really* matter.

Despite its great monetary and cultural value, legacy giving is still a minority activity: today, just 6% of UK deaths result in a charitable bequest[4] and those bequests represent just 3% of all the money left in estates.[5] The challenge for fundraisers, working both as individuals and together as a sector, is to inspire more people to leave a gift in their will.

As every legacy marketer knows only too well, legacies often don't get the airtime that other forms of fundraising enjoy. In 2016 Legacy Foresight carried out an analysis of 36 leading charities, comparing and contrasting the ways they are investing in legacy marketing and how effective they are in generating a response.[6] The study showed that despite legacies generating 38% of all fundraising income for those charities, spending on legacy marketing represented just 3% of their total fundraising budgets.

1

Legacy income trends: A long-term perspective

The value of the legacy sector is tightly entangled with the state of the UK economy, which is not surprising given what legacies are made up of: people's houses, investments and belongings. Over time, much of the growth – and at times the decline – in legacy income is related to the peaks and troughs of the economic cycle.

Figure 1.1 illustrates the cyclical nature of legacy incomes over the past 25 years, with incomes flat or falling during the early 1990s and late 2000s recessions, but climbing quite strongly during the periods of economic expansion – i.e. the late 1980s, the period from 1995 to 2008 and the four years 2013–2016.

FIGURE 1.1 TOTAL INFLATION-ADJUSTED UK LEGACY INCOME, 1988–2016[7]

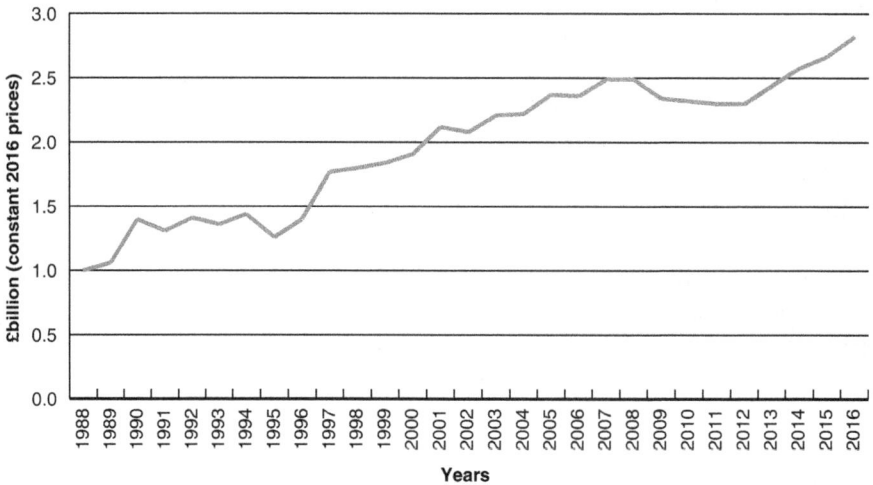

However, underlying these booms and busts, other factors are at play. How many people are dying? What are their family circumstances? How much of their assets do they expend in retirement, whether on having fun or paying for care? How do they balance their responsibilities to their family with their legacy to the wider world around them? And – a key question for legacy marketers – what impact do the myriad communications they receive from charities throughout their lives have on their behaviour?

What drives legacy giving? Lessons from abroad

One way to understand what influences legacy giving over time is to examine the commonalities and differences between countries.

Since Legacy Foresight launched the Legacy Monitor Netherlands benchmarking programme in 2014, the organisation has been approached by legacy fundraisers in other countries about setting up local benchmarking programmes. These conversations have prompted my colleagues and me to think about what drives legacy incomes around the world. Are all markets the same, albeit at differing stages of development? Or are there fundamental structural and cultural differences which will always apply?

Two important lessons can be gleaned from these international investigations. First, when it comes to legacy markets there are more similarities than differences. And, second, the market intelligence, professional support and collaborative networks in the UK are second to none.

Many similarities

• **It's the economy, stupid.** The level of legacy income charities receive is closely linked to the value of the assets in legators' estates, which in turn is driven by the economy. Across the developed world, economies are increasingly being driven by the same underlying trends. For example, when the global recession struck in 2008, stock markets plummeted, house prices fell and economic growth slowed. Of course, the depth and length of the recession varied from one country to another. But, overall, the trends were the same. When the economy booms, average legacy values rise; when the economy sinks into a bust period, legacy values fall.

• **Cash gifts are the most common, but large residuals have the most impact.** In all countries, most of the gifts charities receive are fixed amounts of cash, but a few large 'residual' bequests (i.e. gifts representing a share of the residue of a person's estate once all other bequests and debts have been paid) dominate charities' income. In the Netherlands, *erfstelling* (residual) legacies over €100,000 account for 7% of all gifts to charities but 50% of their total income; similarly, in the UK, residual legacies over £100,000 account for 6% of all gifts to charities but 55% of their total income.[8]

• **Childless legators are key.** When it comes to large bequests in particular, people without 'natural heirs' (not necessarily direct-bloodline descendants) are far more likely to leave a gift to charity. According to a 2016 consumer survey carried out for Legacy Foresight, 24% of childless people aged 50 or over in the UK have written a charitable will (i.e. a will containing one or more gifts to charities), compared to just 8% of people aged over 50 with children.[9] In the Netherlands the difference is even more extreme: 16% of childless people aged over 50 claimed to have written a charitable will compared to just 4% of people aged over 50 with children.[10]

• **The boomers are on their way.** Although the phenomenon of the baby boomers (people born between 1946 and 1963, who now account for 22% of the UK's population)[11] is more marked in some countries than others, most countries saw their birth rate rise significantly from the mid-1940s to the mid-1960s. And those baby boomers will in turn boost national death rates over the next 20 years, which will eventually lead to a rise in the number of legacies charities receive.

• **Living in a 'risk society'.** The UK is at the forefront when it comes to the privatisation of pensions and long-term health care, with most UK citizens now reluctantly accepting that they will need to fund their own old age. Other developed economies are at different points along the privatisation journey, but they are all heading in the same general direction. Most are also seeing a yawning intergenerational wealth gap, with the boomers considerably more affluent than the generations before or after them. For this reason, the need to perpetually support one's children and grandchildren is top of mind for many ageing European parents, not just those in the UK. Balancing the needs of family with the desire to support a charity is a common challenge for will makers across the world.

Some significant differences

• **Testamentary freedom v. family provision.** Perhaps the most striking difference between England and Wales and most other European countries is that under English/Welsh law a person can leave their estate to whoever they like, whereas in most other European countries the surviving spouse and/or children are entitled to a significant proportion of the estate. This has an important impact on the perceived need to make a will. Survey data from 2016 shows that 79% of respondents over the age of 70 in the UK have written a will, compared to 45% in the Netherlands and 34% in Sweden. Persuading someone to write a will is an important first step in encouraging them to include a charitable gift. The same surveys suggest that 17% of people aged over 70 in the UK have written a charitable will, compared to just 5% of Dutch respondents and 2% of Swedes of the same age group.[12]

• **Leading charity brands.** It is surprising how the mix of charities supported varies from one country to another. In the UK, Victorian charities such as the Royal National Lifeboat Institution have long dominated legacy giving. But in the Netherlands, younger charities command a much higher market share, with post-1950 charities accounting for two-thirds of the top 100 charities' legacy income. In both the Netherlands and Sweden, international brands such as Médecins Sans Frontières, Unicef and WWF feature strongly, but in the UK their share is still low.

• **Levels of infrastructure.** The UK stands out in terms of infrastructure, whether in the form of market intelligence from Legacy Foresight, Radcliffe Consulting or Smee & Ford; support systems such as FirstClass legacy administration software and legacy administration specialists Legacy Link; the Remember a Charity campaign; collaborative networks such as the Institute of Legacy Management and Institute of Fundraising special interest groups; or the publications and events provided by the Directory of Social Change.[13] These bodies provide a rich knowledge base and robust forums for debate, which help to drive momentum across the UK legacy sector.

Spotlight on UK legators

Smee & Ford's probate monitoring service indicates that around 16% of the wills read at UK probate courts[14] include at least one charitable bequest.[15] But, beyond this sweeping statistic, there are some important demographic and cultural nuances, illustrated in Legacy Foresight's donor surveys and beyond:

FIGURE 1.2 PERCENTAGE OF ADULTS WITH A WILL, BY AGE GROUP[16]

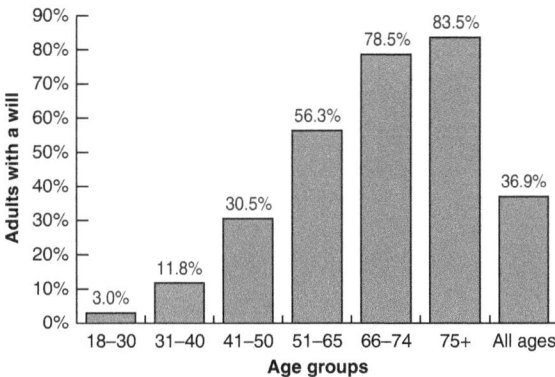

Older people are more likely to leave a legacy, which is not surprising, as the older you are, the more likely you are to get around to writing a will. According to RNLI's latest Charity Monitor survey, nearly 37% of all adults have written a will, climbing from just 12% of people aged 31–40 to 78.5% of people aged 66–74 and 83.5% of people aged 75 or over.[17] For many people, adding a charitable bequest comes later still – at the point when you are putting your affairs in order and thinking about what you want to leave behind.

As figure 1.3 shows, people who engage with charities when they are alive, whether as donors or volunteers, are far more likely to choose to support those causes after they are gone.

People who give significant amounts of money to charity on an ongoing basis are more likely to leave a gift in their will, which probably reflects not only their generosity but also their ability to donate. According to a 2016 survey of UK adults aged 50+, 13% had already written a charitable will. This figure climbed to 19% where the respondent gave at least £50 a month to charity, and 22% where the respondent was a regular volunteer for charities or community groups.[18]

People with more qualifications are more likely to leave a gift, which is probably again a reflection of their greater wealth, but also perhaps results from their appreciation of their own fortunes relative to those of others. As figure 1.3 illustrates, where the respondent had a terminal education age of 19 or above, 21% had written a will including a charitable gift.[19]

FIGURE 1.3 PERCENTAGE OF PEOPLE (AGED 50 OR OVER) OPEN TO LEAVING A CHARITABLE WILL[20]

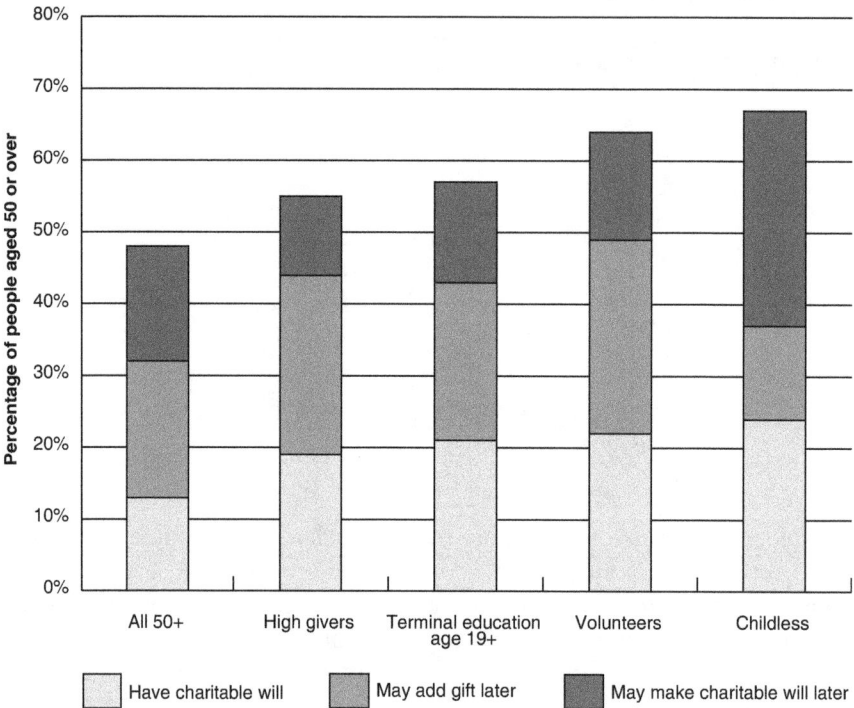

However, by far the most important factor, especially when it comes to residual bequests, is the presence or absence of children. As figure 1.3 shows, 67% of childless adults aged 50 or over are open to the idea of leaving a charitable will (this compared to just 40% of those with children). Furthermore, the survey also found that 23% of those childless people who are open to leaving a bequest would consider leaving a residual gift (i.e. a share of their estate), compared to just 7% of those with children.

Trends by charity type

When the Legacy Foresight team first started analysing legacy giving in the 1990s, a few charities dominated the sector. Back then, the people leaving legacies came from what the Henley Centre called 'the civic generation': born in the early 20th century, and living through two world wars, they were cautious, careful and conservative.[21] The charities this generation admired were the ones they had grown up with: founded in Victorian times, with a focus on domestic poverty relief and supporting disabled people, often with an overtly religious doctrine. Their names say it all: the *Royal National* Lifeboat *Institution*, the *Royal Society* for the Prevention of Cruelty to Animals, the *Salvation* Army, the *Royal National Institute* for the Blind, the *Church* of *England* Children's *Society* and so on. While these charities may have employed legacy fundraising specialists back then, their success came from their high brand recognition, their trustworthy reputation and their status – they were seen as safe places to commit one's largest and most poignant donation.

Back in the 1990s, the sector was concentrated in the hands of these legacy super-brands. And indeed, today the sector is still highly concentrated. Legacy Foresight's analysis shows that the top ten legacy-receiving charities (Cancer Research UK, the RNLI, the RSPCA, Macmillan Cancer Support, the British Heart Foundation, the National Trust, the Salvation Army, PDSA, RNIB and Guide Dogs) account for 35% of the combined legacy income of the 1,000 largest legacy-receiving charities; and the top 50 legacy-receiving charities account for 63%.[22]

However, nowadays it's the smaller legacy-receiving charities that are enjoying the fastest growth. Between 2010/11 and 2015/16, 'medium-sized' legacy-receiving charities (i.e. those with legacy incomes of £1–8 million) enjoyed income growth rates of 8.3% a year – almost twice as fast as the 17 'extra-large' legacy-receiving charities (i.e. those with annual incomes over £20 million), which grew by a more modest 4.6% per annum. (When comparing growth rates by size, however, bear in mind that there is a tendency for larger charities to grow at slower rates as they are growing from a much larger base.)[23]

The same research shows that those charities founded after the Second World War saw their income grow by 7.9% per annum between

2010/11 and 2015/16, compared to just 3.9% a year for Victorian charities and 4.8% a year for those charities formed in the first half of the twentieth century. Many of these smaller, younger charities are investing in legacy fundraising for the first time, sending out fresh messages to their loyal supporter bases. (It is important to add the caveat again here that the newest charities are also the smallest, so, while some of their rapid growth results from novel causes and innovative campaigns, it is also due in part to their growth coming from a smaller base.)

FIGURE 1.4 LEGACY INCOME BY CHARITY SECTOR, 2015/16, %[24]

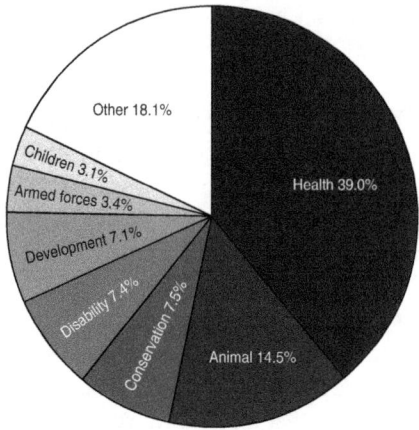

As can be seen from figure 1.4, health charities dominate the legacy sector (accounting for 39% of all income), followed by animal charities (14.5%) and conservation (7.5%). Other important sectors are disability (7.4%) and international development (7.1%), while the 'other' category is boosted by legacy super-brands RNLI and Salvation Army, along with many small faith-based organisations.

Legacy Foresight's analysis of the Charity Commission database shows that over time there has been a significant shift in the type of cause supported – away from the Victorian concerns of disability, domestic poverty relief and the advancement of religion towards contemporary issues such as health, animal welfare and support for the armed services. Other buoyant sectors include air ambulances, hospices, NHS trusts and environmental charities. Many of these smaller organisations have a strong local appeal. Legacy Foresight's analysis of charities by geographic scope showed that over the five years 2005/6 to 2009/10 local charities grew twice as fast as national ones: up by 5.4% a year compared to 2.5% a year.[25]

With an increasingly well-travelled, globally aware donor base, charities with an international outlook are also gaining ground. The same analysis showed that over those five years the incomes of international charities grew at 3.9% a year, compared to 2.5% a year for domestic charities.

Educational organisations, including schools, universities and colleges, are also performing well, especially when it comes to large bequests. On the other hand, most arts organisations still lack the capacity (and perhaps the drive) to invest in legacy marketing.[26] In the face of stringent funding cuts, many smaller arts organisations are focusing their limited resources on short-term income streams. That said, some well-loved, mainly national institutions excel at supporter engagement and receive some very large gifts in response.

FIGURE 1.5 LEADING AND LAGGING SECTORS: SPEED OF GROWTH BY CAUSE AREA

Slow			Fast
Older people	Heritage	Hospices	Armed forces
Advancement of religion	Animal welfare	Environment	NHS trusts
Domestic poverty relief	Overseas development	Medical conditions	Emergency services
Children	Disability	Arts	Education

Economic uncertainties

At the time of writing, the UK is facing an unprecedented period of economic and political uncertainty in the aftermath of the UK's shock Brexit decision in June 2016. This uncertainty is likely to affect legacy values over the coming decade.

The referendum result will cause considerable insecurity over the next few years as the UK negotiates its exit from the EU. Share prices will remain highly volatile for the foreseeable future. Property transactions and house prices, especially in London and the South East, are likely to be depressed. The drop in the value of sterling means that import prices are being pushed up, and so inflation is rising. All these economic factors will impact on estate values and hence on all-important residual legacy values.

Most commentators also believe that the UK's medium-term economic prospects will be weaker outside the EU, if it loses preferential access to its former European trading partners. It will take time to strike new trade deals with non-EU countries such as Australia, Canada, China, India and the USA – and of course there's no guarantee that these deals will be as good.

In the long run, however, no one truly knows how the UK's fortunes will develop outside the EU. Some commentators argue that the UK will be better off without the bureaucracy and inertia today's 28-strong EU generates. The lower sterling may make the UK's exports more competitive and reduce imports (perhaps encouraging greater self-sufficiency in goods and services), so boosting GDP.

The future is not yet clear, but what is certain is that by the time the *next* edition of this book has been published, the economic situation in the UK and beyond will have changed yet again.

The baby boomers are coming...

Since the 1980s, the number of deaths in the UK has been gradually falling, thanks to better living conditions and health care, leading to increases in life expectancy. However, the number of deaths has now started to climb, mainly due to the demise of the sizeable baby boomer generation. Between 2020 and 2050, the number of deaths in the UK will rise by over a third, reaching almost 800,000 in 2050.

FIGURE 1.6 PROJECTED NUMBER OF DEATHS IN THE UK BY GENERATION, 2010–2050[27]

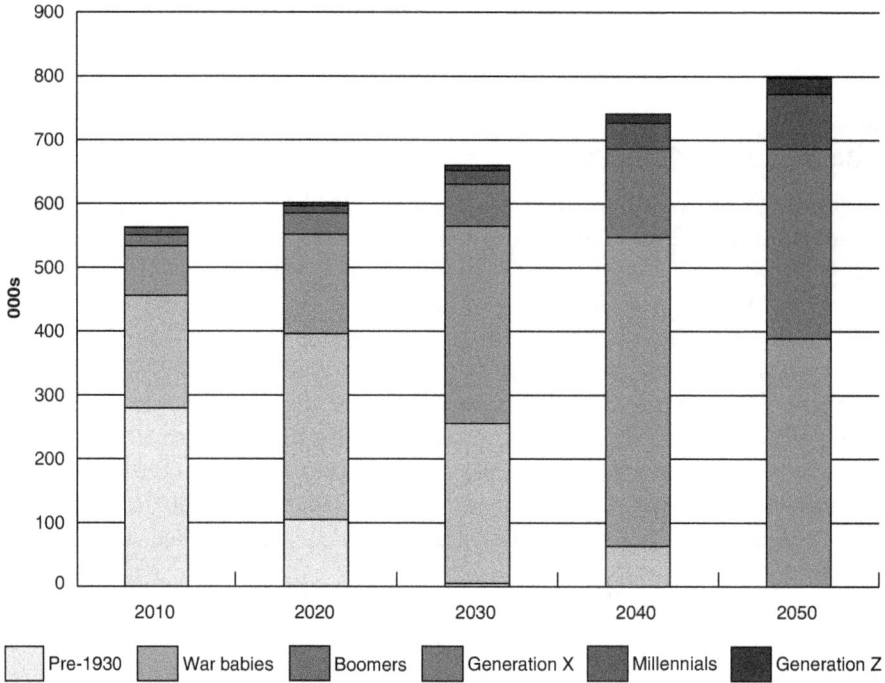

A rise in the number of deaths implies an increase in legacy numbers, even if the proportion of the population leaving a legacy remains unchanged. In fact, Legacy Foresight's consumer surveys and focus groups suggest that the baby boomers are more open to the idea of leaving a charitable legacy than previous generations, which could make the number of gifts received, especially discretionary cash gifts, rise still further. Legacy Foresight's online survey commissioned from Populus showed that 48% of baby boomers (born 1946–1963) are open to the idea of leaving a gift to a charity in their will, compared to 44% of 'war babies' (born 1930–1945).[28]

Looking further ahead, from 2030 onwards the percentage of people dying childless will start to climb sharply, boosting legacy numbers still further. This is because the members of the 'shadow boomer' generation (born 1958–1963) are significantly less likely to have had children than their 'core boomer' (born 1946–57) and war baby predecessors. For example, at the age of 45, 19% of shadow boomer women were childless, compared to just 14% of core boomers.

FIGURE 1.7 PERCENTAGE OF WOMEN AGED 60 OR OVER DYING CHILDLESS, 1990–2050[29]

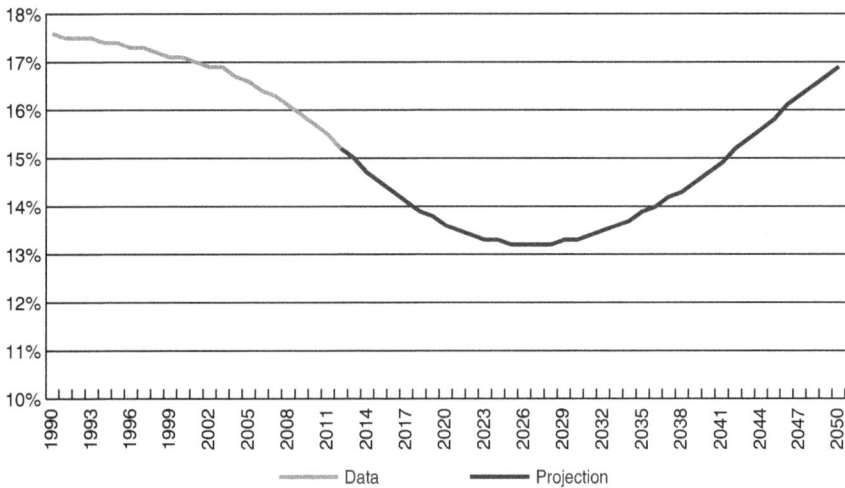

The boomer generation is significantly more affluent than previous generations. They have enjoyed increasing levels of home ownership and seen house prices rocket in real terms. They were the main beneficiaries of the golden age of the welfare state, gaining access to universal secondary education and public health services, and many have also accumulated private pension assets, whether through occupational or personal schemes. Legacy Foresight believes that the sheer scale of the boomer generation and their considerable accumulated resources mean that legacy incomes will grow steadily from 2020 onwards.

That said, research by Legacy Foresight shows that – contrary to popular belief – boomers in the UK are not 'spending the kids' inheritance' (a phrase that has led to some commentators calling this generation SKIers). While they are looking forward to an active retirement, future uncertainties (about long-term care and pension provision) together with relatively modest lifestyles are constraining extravagant spending for most.[30]

Indeed, the boomers are concerned about their children's – and particularly their grandchildren's – future. There is almost universal agreement that for future generations, life will be harder financially, emotionally and practically than it was for the boomers. As a result, many are giving considerable sums of money now to ensure their offspring's happiness before they die. According to a 2013 Legacy Foresight survey, two-thirds of people currently aged 55 or over with children are supporting adult family members financially, whether by buying a large household item (such as a car), paying a deposit on a property or paying university fees, or helping with living expenses on a regular basis.[31]

While this is a significant change in behaviour, it is important to recognise that people with children are not legacy fundraisers' most important audience. While they may consider giving cash gifts or small residual bequests to charity, most people with children – and particularly those with grandchildren – choose to leave the bulk of their estate to their family.

Compared to earlier generations, however, boomers hold different values. They are more willing to challenge conventions about who their money should go to, favouring friends and trusted brands over distant relatives. Given the era they grew up in, they support international development and environmental and human rights organisations over more traditional domestic and religious causes.

At the same time, the boomers pride themselves on being confident and demanding donors. They expect a personalised service and need to feel in control. They want information to aid their choices, and they appreciate straight-talking rather than flattery. When it comes to legacies in particular, they desire proof that a charity intends to spend any money given in a will wisely – the boomers' natural scepticism means that charities will have to work harder to prove the value and effectiveness of their actions.

For these reasons, to communicate effectively with boomer legators, charities need to use a new tone of voice and a new set of messages. The final report of the Commission on the Voluntary Sector & Ageing is well worth reading on this subject.[32] The report concludes that charities need to move on from an ethos of 'you give, we do' to build lifelong mutually beneficial relationships with their supporters. It also states that the sector needs to be smarter at communicating with donors, articulating the cause and explaining why people should donate. These lessons apply to legacy fundraising perhaps more than to any other form of fundraising.

Conclusion

Legacy giving is a vital and vibrant part of our sector, representing 5% of UK charities' total income. Over the next 30 years the number of gifts in wills is set to rise strongly, thanks to significant demographic and cultural changes. Whatever your charity's size, age or cause area, you have the potential to grow your legacy income, providing you can communicate a unique and powerful legacy vision.

Legacy fundraising doesn't require huge budgets or teams, but the whole organisation needs to get behind the idea – the role of the legacy fundraiser is about championing legacy giving with both supporters *and* colleagues.

And it doesn't need to be isolating. In my and my colleagues' view, UK legacy fundraising is one of the most collaborative sectors in the world. By working with other charities, through your trustees and volunteers, and with the wider public, you can truly leave the world a better place.

Notes

1   *Legacy Giving 2017* [PDF], Legacy Foresight, 2017; a copy of the report can be requested via www.legacyforesight.co.uk/documents.
2   Claire Benard, Gareth Lloyd, Jack Egan, Joy Dobbs, Lisa Hornung, Marc Lawson, Nick Ockenden and Véronique Jochum, *The UK Civil Society Almanac 2017*, London, NCVO, 2017 (figures available at https://data.ncvo.org.uk/a/almanac17/income-data).
3   *Legacy Giving 2017* [PDF], Legacy Foresight, 2017; a copy of the report can be requested via www.legacyforesight.co.uk/documents.
4   *Legacy Trends: Discovering potential thorough data* [PDF], Smee & Ford, 2017, https://smeeandford.com/whitepaper, p. 2, accessed 30 December 2017.
5   Percentage calculated using *Inheritance Tax Statistics: Table 12.4 – assets in estates by range of net estate and tax due* [PDF], HM Revenue & Customs, 2017, www.gov.uk/government/statistics/inheritance-tax-statistics-table-124-assets-in-estates-by-range-of-net-estate-and-tax-due, accessed 30 December 2017.
6   Legacy Marketing Benchmark Project, Legacy Foresight, 2016 (analysis conducted for a consortium of charities; research results available to consortium members only).
7   UK Legacy Market Model, Legacy Foresight, 2017 (internal forecasting model).
8   Legacy Monitor UK, Legacy Foresight, 2017 (internal programme).
9   Populus online consumer survey conducted for Legacy Foresight, 2016.
10 *Legacy Monitor Netherlands* [PDF], Legacy Foresight, 2016, www.legacyforesight.co.uk/resources/Dutch%20Legacy%20Market%20Snapshot%202016.pdf, p. 2, accessed 27 February 2018.
11 Legacy Foresight's analysis of data from the Office for National Statistics' population estimates (see www.ons.gov.uk/peoplepopulationandcommunity/populationandmigration/populationestimates).

12   *Ibid.*, p. 3, accessed 4 January 2017; *Insamling 2015 FRII:S Medlemmar* [PDF], FRII (Swedish Fundraising Council), 2015, www.frii.se/wp-content/uploads/2012/08/insamlingsrapport-2015-frii-kortversion.pdf, accessed 30 December 2017.

13   For more information from these organisations see www.legacyforesight.co.uk, www.radcliffeconsulting.org, www.smeeandford.com, www.clear-software.co.uk, www.legacy-link.co.uk, www.rememberacharity.org.uk, www.legacymanagement.org.uk, www.institute-of-fundraising.org.uk/groups/sig-legacy-marketing-and-in-memoriam and www.dsc.org.uk.

14   Wills are read at UK probate courts in cases when a grant of representation has been applied for (known as a probate application), which gives someone the legal right to deal with a dead person's estate. It is possible in some instances to access a person's estate without a grant of representation; for example, if an entire estate was owned jointly with the spouse or if it were to consist purely of cash (so not including any land, property or shares). Wills not read at probate are unlikely to have much of an impact on charitable bequest figures so we can assume that these statistics reflect a true picture of the legacy-giving landscape.

15   Remember a Charity, '10% annual increase in number of charities named in wills' [web article], www.rememberacharity.org.uk/news/10-annual-increase-in-number-of-charities-named-in-wills, 20 April 2016.

16   Biennial consumer awareness and opinion survey, commissioned by the RNLI, 2016.

17   *Ibid.*

18   Populus online consumer survey conducted for Legacy Foresight, 2016.

19   *Ibid.*

20   *Ibid.*

21   Forecasting the value of charitable legacies 1991–2011, study conducted by the Henley Centre for Forecasting for a consortium of major legacy charities, 1996.

22   *Legacy Giving 2017* [PDF], Legacy Foresight, 2017; a copy of the report can be requested via www.legacyforesight.co.uk/documents.

23   *Ibid.*

24   *Ibid.*

25   *Legacy Market Review* [PDF], Legacy Foresight, 2011 (available internally).

26   *Legacy Fundraising in the Arts* [PDF], Legacy Foresight/Arts Quarter, 2016, www.artsquarter.co.uk/reports.html, pp. 6, 17 and 20, accessed 11 January 2018.

27   Legacy Foresight's analysis of data from the Office for National Statistics.

28   Populus online consumer survey conducted for Legacy Foresight, 2016.

29   Legacy Foresight's analysis of data from the Office for National Statistics.

30   *Legacy Giving 2050* [PDF], Legacy Foresight, 2014; a copy of the report can be requested via www.legacyforesight.co.uk/documents.

31   Populus online consumer survey conducted for Legacy Foresight, 2013.

32   *Kate Jopling, Decision Time: Will the voluntary sector embrace the age of opportunity?*, London, New Philanthropy Capital, 2015.

CHAPTER TWO

Who gives and why

Claire Routley and Russell James

Introduction

The previous chapter examined trends in the broad market and their implications for legacy fundraising practice. This chapter considers the specifics of what academic research can tell you about who gives and their motivations.

For many years, legacy giving was the poor cousin of lifetime giving when it came to academic research. However, while there are still fewer studies on legacy giving as compared to lifetime giving, the past ten years have seen real growth both in the number of published studies and in the variety of methodologies used to understand the subject, from surveys to experiments to in-depth interviews, focus groups and even brain-scanning. As a result, there have been significant developments in what is known about who legacy supporters are and why they give. The research can offer you a treasure trove of information to help you know more about your audience and design your strategies appropriately. This chapter will summarise what is known about who gives and why, and offer some suggestions as to what these findings mean for fundraising practice.

Who leaves legacies?

To work out which types of people are most likely to leave a legacy, we can focus on what is known about the demographics of the audience for legacy fundraising. This information can help you to identify those people most likely to leave a legacy, and to focus your time and resources most effectively as a result.

Age

When thinking about the typical legacy donor, the first demographic characteristic that often springs to mind is that they are likely to be an older person. However, the research evidence paints a more complex picture. There is some evidence to suggest that people add gifts to charities in their wills from their mid-to-late 40s onwards; in a study of donors to three large US non-profits, Sargeant, Wymer and Hilton found that the average age of legacy pledgers is 47.[1] Other studies have shown the average legacy-pledger age to be 50–59[2] or in their mid-to-late 60s.[3]

It is important to keep in mind that only the final will a person makes actually determines how assets will be distributed. An Australian study of probate files found that more than 75% of dollars coming from charitable estates were bequeathed in wills signed by people in their 80s or older.[4] Many of these final wills may have incorporated charitable provisions from earlier wills. However, some of the most intriguing findings on age come from a US study which found that 61% of charitable plans were added within the last five years of life – often around the same time that people were reducing their charitable giving and volunteering.[5] This common pattern of ceasing giving and volunteering in the years leading up to the end of life while simultaneously adding a charitable component to the will suggests that charities that communicate with older supporters based only on recency of giving could be making a serious error.

Gender

Although there is some evidence to suggest that men and women are equally likely to *intend* to leave a charitable legacy,[6] in practice, more women than men actually *leave* gifts, perhaps partly because their longer life expectancy means that women are likely to outlive their male partners and thus have final control of how the couple's joint estate is bequeathed. In an analysis of estate data, Atkinson, Backus and Micklewright found that 18% of women with wills that have gone through probate in the UK leave legacies, as opposed to 14% of men.[7] Interestingly, they also found that women are more likely to leave gifts without conditions attached (conditions such as gifts being left to charity if someone else dies first).[8]

Wealth

Analysis of estates shows that, as their value increases, so too, on average, does the proportion given to charitable causes.[9] In a similar vein, in their analysis of UK probate data, Atkinson and colleagues observed a noticeable rise in the number of estates containing charitable bequests around the inheritance tax threshold; estates above the inheritance tax threshold made up 17.5% of all estates but 41.9% of all bequests.[10] You should note, however, that while assets play an important role in bequest giving, potential bequest donors may not have large incomes. Indeed, Brown states that 58% of US bequests are left by donors with incomes of less than $75,000 a year.[11] Potential legacy donors may therefore not always appear as the highest-value donors in your database.

Presence of children

It might seem intuitive that people with children and grandchildren are less likely to leave charitable legacies: after all, most people with children want to provide for them. However, the scale of the impact was highlighted by a study that found that among people over the age of 50 who had already completed a will or trust and were already donating money to charitable organisations in the USA, childless people were five times more likely to leave a gift to a charity than those with grandchildren.[12] Similarly, in the UK, people who are 50 years old or older and do not have children are three times more likely to have written a charitable will (i.e. a will containing one or more gifts to charities) than people in the same age bracket who do have children (24% vs 8%).[13]

What might this mean for fundraising practice?

This information might help you to target your legacy fundraising efforts appropriately and, potentially, to gather more information on your donors that might be useful in legacy fundraising practice.

• Most charitable donors on the typical charity database will be older than their mid-40s and thus, at least in age terms, somewhere on the legacy-giving spectrum. However, any charity considering focusing on younger donors should be aware that research also shows that only 55% of legacies are retained in wills for ten years or longer.[14] You should therefore ensure you have an excellent stewardship programme in place to help retain legacy supporters.

• Particular care should be taken with older donors. The last few years of life are likely to be key for legacy giving but, of course, can also be a difficult time in terms of donor vulnerability. It is therefore vital to ensure appropriate ethical policies are in place. (See chapter 3 for details on the ethics of legacy fundraising.) You should potentially also consider how you treat formerly loyal but now lapsing donors, who may be in the process of deciding on legacy gifts. A specially designed stewardship programme may be appropriate for this audience.

• Although people with children are less likely to give, you might be able to think creatively to develop attractive giving options for people with children. For example, the National Trust mentions the possibility of leaving money in a will to purchase lifetime memberships for children and grandchildren, an option that could benefit both the charity and family members simultaneously.

• The possibility of paying inheritance tax could be a way to open conversations about legacy giving, particularly among more well-off donors. You could make them aware of any charitable exemptions and, in the UK, of the potential to receive an inheritance tax discount when 10% or more of an estate is left to charity.

Motivations of legacy donors

It is vital to understand your donors' motivations. If you know why people leave legacy gifts and recognise their underlying wants and needs, then you can design your fundraising activities in a way that addresses these motivations, resulting in greater donor satisfaction and, ultimately, increased income for your organisation.

The following sections explore some of the key motives of legacy donors. They look at how legacy giving reflects supporters' life experiences, how supporters can use their legacies to live on after their deaths and memorialise others, and the importance of being perceived by supporters as an efficient, effective organisation. They will also explore how legacy donors' decisions are influenced by those of others and, finally, discuss the most appropriate language for a legacy solicitation.

Life experience

As illustrated in the following quotes, when supporters discuss their legacy-giving decisions, it's often possible to see their individual life experiences reflected in their choice of charities:[15]

> [In my will] there's the Youth Hostel Association, first of all ... it's where my wife and I met ... Then there's the Ramblers' Association. We've walked a lot with the local group ... Then Help the Aged – I've got to help the aged, I am one ... Then there's RNID because I'm hard of hearing ... Then, finally, Cancer Research. My father died of cancer and so I have supported them ever since he died. (George, 89)

> The reason I selected Help the Aged ... it was after my mother died ... And I just thought – she'd been in a care home for probably three or four years. And I just wanted to help the elderly ... I'd also support things like Cancer Research ... because people I've known have died ... An animal charity as well ... I had a couple of cats. (Joanne, 63)

This is reflected in a study which showed that of a number of phrases tested on online respondents in the USA to gauge their degree of interest in leaving a charitable bequest, the highest level of interest was generated by making reference to supporting causes that are, or have been, important to the respondent.[16]

The connection between personal experience and legacy giving has been reinforced by James and O'Boyle, who used brain-scanning (functional magnetic resonance imaging) research to understand which areas of the brain are activated when someone is thinking about leaving a gift in a will to charity.[17] They found that two key areas of the brain are activated: the precuneus and the lingual gyrus. These areas are used in internal visualisation and when taking an outside perspective on oneself. Both areas were also simultaneously activated in studies where older adults were shown photographs of themselves taken during life experiences that evoked particularly vivid memories. Therefore, when people choose charities, they can be described as reliving their 'visualised autobiography': looking back over their lives and thinking about the connections between themselves and particular charities.[18]

Our most vivid autobiographical memories are often concerned with the people we love. As the quotes above illustrate, honouring a loved one often appears to be a trigger for a legacy gift. The principle has been tested quantitatively in a research project, first asking study participants to rate their likelihood of leaving a bequest to several organisations, then asking them to recall connections between a loved one and charitable causes, and finally asking about their propensity to leave a bequest to the same organisations but, this time, in tribute to their loved one. The study found that, among those who reported a loved one's connection to a cause, the propensity to leave a tribute bequest increased by an average of 10 points (on a 100-point scale).[19]

Linked to these points, research from Sargeant and Hilton which examined the differences between legacy supporters and lifetime givers shows that legacy donors feel a need to pay back organisations for services or support that they or a loved one have received. The study found that this need was a key factor distinguishing legacy supporters from lifetime givers.[20]

What might this mean for fundraising practice?

• When thinking about potential audiences for legacy fundraising, you could consider which of your stakeholders is likely to have vivid autobiographical connections to your cause. They might be donors but also, potentially, service users, visitors, trustees, volunteers or staff, to name just a few examples.

• You could draw on these vivid memories in your legacy marketing. In practice, this approach has been exemplified effectively by the Red Cross, which asked its supporters 'Do you remember Aberfan?'. More recently, Unicef used this principle in its We Are the Generation campaign.

• You could also offer your supporters the facility to make a legacy gift in honour of a loved one (i.e. a tribute fund) – an option that may well help to lessen the conflict between supporting family and charity in the will.

Living on

The previous section considered the importance of looking backwards over one's life history. However, legacies also involve looking forward – thinking about the impact we will have on the people and causes we care about after our deaths. Psychology offers some useful insights in this area.

As we age, psychologists tell us, we become more concerned with generativity, or 'a desire to invest one's substance in forms of life and work that will outlive the self'.[21] As we move into middle age and beyond, we become increasingly concerned with creating an anticipated ending for our life story which 'ties together the beginning and middle to affirm unity, purpose and direction in life over time'.[22] It is easy to see how leaving a charitable gift in a will could help to achieve this desire. In a single stroke, leaving a charitable legacy could say something about a person's connections to particular causes, their relationships with others, their life experiences, their values and, ultimately, how they want to be remembered.

There is a complementary stream of research in psychology which examines how human beings cope with the foreknowledge of their own death; this research is called 'terror management theory'. The theory suggests that our knowledge of our own mortality could be paralysing but that we have several ways of defending ourselves. Firstly, when we are confronted with thoughts of death, we try to push them away – for example, by telling ourselves that death is a long way off. However, at a deeper level, we have a second layer of defence: we manage the anxiety of mortality through the knowledge that we are 'enduring, significant contributors to a meaningful, permanent world' and put significant effort, throughout our lives, into buttressing this sense of ourselves. Greenberg explains that we can achieve symbolic immortality through, for example, having children, or achieving success in the world of business or artistic endeavour.[23] It would also seem logical that we can achieve symbolic immortality through a charitable gift: we are personally making a difference through our giving, and, at the same time, helping to make the communities we care about better places.

What might this mean for fundraising practice?

• At a basic level, supporters might be reluctant to engage with legacy giving because their first reaction is to push the thought of death away. Integrating the legacy message into other communications – such as newsletters, your organisation's website or supporter surveys – can introduce the subject gently. You could also think about creative, engaging ways of opening the legacy conversation. Since 2009,[24] Remember a Charity has been developing some great examples, including legacy-giving teabags, humorous commercials and offering free taxi rides to members of the public who pass on their words of wisdom (highlighting how important it is in life to pass on things of value).[25]

• In your messaging, you could also focus on demonstrating how legacy gifts make a lasting impact, demonstrating to your donors how leaving a legacy can enable them to live on through their support of your work.

• Similarly, you could also show how legacy gifts are meaningful – how they enable donors to express something of themselves and how much legacy gifts are valued by their community.

Organisational factors

As a legacy fundraiser, you will likely be aware that legacy pledgers can be a more demanding audience than other donors. Sargeant and Hilton found that legacy pledgers are more concerned about organisational performance than other donors, and that they expect both the quality of communication and responsiveness to be of a higher standard than do other supporters.[26] This concern might be linked to the need for symbolic immortality described above: if a donor doesn't believe their money will be spent well, then they won't have any faith that a charitable gift would enable them to continue to have an influence on the world and thus achieve symbolic immortality.[27]

What might this mean for fundraising practice?

• This research points again towards the importance of effective stewardship of pledgers and of other legacy supporters, suggesting that legacy donors will be paying active attention to how they are treated by your charity.

• More generally, however, the research stresses the importance of a good standard of stewardship of the donor base more generally, especially as charities are not always aware of who may be leaving them a gift.

Social influence

An emerging theme in academic research in the last decade is the importance of social influences on the decision to leave a legacy. There are now several studies that have attempted to examine social influence through a series of experiments.

In the UK, research conducted by the Cabinet Office asked people who call a will-writing service to make a will the following question: 'Many of our customers like to leave money to charity in their will. Are there any causes you're passionate about?'. When people were asked this question, the percentage who added a charitable bequest to their will rose from just under 5% to 15%.[28] Similarly, in the academic study previously referred to where researchers tested various statements on online respondents in the USA, adding the phrase 'many people like to leave a gift to charity in their will' generated significantly higher interest (i.e. the hypothetical likelihood of respondents pursuing any given charitable giving arrangement) in making such gifts.[29] However, there is a caveat here in that subsequent research from the Behavioural Insights Team showed that phrasing of this kind (i.e. mentioning social norms) was only effective when people were writing a first will rather than revising their will.[30] Given that the majority (87.8%) of charity donors already have wills,[31] this kind of phrasing may not be optimal in communications with existing supporters.

Also in the realm of social influence, we carried out an online survey in which we tested the effect of a series of different stories on intentions to leave a legacy gift.[32] We found that people who were exposed to stories about other legacy donors were more likely to express an interest in legacy giving than those who saw no stories, and people who were exposed to stories about *living* pledgers were more likely to express an interest in legacy giving than those who saw stories about donors who had already died and left a gift.

What might this mean for fundraising practice?

• The research suggests that sharing stories of other people who have decided to leave a legacy could be a powerful influence on legacy giving.

• However, the research also suggests that you should be careful when using statements based on social norms. Such statements are a powerful tool, but there is still much to be learned about the most effective way they can be applied.

Legacy language

The final point of relevance is the type of language used to discuss legacy giving. In the test of various statements mentioned above, simple or informal words appear to outperform formal words.[33] For example, 23% of respondents said they were currently interested in making a 'gift to charity' in their wills, while only 12% said they were currently interested in making a 'bequest gift' to charity. Sargeant and Shang also found a difference in language between lifetime and legacy giving in their focus group study.[34] Drawing on psychological research which suggests a difference in decision-making over different time frames (temporal decision-making: for example, decisions about tomorrow versus decisions about ten years in the future), they found that, while lifetime giving appears to be concerned with the concrete impact of a gift and the details of the work and immediate need, legacy giving appears to be concerned with the values of the organisation and with the vision and bigger picture of its work.

What might this mean for fundraising practice?

• At a basic level, you should be aware that different uses of language are likely to be optimal for legacy and lifetime giving, respectively. If you regularly write for both audiences, it is important to make an effort to get into the correct mindset for legacy communication.

• When talking about legacies, it is likely to be more effective to focus on the big picture and the long-term vision for the organisation, rather than its immediate needs.

• Avoid overly legalistic language and whenever possible replace a legal term with a simple, everyday one – for example, talk about a 'cash gift' rather than a 'pecuniary legacy'.

Conclusion

As this chapter has shown, while there is still much to learn, we now understand a considerable amount about who leaves legacies and the motivations underlying their decisions. The findings of this research have the potential to feed into your legacy fundraising, helping you to create better experiences for your supporters and, ultimately, raising more money for the causes and beneficiaries who depend on your work.

Notes

1   Adrian Sargeant, Walter Wymer and Toni Hilton, 'Marketing Bequest Club Membership: An exploratory study of legacy pledgers', *Nonprofit and Voluntary Sector Quarterly*, vol. 35, no. 3, 2006, pp. 384–404.

2   Karen Cole, Rachel Dingle and Rajesh Bhayani, 'Pledger Modelling: Help the Aged case study', *International Journal of Nonprofit and Voluntary Sector Marketing*, vol. 10, 2005, pp. 43–52.

3   Adrian Sargeant and Toni Hilton, 'The Final Gift: Targeting the potential charity legator', *International Journal of Nonprofit and Voluntary Sector Marketing*, vol. 10, 2005, pp. 3–16.

4   Russell James and Christopher Baker, 'The Timing of Final Charitable Bequest Decisions', *International Journal of Nonprofit and Voluntary Sector Marketing*, vol. 20, no. 3, 2015, pp. 277–283.

5   Russell James, *American Charitable Bequest Demographics (1992–2012)*, Lubbock TX, Encourage Generosity, 2013, p. 55.

6   Xiaonan Kou, Hao Han and Heidi Frederick, *Gender Differences in Giving Motivations for Bequest Donors and Non-Donors*, The Center on Philanthropy at Indiana University, Indianapolis IN, 2009, p. 26.

7   See footnote 14 on page 14 for details on when probate is required in UK courts.

8   A. B. Atkinson, P. G. Backus and J. Micklewright, *Charitable Bequests and Wealth at Death in Great Britain* [working paper], Southampton, University of Southampton, p. 21.

9   Charles Clotfelter, 'Charitable Giving and Tax Legislation in the Reagan Era', *Law and Contemporary Problems*, vol. 48, no. 4, pp. 197–212.

10   A. B. Atkinson, P. G. Backus and J. Micklewright, *Charitable Bequests and Wealth at Death in Great Britain* [working paper], Southampton, University of Southampton, p. 22.

11   David Brown, 'What Research Tells Us About Planned Giving', *International Journal of Nonprofit and Voluntary Sector Marketing*, vol. 9, no. 1, pp. 86–95.

12   Russell James, *Causes and Correlates of Charitable Giving in Estate Planning: A cross-sectional and longitudinal examination of older adults* [PDF], Association of Fundraising Professionals, www.afpnet.org/files/ContentDocuments/RussellJames_LegacyLeadersReport_EstatePlanning.pdf, 2008, p. 28, accessed 11 January 2018; Russell James, 'The New Statistics of Estate Planning: Lifetime and post-mortem wills, trusts, and charitable planning', *Estate Planning & Community Property Law Journal*, vol. 8, no. 1, 2015, pp. 1–39, table 13.

13   Populus online consumer survey for Legacy Foresight, April 2016, (available to In-Memory Insight Consortium members).

14   Russell James, *American Charitable Bequest Demographics (1992–2012)*, Lubbock TX, Encourage Generosity, 2013, p. 59; Russell James and Christopher Baker, 'The Timing of Final Charitable Bequest Decisions', *International Journal of Nonprofit and Voluntary Sector Marketing*, vol. 20, no. 3, pp. 277–283, table 5.

15   Claire Routley and Adrian Sargeant, 'Leaving a Bequest: Living on through charitable gifts', *Nonprofit and Voluntary Sector Quarterly*, 2014, pp. 1–17.

16   Russell James, 'Phrasing the Charitable Bequest Inquiry', *Voluntas: International Journal of Voluntary and Nonprofit Organizations*, vol. 27, no. 2, 2015, pp. 998–1011.

17   Russell James and Michael O'Boyle, 'Charitable Estate Planning as Visualized Autobiography: An fMRI study of its neural correlates', *Nonprofit and Voluntary Sector Quarterly*, vol. 43, no. 2, 2014, pp. 355–373.

18   *Ibid.*

19   Russell James, 'The Family Tribute in Charitable Bequest Giving', *Nonprofit Management and Leadership*, vol. 26, no. 1, 2015, pp. 73–89.

20   Adrian Sargeant and Toni Hilton, 'The Final Gift: Targeting the potential charity legator', *International Journal of Nonprofit and Voluntary Sector Marketing*, vol. 10, 2005, pp. 3–16.

21   John Kotre, *Outliving the Self*, New York, W. W. Norton, 1996, p. 10.

22   Dan McAdams, 'Personality, Modernity, and the Storied Self: A contemporary framework for studying persons', *Psychological Inquiry*, vol. 7, no. 4, pp. 295–321, 1996.

23   Jeff Greenberg, 'Terror Management Theory: From Genesis to Revelations', in *Meaning, Mortality, and Choice: The social psychology of existential concerns*, edited by Phillip Shaver and Mario Mikulincer, Washington DC, American Psychological Association, 2012, pp. 17–35.

24   'Charities set sights on legacies' [web article], Marketing Week, www.marketingweek.com/2009/03/26/charities-set-sights-on-legacies, 26 March 2009.

25   'Wisdom' powered taxi hits the streets' [press release], Remember a Charity, www.rememberacharity.org.uk/news/wisdom-powered-taxi-hits-the-streets, 30 November 2016.

26   Adrian Sargeant and Toni Hilton, 'The Final Gift: Targeting the potential charity legator', *International Journal of Nonprofit and Voluntary Sector Marketing*, vol. 10, 2005, pp. 3–16.

27   Claire Routley and Adrian Sargeant, 'Leaving a Bequest: Living on through charitable gifts', *Nonprofit and Voluntary Sector Quarterly*, 2014, pp. 1–17.

28   *Applying Behavioural Insights to Charitable Giving*, London, Cabinet Office and Behavioural Insights Team, 2013, p. 22.

29   Russell James, 'Phrasing the Charitable Bequest Inquiry', *Voluntas: International Journal of Voluntary and Nonprofit Organizations*, vol. 27, no. 2, 2015, pp. 998–1011.

30   Michael Sanders, Sarah Smith, Bibi Groot and David Nolan, *Legacy Giving and Behavioural Insights*, London, The Behavioural Insights Team, 2016, p. 9.

31   Adrian Sargeant, Richard Radcliffe and E. Jay, *The Efficacy of Legacy Communications*, Henley, The Centre for Voluntary Sector Management, 2003, p. 13.

32   Russell James and Claire Routley, 'We the living: the effects of living and deceased donor stories on charitable bequest giving intentions', *International Journal of Nonprofit and Voluntary Sector Marketing*, 2016, pp. 109–117.

33   Russell James, 'Phrasing the Charitable Bequest Inquiry', *Voluntas: International Journal of Voluntary and Nonprofit Organizations*, vol. 27, no. 2, 2015, pp. 998–1011.

34   Adrian Sargeant and Jen Shang, *Identification, Death and Bequest Giving*, Arlington VA, Association of Fundraising Professionals, 2008, pp. 42–46.

CHAPTER THREE

Ethics

Sebastian Wilberforce, Daniel Fluskey and Justine Williams

Introduction

All forms of fundraising raise issues around ethical practice, but none more so than legacy fundraising. With often large amounts of money left in wills, potentially vulnerable audiences and of course the inherent connection with death, there are a number of sensitive issues to be aware of and recognise. This chapter seeks to address some of the ethical issues that surround legacy fundraising.

Excellent fundraising is not just about counting the money that is raised and delivering the best expenditure-to-income ratio. It is about fundraising in a way that grows public trust and confidence in your charity and that is rooted in the values and ethos of your organisation's approach. An ethical approach is essential to the long-term success and sustainability of a charity – an approach that concentrates just as much on *how* money is raised as on *how much*.

In legacy fundraising it is essential to be aware of the ethical dimension as you will be dealing with incredibly sensitive issues, bereaved families and often large amounts of money. This means that it is absolutely fundamental to ensure that your charity is conducting its legacy fundraising in a way that is legal and ethical.

Regulation, ethics and law

Since the previous edition of this book, the regulatory framework for fundraising in the UK has changed radically. Following a review of fundraising regulation in the summer of 2015 led by Sir Stuart Etherington,[1] the Fundraising Regulator was formed to be a new independent regulator of fundraising in England and Wales, taking over from the previous body, the Fundraising Standards Board. The Fundraising Regulator sets and maintains the standards for charitable fundraising in the Code of Fundraising Practice, as well as investigating and adjudicating on complaints about fundraising practice.

The Code of Fundraising Practice should be your starting point to understand the rules that you need to follow.[2] It incorporates both legal requirements and the standards that are set by the Fundraising Regulator. If charities are found to be breaching these rules, the Fundraising Regulator will adjudicate and can sanction them.

While charity fundraising has to start with fundraisers and charities knowing and understanding their regulatory requirements, an ethical approach involves more than just tick-box compliance. It is about creating a culture and values in your charity that embed an ethical approach, which will result in a great outcome for donors and supporters as well as give confidence and reassurance to your charity that it is fundraising in the right way.

This chapter explores some of the considerations that your charity should be giving thought to, as well as highlighting points of best practice. (For details on further resources such as the Fundraising Regulator and the Institute of Legacy Management see the appendix.)[3]

The acceptability of legacy fundraising

It is perfectly reasonable to bring to someone's attention the possibility (even desirability) of expressing their support for a charity through leaving a gift in their will. Legacy fundraising is an ethical activity: by actively promoting and encouraging the opportunity to leave a legacy gift, charities give people the choice to support causes that they care about. Questions over the ethics of legacy fundraising are not about whether it is acceptable but about how it is done.

Charity trustees and staff who are new to legacy fundraising often feel uncomfortable about it because they think it involves breaching that great taboo of talking about death. However, in reality, this taboo does not exist. A British Social Attitudes study reported that 70% of people are comfortable talking about death and end-of-life matters. In legacy fundraising it really is not an issue.[4] To quote the legacy fundraising consultant Richard Radcliffe, 'legacies are life driven and only death activated'.[5] It is not a person's death that prompts the gift but how they feel about a cause and how your charity can realise the person's desire to have a continuing impact upon that cause. The same British Social Attitudes study revealed that 13% of people do feel uncomfortable talking about death. There will always be a minority who do not want to engage with a legacy or anything else which reminds them of their own mortality, but clearly there is a very large majority who do want to do this. When you encounter one of those 13%, you will know it because of the words they use, their tone or their body language – but then all you have to do is back off and concentrate on someone in the 70% (or, indeed, the remaining 17% of respondents who chose the statement 'No strong feelings either way').[6] If you are new to legacy fundraising, remember too that if you are talking to someone about a legacy they will most likely be in that 70%.

Another statistic to bear in mind is that people's fear of death peaks in their twenties and then declines with age and psychosocial maturity.[7] If you feel uncomfortable talking about legacies, ask yourself to what extent you are projecting your own concerns about dying onto the donor, and remember two things. Firstly, legacy fundraising is not about talking about death but about sustaining a cause a person supports – often passionately. Secondly, in the great majority of cases, death will not come up in conversation, and when it does it will be in passing – along the lines of 'when I'm gone I want these charities to have some of my money'.

Who might leave a legacy gift and why?

As people age, they realise the proximity of their death. Legacy fundraising is generally directed at people who, by reason of their age, are more aware or likely to be thinking about making a will and sorting out their end-of-life affairs. Older people tend to face the idea of their death, if not with equanimity, at least with an acceptance of its inevitability. While of course this is never an easy time, people may look positively on the idea of getting their affairs in order, making sure that their family and friends are looked after, and ensuring the charities whose causes they care about are supported. Many people actively want advice about this last topic.

But wills are not just for older people. Individuals of all ages may be, for whatever reason, giving consideration to their life and legacy. It may be that they are going through a key life change such as marriage, divorce or the birth of a child, which are often trigger points for people wanting to write or update their will. Or they might be buying or selling a house, have experienced a bereavement themselves, be starting a new job or retiring. There is no reason why your charity should not be mindful of how and when people might be going through times of change. By both making specific legacy asks and embedding information and messages about the possibility of leaving gifts in wills, you can inform individuals of the opportunity to leave a legacy as well as potentially reminding people to write a will in the first place. As wider public policy, this is a positive and worthwhile activity.

Key issues to think about
The subject of death

The subject of death comes up usually during face-to-face or one-to-one conversations with members of the public and in the sense of 'when I'm gone'. It may also arise when couples contemplate whether they are going to die before or after their partner.

If and when you have to refer to death, it is best to do so in a matter-of-fact way, remembering that this is how most older people view the event. In my experience, older people often appreciate a direct attitude that uses words such as 'dying', 'death' or 'dead' rather than euphemisms

– this is particularly the case with people who have been bereaved themselves. Euphemisms such as 'passing on' or 'the other side' should be used only with care, and it is particularly inadvisable to use more humorous euphemisms, such as 'when you've kicked the bucket', even if the person being spoken to uses such terms. They can come across as flippant and can suggest a degree of casualness in the way you or your employer goes about things.

What is absolutely crucial is to be respectful, responsive and sensitive to both the individual and the context of the conversation. Following a script line by line every time is likely to feel cold and impersonal, although having bullet points to help guide you through a conversation or answer specific questions can be useful. Every conversation about a legacy gift should be tailored as much as possible to the individual. Think about their situation and circumstances – this does involve finding out more about them and asking questions. Also think about your particular charity or cause. For example, if you work in a hospice, you may be involved in conversations where death is very close, and it could be completely inappropriate to talk then about a legacy gift. However, if someone is dying in the care of a hospice and does not have a will, they may want to write one and get their affairs in order. The more that you have thought through in advance how best to talk about legacies, the better you will be able to respond to an individual's needs appropriately.

The fundraising message

The fundraising message must be honest and truthful. Facts about the need for legacy gifts must not be exaggerated, nor must the impact that a legacy can have on meeting that need. Particular care is also needed when seeking funding for a specific project or areas of work (see 'Restricted legacy funding', page 32).

The message must be based on factual evidence and you must be able to show independent corroboration for any factual statements made if asked to do so. It must not exploit any vulnerability, credulity or insecurity of any individual and neither must it seek to induce a response based on fear, guilt or coercion.

Particular care needs to be taken over fundraising materials used by third parties (including volunteers). Ideally you should agree all materials beforehand to ensure their accuracy and establish consistency in the message put out across all parts of the organisation and by parties speaking on behalf of the organisation. In practice, this can be difficult – conversations between volunteers and supporters cannot be monitored – but your charity should put in place policies and procedures to ensure as much as possible that legacy fundraising communications are appropriate and done in a way your charity is happy with.

People in vulnerable circumstances

It is important to be aware of and alert to signs that someone is, or might be, in a vulnerable circumstance, and you must never exploit anybody's vulnerability. You must also be aware of issues around mental capacity and an individual's ability to make a valid will (see 'Individuals with low mental capacity' on the following page).

Being older does not in itself mean that an individual is vulnerable, but there are factors that are more prevalent in older age that may mean that individuals need additional care or support. Considered below are some factors or circumstances particularly relevant to legacy fundraising that may indicate vulnerability, but, for more general guidance on responding to the needs of people in vulnerable circumstances, see the Institute of Fundraising's guidance *Treating Donors Fairly*.[8] Your charity will also need to consider whether Disclosure and Barring Service checks need to be undertaken first on any of your fundraising staff before they make direct contact with some key vulnerable groups.

Users of the charity's services

Care should be taken to present any fundraising message in a way that does not deter people from using the charity's services. For example, the availability of a charity's services should not be perceived as being contingent on any donation. It is of course completely acceptable for a service user or beneficiary of a charity to want to leave a legacy to a charity that has provided them with care or support, but this must be free of any pressure to do so.

Terminally ill people

Your charity may decide that legacies should only be solicited from terminally ill people on a face-to-face basis, in the presence of a third party (such as a family member or a staff member of the institution where the person is being cared for), and in light of a careful assessment of the individual's state of mind. Care should also be taken to assess whether any approach (before the face-to-face encounter even takes place) is appropriate in the first place. It is important to be particularly careful as to how your actions could be interpreted by the prospect's friends or family. The presence of a solicitor or will writer can help to ensure that any conversation about a legacy gift is appropriate, but make it clear that you will leave the room at the right time in the conversation, so the lawyer can establish that any legacy to your organisation is freely given, without any coercion or undue influence.

People who are bereaved

You should be aware of the grieving process and how individuals may react differently or need more time before engaging them in any conversation about a legacy. If you encounter a bereaved individual, it is vital to be sensitive to their loss and careful about how to approach any conversation. Any sense that the person is being pushed before they are ready must be avoided. However, the gratitude of a charity, properly expressed, for the compassion shown by the deceased in leaving a legacy to a charitable cause may be a comfort to the bereaved and, in some cases, may even help people with their grieving process.

Next of kin

In addition to the considerations noted above, you will need to allow a suitable interval to pass before seeking to communicate with any next of kin. This period should at least encompass the time it takes for the size of the legacy of the deceased person to become known (if not actually paid) and for any factors relevant to developing a relationship with the next of kin to come to light during the administration. You should also be aware of any potential resentment that a family member may have that what they might perceive as their inheritance has benefitted a charity at all.

Related to this topic is the question of how your charity should communicate with the executors of estates of which it is a beneficiary. Particularly where executors are private individuals, for instance family members of the deceased, great care and sensitivity are required in the choice of words used in communications from the charity, and in their timing. In this respect, Smee & Ford has on its website a very useful webinar titled 'Dear executor: communicating with executors personal & professional'.[9]

Individuals with low mental capacity

While this is more a matter of law than ethics, you will need to be aware of the tests in law of the mental capacity to make a will. This is particularly relevant in face-to-face fundraising. When making a will, individuals must be of sound disposing mind, meaning that they must understand the act of what they are doing in making a will, and the effects of doing so. They must also understand the extent of the property at their disposal and the claims of those to whom they might bequeath their estate.

Undue influence

Be aware that gifts in wills can be set aside if a claim of undue influence (i.e. of the individual having been coerced into giving a legacy) is successfully established. Your charity must recognise when a person's weak health or state of mind could render them susceptible to influence in an unacceptable manner, and know when to refrain from asking for support. In cases where you are unsure, you should make a written note of what passed between your charity and the individual and of matters you consider might be relevant to the issue of susceptibility to influence. Your employer should retain these until the individual dies and only destroy them after obtaining legal advice as to whether to do so.

Restricted legacy funding

A difference between legacy fundraising and other fundraising is that whereas, with other types of fundraising, gifts can be restricted for particular projects, the scope for doing so with legacies can be very limited. This is because a legacy is a future gift whose date of receipt cannot be accurately predicted. It may be paid out many years after the will containing it is written, at a time when the recipient charity may not be performing the activity in question or may not need the funds for that purpose.

There is a win-win approach you can suggest to your supporters, one that meets the charity's need for practicality and the supporter's wish to make a gift to a particular area of work. In this approach, the individual's will specifies a gift for the charity's general purposes but expresses the wish that the legacy is used in the area that the individual wishes to support. In this way, the individual can signal to the charity where they would like their funds to go, but, if for any reason the charity cannot use them in that way, they can be used to meet some other need at the time they are received. Charities are under no legal obligation to take this approach, but there are strong moral arguments for them to do so. Wills containing gifts like this must be correctly worded, which will require them to be drafted by a professional.

Getting a legacy written into a will

It is common practice and entirely acceptable for charities (having taken legal advice) to provide an accurate standard wording to be used by their supporters who wish to leave them gifts. However, while it is permissible for legally qualified charity employees to write wills for their supporters, this should only be undertaken purely as a service, where no fundraising or gift to the charity is concerned. You must not be present at any time during the preparation, drafting and signing of a will containing a gift to your charity, to avoid any potential issues of undue influence.

If the will maker wishes to include a legacy to the charity then, as a general rule, the charity should decline to write the will. Ideally, the will maker should be persuaded to go to a solicitor or will writer who is not connected with the charity, to prevent allegations of undue influence on the part of the charity or want of knowledge and approval on the part of the individual. Unfortunately, though, there can still be individuals who insist that the charity writes the will (or pays a solicitor's fees for doing so) if it wants to receive the potential legacy.

Free will-making schemes are increasingly being promoted by charities to the public (with the charity paying the solicitor's fees) in the hope
that legacies to the paying charity may result. Your charity should ensure
that such schemes do not include any conditions that the charity must be
named in the will. Readers should consult the Charity Commission's
detailed guidance on the subject in its publication 'How to legally raise
money for your charity through legacies and wills', available on its
website.[10]

Providing individuals with lists of solicitors from which to choose a
firm to write their will is acceptable, but charities need to be careful not to
be seen in any way to be endorsing those firms, and so you should provide
a list of no fewer than two firms. Charities are advised to have nothing to
do with will writers who do not possess as a minimum full training in
will-writing and the qualifications of legal executives or solicitors.

Motivations for support

In England and Wales an individual is entirely free to dispose of their
estate as they wish, subject to legislation such as the Inheritance (Provision
for Family and Dependants) Act 1975.[11] However, it is known that some
legacy gifts to a charity are done with a desire to disinherit a relative.
Where your charity knows during the lifetime of the will maker that this is
the reason for a bequest, you should at least advise the individual to review
their will regularly, to ensure that it still reflects their settled intentions.

Internal family politics can be notoriously complex and subject to
change: wherever possible, your charity should not get involved in them.
Encourage will makers to discuss their intentions with close family
members if they mean to make little or no provision for them. You should
also recommend the will maker to seek their own professional legal
advice; this recommendation should be recorded in a letter with a copy
kept on file, and you should additionally recommend the will maker to
keep a copy and explanatory note with their will.

Face-to-face communications

A number of issues arise from face-to-face work. With lonely supporters it
can be difficult to draw the line between business and social involvement,
particularly if you like the individual. If you wish to see the supporter
socially, it is very important to consider at the outset the potentially negative consequences for the charity if the social relationship goes wrong.

In the same context, your charity must have policies covering legacies
made by supporters to charity staff and volunteers themselves (including
wider policies regarding the Bribery Act and the Fundraising Regulator's
Acceptance and Refusal of Donations), and include this in the contract of
employment or volunteering terms and agreement.

Competition and collaboration with other charities

The average charitable will contains legacies to three different charitable organisations,[12] which indicates that donors like to support a range of charitable causes. This is positive in that it shows individuals are committed to a variety of causes, but also means that there is a mutually beneficial impact of good legacy fundraising across the whole sector. It also means, however, that you must be aware of people's desires and preferences. Starting a conversation with an individual about writing a will may lead to another charity receiving a legacy gift. It is important to accept this and put the needs of the potential donor at the heart of the conversation.

Conclusion

Being ethical in legacy fundraising involves a combination of a number of individual things. It means being aware of the rules and regulations; it entails being sensitive, aware and responsive to the needs of different people and supporters; and it requires your charitable organisation to think through its approach, policies and values regarding how it wants its fundraisers to work.

Legacy fundraising is about every organisation taking the time to think about adopting an ethical approach to its fundraising, and realising that sometimes there are no easy answers. The more that your charity thinks through its approach in advance, supports and guides its fundraising teams, gives individual fundraisers the space to make their own judgements and decisions, and recognises that the needs of the supporter or donor come first, the more likely it is that you will be fundraising in the right way.

Notes

1   'Review of fundraising self-regulation' [web page], The National Council for Voluntary Organisations, 2017, www.ncvo.org.uk/fundraisingreview, accessed 30 November 2017.

2   *Code of Fundraising Practice* [PDF], Fundraising Regulator, 2017, www.fundraisingregulator.org.uk/wp-content/uploads/2016/06/Code-of-Fundraising-Practice-v1.4–18102017.pdf, accessed 30 November 2017.

3   See also *Treating Donors Fairly: Fundraising with People in Vulnerable Circumstances* by the Institute of Fundraising. At the time of writing, the PDF is available to download at www.institute-of-fundraising.org.uk/library/treatingdonorsfairly.

4   *Dying: Discussing and planning for end of life* [PDF], British Social Attitudes (NatCen Social Research), 2017, www.bsa.natcen.ac.uk/media/38850/bsa_30_dying.pdf, p. 1, accessed 1 December 2017.

5   'What is a legacy?' [web page], Radcliffe Consulting, 2017, http://radcliffeconsulting.org/legacy-define, accessed 1 December 2017.

6   *Dying: Discussing and planning for end of life* [PDF], British Social Attitudes
     (NatCen Social Research), 2017, www.bsa.natcen.ac.uk/media/38850/
     bsa_30_dying.pdf, pp. 1–2, accessed 1 December 2017.

7   R. J. Russac, Colleen Gatliff, Mimi Reece and Diahann Spottswood, 'Death
     Anxiety Across the Adult Years: An examination of age and gender effects',
     Death Studies, vol. 31, no. 6, 2007, p. 1.

8   *Treating Donors Fairly: Fundraising with people in vulnerable circumstances*
     [PDF], Institute of Fundraising, 2016, www.institute-of-fundraising.org.uk/
     library/treatingdonorsfairly, accessed 1 December 2017.

9   'Dear Executor: Communicating with executors personal & professional'
     [webinar], Smee & Ford, 2016, http://smeeandford.com/webinar/
     watch?title=dear-executor-communicating-with-executors-personal-professional-
     &id=756&watch=0, accessed 1 December 2017.

10   'Raising funds through wills and charitable legacies' [web page], Charity
     Commission, 2013, www.gov.uk/guidance/wills-and-charitable-legacies, accessed
     1 December 2017.

11   'Inheritance (Provision for Family and Dependants) Act 1975' [web page], UK
     Government, 1975, www.legislation.gov.uk/ukpga/1975/63, chapter 63, accessed
     1 December 2017.

12   *Legacy Trends 2017 Update: Discovering potential through data* [PDF], Smee &
     Ford, London, 2017, http://smeeandford.com/whitepaper/index, p. 12, accessed
     9 January 2018.

CHAPTER FOUR

Developing a strategic approach to legacy fundraising

Chris Millward

Introduction

Strategy is, in my opinion, more of an art than a science. It is also something that used to slightly daunt me. But, it turns out it is something I was already doing on a daily basis. There is no such thing as the perfect strategy. They can take many forms – the shortest I ever saw was only three words – and can be expressed in many ways.

Put most simply, your legacy fundraising strategy should be a statement of intent: a road map setting out – based upon insight, resources and buy-in – how you are going to get from where you are to where you want to be.

This chapter sets out several key principles for you to consider to empower you to develop the best strategy you can. Whether you are establishing a legacy fundraising strategy for the first time or refreshing an existing one, these principles will help shape your thinking and enable you to ask the right questions of yourself, your organisation and your supporters.

Legacy fundraising strategy

Are you ready?

The role of legacy fundraiser is not an easy one. However considered your final strategy, your greatest challenge will be engaging others – both internally and externally – to achieve your goals. Tenacity is your watchword. As such, it is important to take a moment towards the beginning of the process to check in with yourself mentally and physically to ensure that you are in good shape for the task ahead. You need to cultivate the best possible mindset to be the most effective ambassador you can be for the organisation and beneficiaries you represent. You also need to ensure that you are mentally ready for the long-term and often frustrating process of bringing the rest of the organisation with you on the journey.

One of the most useful pieces of writing I have seen in this area to best prepare yourself to deliver a successful strategy is Daniel Goleman's book *Emotional Intelligence*.[1] It offers the tools not only for understanding and managing your own emotions but also for how to develop the ability to better understand other people's emotions. This in turn helps you to persuade others, but in an effective way that they welcome, to support you in delivering strategic objectives.

Having a supporter-centred approach

Legacy giving is fundamentally personal. It may be triggered by the death of a person but it is very much a reflection of life. It is an expression of the values an individual holds, the way in which they see the world, the people and causes close to their heart, and how they want others to remember them. Given these very personal considerations which lie at the heart of legacy giving, your approach naturally needs to be as sensitive and personal as it can be.

I have observed a transformation for the better in legacy fundraising in the past decade. Rather than using organisationally driven metrics, it's moved towards a more donor-centred, insight-based, choice-led and collaborative way of working.

The evolution of the supporter journey

This shift towards this supporter-centred approach was precipitated by Remember a Charity's adoption of terms originally used by Prochaska and Velicer in their theoretical model of behavioural change.[2] Although this model is based on insight from a different sector – it was applied by scientists in clinical trials relating to smoking cessation – it provided helpful terminology to describe the process of behavioural change that could be applied in different fields. When the Remember a Charity consortium commissioned research to explore behavioural change, the researchers picked up on this study's approach, and the consortium chose to employ these terms in the context of the legacy fundraising journey.[3]

The model consists of the following five stages:

1. pre-contemplation;

2. contemplation;

3. preparation;

4. action;

5. maintenance.

It should be noted that, as with ceasing smoking, people can fall back as well as move forward along the stages and once in the final stage (maintenance) may not stay there.

I believe that the adoption of this model has helped to cause a shift from using language that implied a charity-centric view of what a supporter had or had not done (i.e. enquirer, considerer, intender, pledger) to a supporter-centric view that focuses on people's mindset. The implication of these terms (which are still used as standard within the technical legacy data and research worlds) is more as a result of how they've been historically employed in the sector, rather than their inherent meanings. The old focus was on counting responses and increasing numbers via an approach of sending a booklet to supporters, which allowed charities to tick a box noting these supporters as 'enquirers'. This led to dangerous and often false measures on impact.

The new model has become the gold standard in legacy activity. It has allowed fundraisers to approach legacy fundraising as a softer, two-way discourse where they can create opportunities and help others to be aware of, and to contemplate, the idea of leaving a gift to charity.

At the NSPCC in 2010, I recall Stephen George leading a new approach, based on this model, recommending the terms 'conversation' and 'consideration' for legacy fundraising. In terms of conversation, he proposed an increase in two-way communication, particularly (where appropriate) face-to-face communication. In terms of consideration, he promoted that supporters should be stewarded as part of a longer-term journey across the five stages – rather than their status remaining, as it did historically, static.

I have observed that the most successful charities are the ones that have placed this model at the heart of their legacy strategy and shifted from an organisational narrative to a more supporter-centred one. Legacy fundraisers from these charities approach the supporter relationship through a wide definition of 'conversation': from a note on a campaign letter to face-to-face meetings.

Optimising the journey

Through the communications you have with your supporters, you can determine at which stage they are in their personal journey. This will allow you to plan better interactions to help them move forward, closer to acting and writing a will or pledging a legacy gift. Over time and through many conversations and other interactions, you can gain the insight and experience to better understand what is most likely to encourage your donors to move forward: based on supporter insight rather than false metrics. You can also learn from the times when they fall back in the model to an earlier – less engaged – stage.

Understanding your world

To articulate a strategy, the first thing you need to do is understand the external environment in which you are operating and then gain an understanding of your internal environment (your own organisation's capabilities) – the issues that will directly have a bearing on your legacy marketing strategy. Be sure to explore these areas with a number of people so you can get the benefit of different perspectives and experiences.

The external environment

A good starting point for any strategy development work is a clear understanding of the external environment in which you are working. What sources of information are available to help you better understand this?

A picture of the legacy marketplace at the time of publication is shared in chapter 1, which is informed by experience from Legacy Foresight, a commercial organisation which offers market insight, bespoke forecasting and tailored research. Legacy Foresight publishes regular updates on the performance of the legacy marketplace and is one source of information that can help you understand the context in which you are working.

Another useful organisation is Smee & Ford, which provides a subscription notification service for charities allowing them to be aware of any legacy gifts they have been left. Smee & Ford can also provide information on legacy trends and bespoke analysis to help inform your strategy development.

In addition, the Remember a Charity campaign is a consortium of charities working together to try to normalise legacy giving in the UK. Remember a Charity works with charities, solicitors and consumers to build greater understanding and increase participation in will-writing and legacy giving. Your charity can gain a helpful source of insight by being a member of the consortium.

Whichever sources of information you decide to use, you will be looking to gather information on, for example:

• demographic changes affecting legacy giving;

• current economic factors that may have an influence;

• relevant perceptions and attitudes.

The internal environment

The performance of your organisation and how it is perceived by others can have a fundamental influence – for good or bad – on your legacy strategy. You will need to consider how this might affect your overall approach. Questions to ask include:

• What does the overall organisational strategy look like, and how can a legacy strategy fit with and support this?

• How is your organisation perceived externally, and how might this influence or impact on your legacy strategy?

• How established is your organisation's fundraising programme, and what opportunities or threats does this present?

• What level of internal support is there for legacy fundraising, and how might this impact upon your activity? How can you overcome this?

Organising your analysis

One of the simplest ways to organise and interpret the information you've gathered about your internal and external environments is by using a SWOT (strengths, weaknesses, opportunities and threats) analysis.

Figure 4.1 shows an example SWOT analysis with a few thoughts based on some current conditions in the external environment and a few hypothetical internal issues. These examples are, of course, just for illustration and aren't intended to form a prescriptive template.

If you would like to explore external factors further, you can also use a SLEPT analysis, which is focused purely on external factors (social, legal, economic, political and technological).

The completed SWOT analysis can help inform your objectives and your tactics (see 'Setting your objectives' and 'Choosing your tactics' below): you might be able to solve some of the issues you identify by taking advantage of your strengths or of untapped external opportunities. In addition, you may need to invest time or money in training or other solutions to fill in the gaps that will allow you to achieve your objectives. For example, from this SWOT analysis there's an opportunity to influence the organisation's short-term financial thinking by taking advantage of good supporter data. The current lack of data analysis capacity is then a gap that would need to be filled to achieve that objective.

FIGURE 4.1 AN EXAMPLE SWOT (STRENGTHS, WEAKNESSES, OPPORTUNITIES AND THREATS) ANALYSIS

Strengths (internal)

- A strong organisational brand: good brand recognition (24% spontaneous awareness and 67% total awareness) and known for being ethical and effective
- Trustees and leadership team open to change and influence
- A small but strong legacy team with a compelling legacy message
- Widely and consistently recorded data on supporters
- Good training skills and experience within the legacy team

Weaknesses (internal)

- Not enough resources allocated to legacy fundraising as a result of our organisational strategy's priorities
- Short-term financial thinking
- No current capacity to conduct data analysis to identify the best audiences to target
- Legacies are not integrated across the organisation
- Lack of understanding of legacies in other teams and reluctance to engage (due to lack of knowledge)

Opportunities (external)

- Changing demographics: realisation of legacy income owing to age of baby boomers
- Projected increase in women aged 60 or over dying child-free (known factor of higher likelihood of legacy giving)
- Baby boomers' different perceptions from previous generations: more willing to support charity, not only distant relatives
- Increase in percentage of supporters writing wills overall thanks to Remember a Charity campaign/legal will-writing services

Threats (external)

- How people perceive 'legacies' – a lack of understanding and reluctance as a result
- Perception of not having money to leave to charity because of family and/or care costs
- Changing attitudes to charities owing to negative media stories of charities haranguing supporters
- Unknown ramifications of Brexit: impact on estate values and therefore residual legacy values
- Only half of legacies remain in wills for ten+ years

Defining your strategy

Establishing your mission

To be the most effective legacy ambassador you can, it's vital to establish not only a shared plan of action but also a unifying purpose for that plan. Simon Sinek, in his Ted Talk 'How Great Leaders Inspire Action', looks at both this issue and why some organisations are more successful than others. His thesis is that the most successful leaders and organisations are the ones that have a clear sense of purpose or mission: their 'why'. In all that they do, they focus on that shared purpose rather than the 'what' or the 'how' of their business – as Sinek terms it in his book of the same name,[4] they 'start with why'.

41

This way of working reflects the way in which our brains work biologically. Our limbic brain – the part of our brain responsible for all human behaviour and feelings such as trust and loyalty – corresponds to the 'why' and the 'how' of Sinek's model. The neocortex – responsible for rational and analytical thought – represents the 'what'. When you start with why, you talk directly to the part of the brain that controls behaviour, and you are more likely to influence change. While charities naturally grow from a sense of mission, I believe that legacy fundraising has become too preoccupied with the mechanics of what we do rather than the why of our inspirational purpose – something which we all need to remember.

The internal legacy mission I put in place while at Save the Children was:

> To ensure **everyone** who believes in our cause has the opportunity to **consider** supporting our work with a gift in their will.

This simple expression of our purpose created a clear focus for our activity by setting out the scale of our ambition and highlighting some of the key principles by which we would work.

In turn, you can express this as a vision: your view of the future that you want to see. So, in this case:

> A world where everyone who believes in our cause has considered supporting our work with a gift in their will.

Setting your objectives

It is important to set clear objectives for any strategy. What does success look like? What milestones will you need to achieve along the way? It is important when setting these objectives to speak to internal colleagues – fundraising, finance, data, legal – to ensure shared understanding and ownership. A few potential objectives could include the following:

• Increase overall legacy income (e.g. X no of legacies from Y people).

• Grow the level of support from existing supporters (e.g. optimise current channels to provide opportunities for consideration).

• Increase the pool of support through external acquisition (e.g. consider will-writing schemes, consortia, digital activities and events to reach new audiences).

• Increase engagement with and stewardship of existing prospects (e.g. undertake tailored activities for supporters at different stages to optimise conversion of support to a gift).

• Increase knowledge and understanding of donor motivation and commitment (e.g. looking further than transactional measures – such as recency, frequency and value[5] – to identify prospects).

The objectives you set will depend upon your overall organisational strategy, the opportunities and threats you identified as part of your SWOT analysis, the donor and market insight available to inform your planning and the scale of the vision you have set. Review progress on an ongoing basis and revise objectives as necessary based upon new insights and learning.

Choosing your performance measures

As with any strategy, it is important to be able to measure the impact of your work. Measurement of the effectiveness of legacy campaigns has historically been difficult, and it has especially been tricky to draw causal links between marketing spend and legacy income. It is important, however, to measure whatever you can in order to be best informed about the impact you are having. Your ability to better demonstrate the impact of your work will increase your ability to influence internally and to secure buy-in and resources to further your efforts.

Measurement of legacy activities should take place over the short, medium and long term. Identify the things you want to be able to report on, and if you can't already measure them look for creative ways to do so. Whatever you choose to measure, make sure you do this consistently over time: legacy impact reporting is a long-term project. Some potential measures are shown in table 4.1.

TABLE 4.1 EXAMPLES OF SHORT-, MEDIUM-, AND LONG-TERM MEASURES OF LEGACY ACTIVITIES

Short	Campaign-specific measures such as numbers relating to:
	• reach;
	• open rates;
	• interaction;
	• responses;
	• people at each stage of consideration in the legacy supporter journey (pre-contemplation, contemplation, preparation, action, maintenance);
	• cost per response.

Medium	Measures concerning the impact of the marketing activity. For example: • reach (in terms of how many people on your database have seen a legacy message (directly or indirectly)); • number of responses; • percentage of supporters at each stage of the legacy supporter journey; • number of positive (and negative) moves over time between categories, for example progressing from preparation to action, or falling back to contemplation after having taken action); • cost of activities to get supporters to action stage.
Long	Measures such as: • number and value of gifts; • percentage of legacy gifts from those people known to organisation; • percentage of legacy gifts from those people known to the legacy team (your reach will always be wider than your known pool); • ages of pledgers or legators; • locations of pledgers or legators; • profiles of pledgers or legators;[6] • conversion rates to legator. This stage requires close collaboration between the fundraising and administration teams to bring both sides of the legacy-giving journey together. Legacy fundraising and legacy administration are two sides of the same coin and you need to measure and record findings on both sides (see chapter 20 for detail on legacy administration). Don't think about key performance indicators in isolation.

Choosing your tactics

Having established the objectives of your legacy fundraising strategy and how you will measure success, the next step is to decide which activities (tactics) you will undertake to achieve those objectives. The plan you put together will be enabled or limited by a number of things, including the resources you have available and the access you have to existing supporters and communications channels. You will have already considered these aspects in your SWOT analysis in the context of your organisation's strengths and weaknesses.

Here are a few simplified examples of activities, using the objectives outlined above as a starting point:

• To grow the level of support from existing supporters, we will use our in-house data expert to identify the audience groups we should communicate with for more effective engagement.

• To increase our pool of support, we will join and take part in the Remember a Charity consortium activities, including the Remember a Charity week.

• To increase engagement with and stewardship of existing prospects, we will use dedicated mailings for pledgers as well as those individuals who have visited our charitable projects.

• To increase knowledge and understanding of donor commitment we will look at how long supporters have been on our database, the ways individuals have supported our cause and how actively they have engaged or responded to our communications.

• To increase knowledge and understanding of donor motivation, we will ask people who have decided to support our charity (in any way) or to leave gifts why they are doing so; we will do this for legacy gifts already received by asking next of kin via our legacy administrator.

Case study: Building trust with branches

As Head of Legacies at Save the Children I was aware of the critical role community fundraising teams played in supporting conversations with some of the charity's warmest and longest-standing supporters – some of the most committed of whom were members of local branches of the charity.

Historically, engagement between community fundraising, and branches in particular, and the legacy team had been problematic – leading to feelings of mistrust and resentment. Our team identified this as one of our internal weaknesses, and as a result made it a priority to rebuild trust and work out how best we might support each other. With the community fundraising teams, we identified two key ways in which we could work more collaboratively.

Through responses to a branch survey we discovered that one-third of members who had responded to our survey had already included a gift in their will to Save the Children. As a result, we focused our resources on helping the community team to acknowledge this vital support and to demonstrate the potential future impact of these gifts. This was of mutual benefit both in terms of how engaged and recognised current branch members felt and the safeguarding of future legacy income potential.

In addition, the community team led on an overall review of branches and identified that some branches were financially viable and others had declining income. As a result, the community team created a new strategy – part of which supported the managed decline of the less sustainable branches. Given the previously identified pool of potential future legacy gifts from branch members it was vital that this was done in such a way as to safeguard the pledged gifts and potential future income. The legacy team responded by seeking new ways to help branches and, as a result, dealt with the administration of gifts received from former members and took responsibility for the ongoing communication relating to closed branches.

Harnessing your means

Internal collaboration

Internal communication plays a vital role in helping others to understand the critical contribution legacy gifts make. Be sure to communicate your internal mission and vision for legacy giving (see 'Establishing your mission', page 41) in order to help others to understand how they can best support your strategy and the outcomes you are trying to achieve.

A good overall approach when working with others, is to think about the positive benefits they and their audiences can gain from engaging with legacy giving. How can you help them to achieve their objectives? By considering the needs of others first, you are more likely to be able to influence their ways of working and agree goals that they will want to achieve.

Influencing fundraising colleagues

All charity employees have a critical part to play in supporting legacy fundraising activity, but in particular, other fundraising colleagues as regards access to and influence of existing supporters. It is important that internal communication activities are undertaken to help raise awareness and increase general knowledge and understanding of legacy giving. The aim should be to create informed ambassadors who can help to support your overall strategy.

Influencing key stakeholders

When discussing the impact of legacy gifts with other internal stakeholders, it is important to tailor your message according to the audience. For service colleagues, the message will centre on the critical contribution they make;

for finance colleagues, the message will concern the usually unrestricted nature of the gifts and the operational flexibility this brings; and, for fundraising colleagues, the message will emphasise the valuable contribution legacy gifts can make in terms of overall income. Finding the right stories to tell will help you to create a positive internal climate which will work in your favour when trying to secure future buy-in and resources.

Case study: Internal awareness campaign

As Legacy Promotions Manager for Macmillan Cancer Support, I ran an annual internal awareness campaign for legacy giving to engage staff. As many of our colleagues were younger and therefore may not have thought about legacy giving before, in our first year we focused on raising the profile of the legacy team and general levels of understanding in relation to legacy-related issues.

In our second year the legacy team provided all staff with the opportunity to have their will written in the belief that those who had been through the process were more likely to have a better understanding and be better able to talk to others about it in a more informed way.

In year three we set targets for specific groups to drive activity and encourage staff to have proactive conversations with supporters about legacy giving.

Internal campaigns proved a great way to build awareness and understanding of legacy giving.

External resources

Remember a Charity

The Remember a Charity campaign is a consortium of approximately 200 charities working together with pooled resources and a collective voice with the aim of growing the UK legacy market. The campaign's ambition is to make legacy giving a social norm – something it believes no single organisation can achieve on its own. It runs an annual awareness campaign and also a solicitor engagement programme which, among other things, encourages solicitors to sign up to its Campaign Supporter Charter, which includes making their clients aware of the possibility of leaving gifts to charities. To support these campaigns and programmes it provides content and platforms that charities can piggyback their own activity onto and make use of their supporting materials (for example creative executions, toolkits and so on). Remember a Charity also supports member charities' activities by providing a platform for legacy fundraisers to talk internally about legacy giving to inform and influence senior stakeholders and colleagues.

Will-writing schemes and working with solicitors

Solicitors play a critical role in the legacy-giving process through prompting potential donors to leave gifts in their wills but also through their involvement in the administration of estates. As a result, many charities choose to form partnerships with firms of solicitors to encourage people to write their wills, providing a practical solution to overcome the barriers to will-writing. These partnerships can take several forms:

• individual schemes between charities and firms – such as Cancer Research UK's Free Will Service;[7]

• groups of charities working together as a consortium – such as Will Aid;

• groups of charities through initiatives such as Free Wills Month and the Free Wills Network (run by Capacity Marketing for Charities);[8]

• online or digital campaigns.

Will-writing schemes aren't for every charity. Think carefully about what might work best for you and your supporters. Further guidance on charities paying for will-writing is available from the Fundraising Regulator and the Charity Commission.[9] It is also worth consulting guidance on HM Revenue & Customs' donor benefit rules, a clear and helpful version of which can be found on the Institute of Fundraising's website.[10]

Legacy marketing strategy

Understanding your audience

It is important to understand the various reasons why people support your cause as this will have a fundamental impact upon the approach you use to engage them in legacy giving. For example, how might the approach of a charity related to causes of death, such as Macmillan Cancer Support, differ from that of a loved-in-life organisation such as the RSPCA? What impact might this have on target audience, channel selection, and the tone and content of messaging? You will need to think carefully about who you are talking to and how best to engage and inspire them.

Differing generational attitudes are also important to consider when deciding upon your campaign messages. You may be communicating with and seeking to influence the behaviour of several generations across the stages of the legacy journey or targeting particular groups. Questions to consider include:

• How should you be communicating with the civically responsible and duty-driven older generation?

• How can you best reflect and meet the needs of the baby boomer generation? This generation tends to seek greater control and a desire to define their deaths – as they have their lives – in their own way.

• What approach should you be taking to engage with the millennial generation? What new channels and propositions do you need to develop to secure their future support?

• How does each of these groups want to be recognised and thanked – if at all – for their gifts?

Acknowledging these differences will help you to optimise the legacy journey for each of these groups, increasing the likelihood of their consideration and ultimately of them leaving a gift in their will.

Personalising your message

In his presentation 'Planned Giving and the Brain', Russell James outlines his fMRI experiment, in which researchers scanned men's brains while they were contemplating decisions on charitable giving, volunteering and leaving legacy gifts. He reported that the core areas of the brain which are activated are those used when people visually recall vivid personal events in their lives from a third-person perspective. He terms this a 'visual auto-biography'. These areas of the brain are also activated when people recall memories of a loved one who died recently, and generally by reminders of death.[11] This research shows how legacy giving is different from other forms of giving: the contemplation of it evokes fundamental and powerful emotions about people's lives, decisions and loves.

Inspiring supporters

The potential implications Russell James notes that are worth considering when planning legacy marketing strategies are that you should:

• focus on a person's significant life experiences as opposed to your charity's or beneficiaries' needs for the funds;

• take into account the idea of having symbolic immortality (and the link of this desire with those who do not have children) and how this can apply to people leaving money in the name of a deceased loved one (as a tribute gift) or leaving a lasting gift to an established organisation in the form of an endowment, a named building, a fund and so on.

This research is backed up by James's later research, outlined in chapter 2, which underlines the importance of appealing to people's life experiences and, to a lesser but still important extent, to the idea of living on by creating an impact after death.

In these ways, it is important to ensure that the legacy fundraising process is a personalised one. You must reach out to and communicate with people in such a way that inspires them to want to support your cause with a gift in their will. Focusing on the mechanics (i.e. how to write or update a will: the 'what') will leave people better informed about will-writing and legacy giving and remove some barriers (as outlined in the next section) but it will not necessarily result in behavioural change.

Creating impact through your language

It is important to remember the powerful impact language can have. You make an impact on people at a personal, not organisational, level and by using collaborative language (rather than a one-way monologue). When communicating with donors, be mindful of the language you use: less 'we' and 'our' and more 'you' and 'your' (for more on the use of language see 'Legacy language' on page 23). Legacy strategies, and the communications that are rooted within them, should seek to promote a two-way dialogue between charity and donor and provide opportunities for engagement and feedback. Building insight through more two-way communication with donors and other key stakeholders will enable you to provide a more personalised approach – one which is most likely in the longer term to produce positive results.

Overcoming barriers

While the removal of barriers may not move someone to take action, it will reduce the probability of people putting off making a will and the opportunity to include a legacy gift. In addition to helping people understand how to make or update a will you can make use of the following approaches.

Making use of time limits and appointments

One of Russell James's recommendations as a result of his fMRI study is that we need to be aware of the likelihood that people will want to avoid or postpone dealing with the subject of mortality, so it is wise to use tactics such as using deadlines, making appointments with prospective pledgers and having campaigns with time limits. Will Aid, which only runs for one month a year in November, is a good example of a time-limited campaign.

Repositioning the legacy ask

Historically, legacy gifts have been positioned as 'the most significant gift someone can make'. Instead, legacy giving should be positioned as 'the next logical step in someone's support' or 'the best way to continue your support after you have gone' so as to normalise and overcome perceived barriers to consideration. It should be something that everyone has the opportunity to consider. If you are still using the historical approach, consider how you can ensure legacy gifts become part of every donor's journey.

For more details on this subject, see 'The barriers and motivators to legacy giving' on page 151.

Targeting your legacy marketing approaches

As a starting point, the best responses to your legacy marketing approaches are likely to come from those donors you already have an existing relationship with. Think of this process like an onion, starting with your strongest supporters (regular or one-off cash givers) followed by supporters in your wider networks (community, retail, committees, etc.). In terms of targeting, thereafter it is about finding the people who are the most likely to have an affinity with your cause and approaching them using the most appropriate channel, depending on the audience.

To optimise your approach, think about what has worked well before. Review any available communications histories and campaign results to inform your activity. The learning and the resulting approach will be unique to your organisation and your supporters. Do what feels right for you; don't feel you must follow the crowd.

Choosing your channels

Start by understanding what existing donor communications channels there are within your organisation. Utilising these to share your legacy message not only is cost-effective but also will help to ensure that your legacy messaging is incorporated into ongoing communications, helping to normalise it within supporters' minds. Newsletters, websites, events and annual reports are all great opportunities.

Depending upon the objectives of your strategy and the resources available to you, the most logical next step is usually to think about stand-alone legacy-specific activities. Each channel has its respective pros and cons – reach, level of engagement, response rates, etc. – and you will need to think about which is the most appropriate. A few thoughts on the respective merits of each follow.

Email

- Pros: cost-effective, interactive

- Cons: low response, disposable, low-level interaction

Mail

• Pros: a method supporters are likely to be familiar with, cost-effective, scalable

• Cons: low open rates, highly competitive (has to stand out from other items that fall onto supporters' doormats), low response, less engaging and interactive

Telephone

• Pros: quality interaction, conversational, personal, tailorable, high response rates

• Cons: costly, potentially intrusive, restricted by data permissions (such as via the Telephone Preference Service)

Events

• Pros: quality face-to-face contact, provides an opportunity to use a show-and-tell style and to engage with supporters on a more emotional level

• Cons: doesn't work for all causes, can be resource-heavy, may be good for awareness but not action, often requires the buy-in of others (such as services, community and volunteering) to deliver

Informing your targeting and channels with data

Data is an important tool which can help to inform your marketing approaches. It can provide insight but ultimately it's down to you to make decisions about how you use it.

Data is traditionally used to narrow selections down to identify your best prospects. But it can also be used to inform channel selection, i.e. which channels you will use to communicate with supporters such as newsletters, email, events and your website – allowing the greatest number of people to be reached in the most cost-effective way. Lower-cost channels, such as email, provide an opportunity to increase the number of supporters you can contact while higher-cost channels such as telephone can be reserved for the prospects identified as having greatest potential.

Transactional metrics such as recency, frequency and value are useful but they give no indication as to the motivation behind someone's support or the depth of their affinity. Think about what other forms of data you could look at to allow you to make more informed selections. Examples include how long supporters have been on your database, the number of different ways in which individuals have supported your cause (for example, do they just give money, or have they also volunteered or supported in other ways?) and how actively they have engaged or responded to your communications).

For an in-depth exploration of using data analysis to target potential pledgers, see chapter 9.

Integrating your message

Legacy messaging should be integrated across all communications channels to normalise it alongside other forms of support. Once donors have engaged with legacy messaging, you must ensure their experience remains consistent. So I recommend as best practice, if possible, that you don't withdraw your established communications with pledgers or contemplators by replacing them with new stand-alone legacy communications programmes. If they are used to the communications they already receive from you and they are clear, don't muddy the message. Instead, that new legacy message needs to be woven into existing communications.

But you do need to acknowledge the additional commitment they have made and include thanks for this within ongoing stewardship activities and via communications that reach the donor. Consider creating legacy segments within existing programmes so that people with a known legacy status can be treated appropriately and content tailored to them accordingly. It is also worth reviewing how to further enhance the experience of this group through cross-selling of other products (special events, thank-yous, impact reports, etc.).

Case study: Integrating major donor and legacy fundraising messaging

While I was Head of Legacies at Save the Children, I implemented a joint strategy in collaboration with the major donor team to ensure legacy-related messaging was considered as part of the initial planning process for stewardship of major donor prospects. This was established by influencing colleagues, including the Director of Major Donors and his team, to include prompts in internal documentation used by the team to plan the stewardship of individual major donors. This didn't guarantee that the major donor team would incorporate a legacy ask for each major donor prospect but it did mean that individual major donor officers had to consider whether or not it might be appropriate at any point in the plan to make such an ask as part of their overall solicitation.

We also investigated the overlap between legacy pledgers and major donor prospects. This allowed us to identify around 200

53

donors who were both within the major donor stewardship programme and who were known to be considering leaving a legacy to Save the Children.

This collaboration enabled the legacy and major donor teams to consider the overlap in roles and in our potential donors and pledgers and to establish a joint stewardship programme, allowing the major donor fundraisers to lead the relationship but also for legacy messages to be incorporated appropriately. Major donor events were also used, where appropriate, as stewardship opportunities for legacy prospects. It was a great way to enhance their knowledge of Save the Children's work, increase their engagement and demonstrate the potential impact of their gift.

Implementing your strategies

The importance of consistency

It is important to ensure – as far as possible – a consistent approach in the implementation of your legacy fundraising and marketing strategies. Changes in personnel all too often result in the review and subsequent revision of the approach. Only by retaining consistency will you ever be able to see the true impact of your work and in time draw causal relationships between your legacy marketing activity and income.

Communicating the strategies clearly

You need to make sure that your strategies are robust and concise enough for you to be able to explain them in a clear, succinct and (most importantly) compelling way to others. Think about how you want to engage and influence specific groups and what messages may be most appropriate for them. Depending upon who you are talking to you are likely to want to focus on different parts of your overall strategy. For instance, the members of your senior leadership team are likely to want to know about different things than, say, your volunteers.

Continuing to learn and innovate

When you are implementing your strategies and delivering activities/ tactics, it is important to keep both fresh by continuing to gather insight and then applying what you learn. Your overall approach may need to evolve in response to organisational, marketplace or donor changes. Evolving in this way will help you to optimise the impact of your work for current beneficiaries and to ensure you continue to engage and inspire future generations of supporters.

Case study: Virtual visits

Save the Children's legacy team was one of the first to use online virtual visits as part of its stewardship programme. The team used these as a conversion tool for those who had previously indicated that they would consider leaving a gift in their will but had taken no further action.

Supporters logged into a website via which they were taken on a guided tour of projects by one of the field workers (who joined by telephone from the host country). Video, pictures and commentary were used to create an interactive experience to engage and inspire supporters to take the next step on their legacy-giving journey.

Case study: Digital acquisition

When I was at Save the Children, having initially concentrated on the promotion of legacy giving to existing supporters and through the charity's networks, in the third year of our strategy my colleagues and I expanded the programme to incorporate acquisition activity. We used digital banner advertising and affiliate marketing to achieve this. Using these channels meant we could gather insights quickly and scale up or down as required based upon the results.

This proved a highly successful campaign, attracting many new potential donors to Save the Children – over one-third of whom signed up to receive further information on other ways of giving and our services.

Conclusion

To conclude, the following checklist may help you to formulate your legacy fundraising and marketing strategies.

Lay strong foundations

• Am I ready?

• Have we put supporters at the centre of our strategy?

• Do we have ways to manage the responses and insight we're going to gather from supporters?

• Have we thought about how we will optimise the donor journey?

Know where you're starting from

- Do we understand the external environment?

- Do we understand the internal context?

- Are we familiar with the most recent research and insights in legacy giving?

- Do I have a way to organise the information I've gathered with my team?

Establish a shared purpose

- Can we clearly express our legacy mission and vision?

- Are others on board with what we're trying to achieve?

- Do we know how we're going to sustain resources and buy-in from others to ensure consistency?

Know where you're heading

- Have we set clear objectives?

- Do we understand how these fit with our organisation's wider strategy?

- Have we identified the right activities to achieve our objectives?

Measure and communicate your impact

- Have we established clear measures of success for our campaign?

- Are we measuring impact in the long, medium and short term?

- How will we share success with internal stakeholders?

Build networks and influence

- How clearly do we understand the objectives of our colleagues?

- Can we clearly express the benefits of engaging with legacy giving for our colleagues?

- How are we collaborating with others to achieve our objectives?

- Are we best using external consortia and initiatives to the benefit of our organisation?

Understand your supporters

- Do we understand the motivations of our donors?

- Do we understand how to communicate differently to separate audiences?

- What can we learn from historical activity to inform our actions?

Keep it personal

- Have we developed an inspirational donor proposition for legacy giving?

- Are we talking about legacies in a way that removes rather than reinforces barriers for supporters?

- Are we using the right language in our communications to create the most impact?

Tailor your approach

- What do we know about our prospects and donors that would allow us to tailor our messaging?

- Do we understand the channels available to us and their respective pros and cons?

- How can we use data and insights to inform our targeting and channel choices?

- Is legacy messaging integrated across all communications channels?

Implement and keep it fresh

- Are we being consistent and communicating our strategies clearly?

- How have innovation and testing activities been incorporated into our plan?

• Are we seeking out new developments and insight and evolving as a result?

• How can we continue to optimise the conversion of donors from contemplation to action?

Notes

1   Daniel Goleman, *Emotional Intelligence: Why It Can Matter More Than IQ*, London, Bloomsbury, 1996.
2   James Prochaska and Wayne Velicer, 'The Transtheoretical Model of Health Behavior Change', *American Journal of Health Promotion*, vol. 12, no. 1, 1997, pp. 38–48.
3   The Commission on the Donor Experience, 'CDE project 10 section 3: putting the donor-led experience at the heart of legacy fundraising growth' [web article], SOFII, http://sofii.org/article/cde-project-10-section-3, 28 April 2017.
4   Simon Sinek, *Start with Why*, London, Penguin, 2011.
5   A supporter list can be segmented by these metrics: (1) when a donor last gave, i.e. recency; (2) how many interactions the donor had with the organisation over a given timescale, i.e. frequency; and (3) the individual donation amount, i.e. value.
6   See, for example, 'What is Acorn' [web page], CACI Ltd, https:// acorn.caci.co.uk, accessed 9 January 2017; Acorn is a segmentation tool which provides information to organisations to allow them to target prospects more effectively.
7   'Free Will Service' [web page], Cancer Research UK, 2017, www.cancerresearchuk.org/support-us/donate/leave-a-legacy-gift-in-your-will/ free-will-service, accessed 6 December 2017.
8   'Legacy Marketing for Charities' [web page], Capacity Marketing, 2017, https:// capacity-marketing.com, accessed 1 December 2017.
9   'Raising funds through wills and charitable legacies' [web page], Charity Commission, 2013, www.gov.uk/guidance/wills-and-charitable-legacies, accessed 1 December 2017.
10   'Benefit rules' [web page], Institute of Fundraising, 2017, www.institute-of-fundraising.org.uk/guidance/fundraising-essentials-legislation/tax-effective-giving/ gift-aid/benefit-rules, accessed 6 December 2017.
11   'Planned Giving and The Brain', presented by Russell James for the Department of Personal Financial Planning, Texas Tech University, at Erasmus University Centre for Strategic Philanthropy, Rotterdam, The Netherlands, 2 April 2012.

CHAPTER FIVE

Integrating legacies into your overall fundraising strategy

Stephen George

Introduction

The subject of integration in charity fundraising has become a key topic that is widely discussed and considered. For many, integration of fundraising across the organisation feels like a sort of holy grail – desirable but out of reach. In my experience, most people, if asked, would say a cohesive approach is not only right but also necessary.

Overall, charities are realising that to be truly successful with legacy fundraising they need to ensure that legacies are integrated into their wider fundraising strategy so that the whole organisation, including non-fundraisers, can talk about the issues surrounding legacy giving with confidence. However, with the perceived taboos surrounding death and money, this can be difficult to achieve.

This chapter will focus on practical steps you can take to help your organisation achieve the level of integration it needs for success.

Integration at an organisational level

What is integration?

What is meant by integration in this context? At its very simplest, it is about taking a joined-up approach and aligning an organisation's values with those of the people who work in it.

In the commercial sector, a product requires an integrated approach within a company so that it can be moved in a streamlined way from inception to creation, then through distribution centres and sales outlets to the customer.

Many commercial operations have few conflicting demands. The company's purpose is to make a profit through the distribution of its services or products, and creating the right customer experience is often crucial to the profitability of the company. Companies that have a joined-up approach, with the customer at the heart, offer a consistent service and experience so that each part of the organisation is working towards the same end goal: namely the customer's satisfaction and the company's profit.

Despite this relative lack of conflicting demands, however, it can be difficult to create such a level of integration of values within companies. A survey of over 50,000 employees worldwide, for example, found that 33% don't believe their company's core values align with their personal values.[1]

Charities have a natural advantage over commercial organisations in that they are created with an explicit mission to make a positive change in society. Many people are drawn to work for a particular charity because their values align with the organisation's. Nevertheless, charities are complex, with conflicting demands, diverse audiences and complicated infrastructure. Staff often end up working in silos and can lose sight of the organisation's overall purpose and how all parts of the charity need to be working together to achieve the same aim. In this way, it is similarly difficult to create an integrated environment as it is in commercial organisations, even when the leadership is in in place with the intention and means to try.

The costs of a lack of integration

For both the commercial and charity sectors, a lack of integration can lead to a lack of co-ordination and to waste, inefficiency, increased costs and poor service. A lack of a cohesive approach to behaviours, policies and the organisation's purpose and values can also cause a low level of staff engagement and, as such, reduce how effective organisations can be at realising the outputs and outcomes they want to achieve. Having a system to unify these elements is crucial to delivering a successful customer or donor experience.

Starting with your charity's purpose and values

To have the highest chance of creating the type of environment that produces a well-integrated donor experience, you will need to focus on aligning the values of your staff and volunteers with the *why* at the very heart of your charity's mission and its values. You will also need to link your charity's overall purpose to your legacy fundraising purpose and the strategic reasoning behind it (as outlined in building block 1 below).

This link needs to be regularly reinforced so that staff are reminded of why they do what they do. This should be done through all areas and departments and, most importantly, through leadership.

Integration of fundraising

Fundraising is a natural area where charities can integrate their various approaches effectively. The organisation's need for income to achieve its mission should be a paramount concern and unifying opportunity, and therefore the whole organisation should contribute in order to deliver fundraised income. But, even within a relatively cohesive environment, fundraising techniques can operate in ways that don't seem joined up.

the population is projected to continue ageing, with the average (median) age rising from 40.0 years in 2014 to 40.9 years in mid-2024 and 42.9 by mid-2039.[5] In mid-2016 there were 1.6 million people aged 85 and over; by mid-2041, it is projected that this number will double to 3.2 million.[6]

These figures can help everyone in your organisation to realise there is a crucial opportunity where they can offer supporters in these groups the chance to leave a gift to your charity in their will. This is particularly important for your organisation's older supporters.

In addition, given that the number of supporters at an older age will continue to grow, the opportunity for raising money is not just a long-term goal, important as that is. The more this way of giving feels normal, available and accessible to your supporters, the more likely it will be that you start raising money sooner. The important strategic goal is to build future value today within the changed market of firstly more people, and secondly an increased ability to give. Future value, not short-term cash must be the goal.

2. Increasing amounts of wealth

The second driver is the wealth of these people. Strategy& and Pricewater-houseCoopers estimate that 36% of the UK's total liquid wealth (£1.7 trillion) will be in the hands of retirees between the years 2017 and 2027.[7]

If we place charity and leaving a legacy as a compelling proposition and a new social norm alongside the rightful transfer of assets to family and friends, we – all of us working within and with charities – could transform giving and charitable impact sooner rather than later.

3. Higher levels of technology use

The third driver is technology. According to the Office for National Statistics, internet use among 65- to 74-year-olds in the UK increased to 78% in 2017 from 52% in 2011[8] and one in four over-65s in the UK are now using social networking sites.[9] While there is an increase in the tech knowledge of the existing older demographic, the members of the generation that will become the oldest generation in the next 30 years are already tech savvy. For them, this is the norm.

The availability and access to this technology and social media provide a huge chance to develop a soft, conversational approach around stories and information about legacy-giving, and to inspire people to leave charitable legacies in their wills.

4. Motivation to do good and be remembered

The fourth driver is motivation to do good and to be remembered: powerful factors in driving the wider concept of legacy. With people aged 65 to 74 being the most likely to volunteer at least once a month,[10] the spirit of giving and the motivation to give are strong for the baby boomer genera-tion, and the generation before. This suggests that people in these generations are likely to welcome being given the opportunity to leave a gift to charity, and also that staff in your organisation will naturally have an affinity with supporters regarding these motivations.

5. Changes in donor behaviour

The final driver is donor behaviour. In terms of legacies, there has already been an increase in those considering leaving a gift in their will (see 'Will-writing analysis on page 103) and a rise in those who do so.[11] Alongside this, I have observed changes in other behaviour, especially in baby boom-ers. Specifically, people want more choice and value, transparency and engagement, and they are using the internet to conduct research and engage with organisations.

By understanding this behaviour and realising that there is a growing trend in leaving gifts in wills to charities, staff can be both reassured that this form of giving is steadily becoming normalised and staff are increas-ingly becoming equipped with the knowledge of how best to inspire and engage with this generation.

These five factors can be used to demonstrate that opportunities and a market exist for legacy fundraising, and that your charity needs to have in place a plan and a strategy to take account of these possibilities.

Building block 2: Communicating strategic reasoning through leadership

To successfully articulate the purpose and reasoning around why integra-tion is right for legacies, your organisation needs to ensure that everyone is pulling together. Without leadership from the board down, and the message that it is everyone's responsibility and duty to contribute, individuals will remain focused on their narrow roles. To embed the message at all levels in your organisation, then, you will need an approach where staff and volun-teers are given the permission and authority to act on legacies at every level.

Securing support via conversations within your organisation

As a first step, you should try to secure support for an integrated approach to legacy fundraising through top-down leadership (driven by strategic reasoning) and simultaneously a bottom-up cultural approach (outlined in building block 3). The right strategic framework is critical in terms of posi-tioning legacies positively within your organisation and receiving permission to allocate resources and priorities.

To secure this support, you will need to be on the same page as direc-tors and heads of fundraising when it comes to the practical aims of the legacy fundraising strategy. It is crucial to agree, first and foremost, what can be done and what can't be done. This will determine where to begin with your plans to engage in a conversation about legacy fundraising within your organisation.

There are three levels of conversation that can take place:

1. upwards to the CEO, directors and board;

2. sideways to other fundraising leaders, heads, departments and functions;

3. downwards to teams and individuals in key areas.

The sort of conversations you have with people at these different levels depends on your circumstances and your priority, but you should aim to talk to all three groups. Having conversations upwards sets the tone for legacy leadership by creating a strategic context which helps the strategy for legacies trickle down with a mix of authority and confidence. A conversation sideways helps to ensure fundraising leaders, heads, departments and functions buy in to the strategy to secure access to resources. And finally, by talking with teams and individuals you can find allies, openings and opportunities. Each level prompts further opportunities. Once you've had conversations with these groups, it's helpful to ask yourself: Do we need to consult any further? Are there any practical issues we need to identify? What are the next logical steps given this?

Using the organisational and legacy purposes as a foundation, and backed by the strategic purpose for legacy fundraising and the organisational information you have gathered (such as performance and trends), a case for an integrated strategy can be made. Following engagement and feedback with these three groups, you can then further refine what an integrated plan and strategy might look like (see also 'Refining and presenting your plan' on page 70).

Additionally, there is a need for a fundamental shift in the way legacies are measured and how these groups perceive and value them. Because most people are focused on fundraising, which is driven by targets within the current financial year, priorities are often built around cash-driven objectives. Legacies are a medium- to long-term source of funds, but can be a highly significant one. As such, objectives and targets related to legacies need to be shifted away from a focus on simply cash towards measuring the number of engagements with supporters (but not discounting the underlying financial benefit that underpins the strategic reasoning for legacies, which can be used to focus on building future value).

Furthermore, given that the process of engagement is slow – the aim of engagement is to create a climate in which legacies feel normal, where potential legators can open up the subject so that they can consider making a gift and then take action – the nature of legacies requires a softer approach and a mindset of a longer time frame than other types of fundraising. To change this mindset, members of the legacy team need to communicate to internal stakeholders the reasoning behind and purpose for integrating legacies into the organisation and then provide ongoing support in implementing this new way of working.

Using measures to shift mindsets and evaluate engagement

To help shift your organisation's thinking and attention away from money to engagement through conversations, you need to introduce some measures. Some organisations focus their attention on initiating a top-down strategic set of measures that everybody is required to deliver. As an example, one organisation asked every member of staff to commit to having two legacy conversations with potential legators annually. While two conversations do not seem like much, the aim was to influence behaviour by getting everybody to demonstrate commitment and contribution and gain experience. For other organisations, there is no hard number. Instead the objective is to encourage teams to have a series of conversations themselves and to report on the outcomes of these conversations. Both approaches are designed to drive individuals to actively engage in speaking about legacies. This significantly helps to change cultures.

Another key measure or outcome to track will be to identify the number of enquiries generated through legacy-related messages being attached to existing channels and networks. For example, local voluntary groups may require legacy information brochures; an article in your organisation's newsletter may generate several enquiries; or a tick box in the community fundraising department's set of materials may generate further enquiries. These enquiries which are measured are close in nature to direct response marketing. They are not, however, income generating. In line with the strategy and purpose, they are ways to measure engagement. This engagement may be passive, in the sense that there will be people who are influenced to leave a gift but you will not receive any indication of their intention. There will equally be other people who will engage with your organisation and actively seek information, and in so doing will provide your organisation with their details. The purpose is to influence and engage, and it is this that is measured.

Another key measure is to assess people's attitudes towards legacies both before and after an activity takes place. If you have an external campaign, delivered through media channels such as PR, press, social media, radio or TV, this can be done through a simple survey or polling of the public or target markets.

Building block 3: Creating the right culture through behaviours

No amount of direction, even with a sound strategic purpose and reason, can create all the right conditions required for legacies to be embraced. If your charity has clarified its purpose and strategic reasoning, and communicated these through leadership, the next building block is to focus on the way your staff and volunteers behave, and the climate and environment in which legacies can be engaged. When organisations culti-vate the right behaviours, they create the right culture and, as a result, are far more likely to achieve their objectives and aims. Integrating legacies is highly dependent on this approach, because the approach can directly address the barriers to embracing legacies.

The key question then is how staff and volunteers who are not directly responsible for legacies should behave, which is essentially to be confident about having legacy conversations. When staff and volunteers understand legacies and are not afraid of having conversations about them, then they can contribute to creating an environment where these conversations feel normal and accessible.

In the right culture and atmosphere, less time is spent asking people to leave a gift and more time is spent asking people to consider doing so. This is a softer approach and one in which most people can feel confident. In this way, helping people to understand legacies and actively engage in legacy conversations by increasing their knowledge, directly addressing barriers and inspiring donors are the key ways that can transform how an organisation embraces the legacy opportunity.

Case study: Giving staff the knowledge

When I was at the NSPCC, my colleagues and I in the legacy fundraising team spoke to a range of staff across many different functions through both focus groups and surveys. We wanted to know and understand what it took for others have a legacy conversa-tion. We asked what stood in the way and what was needed to help the organisation deliver more legacies.

The results were simple and clear. Staff and volunteers – those in fundraising and beyond – all concluded that they needed to have knowledge, tools and confidence. They wanted a certain basic level of knowledge that would be sufficient to have a legacy conversation, but they also wanted to know that there were other more specialist people who could help them when needed.

They wanted the right tools, which meant simply having a legacy brochure, a web page, social media and the ability to signpost people to other information. Having these two contributed to the third factor: confidence. They stated that their confidence was raised by practising, learning, and feeling comfortable in either raising the subject of legacy gifts or responding to enquiries or opportunities related to them, even when these areas were not ones they would normally engage in.

To create the right culture and behaviours, it is important to remember that staff need to be briefed, to be trained and to have some space to practice.

Delivering internal campaigns

Another factor in creating the right culture is building the right environment for legacies by creating noise about them, thereby making the idea of legacy-giving more visible. You can do this by providing content that gives people things to talk about and engages them in a fun and inspiring way. One way to deliver this is to create an internal legacy-promotion campaign with a theme to promote giving or to establish a launch or strategy. Here are ten practical ways to deliver an internal campaign:

1. Hold a staff briefing and presentation.

2. Offer free wills to staff.

3. Hold a supporter event and invite staff.

4. Launch an external legacy campaign or product.

5. Give away free gifts or materials, such as mugs, badges or mouse mats.

6. Create visibility, for example through posters in the lift or kitchen, or each floor.

7. Launch a training programme on legacies for all staff.

8. Run a creative competition or get people to sign up to a agree to have a legacy conversation.

9. Create legacy 'champions' from various teams who engage people and lead the way in promoting legacy-giving to all staff (see next section).

10. Create a social media campaign where everyone can share something together.

Engaging champions

Having built a platform for your integrated approach through several layers of engagement and feedback, the next step is to identify those individuals who are willing to offer their support. There are two options available here. The first is to pull together a more formal champions structure in which the champions represent their individual teams and departments. The second option is to have a looser group of people who are naturally willing to engage with legacies and around whom a tribe of enthusiasts can be built who will help to integrate the plan.

Be sure to give your champions clear roles and steps to take, and make sure they are trained and well briefed. They could run a campaign, help launch a product, or implement legacy giving with their colleagues or team. Many staff would welcome the opportunity to add some legacy fundraising experience to their portfolio or CV, and this is one way in which they can do so.

Case study: Bringing about behavioural change

In 2013, the NSPCC commissioned a piece of research motivated and guided by the aim of bringing about behavioural change.[12] The researchers aimed to identify ways in which the supporter care team (which was receiving calls about a whole range of subjects, including changes of details and addresses) could alter its procedures and operations to introduce the subject of legacies. Having identified all the key questions the supporter care team might be asked, they formulated a series of responses for the team. Scripts were then changed and staff were trained to be able to introduce legacies in a conversational way. As a consequence, the team changed its own procedures and processes.

Having practised for a week, team members then began introducing legacies as part of normal conversations. They uncovered a significant interest in legacies and were able to distribute several brochures to enquirers and also hand on details to the legacy team for follow-up.

These practical ways to embed a legacy engagement programme in everyday operations follow naturally from setting out purpose and strategy, and then building a culture and behavioural environment in which legacies are discussed and are then turned into an operational plan for delivery.

Building block 4: Establishing operational systems and plans

Re-engineering key touch points

With purpose and leadership and then behaviours and culture in place, the final building block your charity needs to consider in order to deliver integrated legacies is operational. Whatever the size of your fundraising team or organisation, getting the operational side of an integrated strategy working requires firstly identifying all the key touch points (i.e. points of contact and interfaces with the organisation) within which legacy messaging can be placed. You will need to identify both internal and external touch points.

Internally, look for all the areas in which staff, volunteers and key stakeholders are engaged. These could involve emails, staff newsletters, weekly team meetings, database protocols, and supporter care policies and procedures. Externally, identify all the moments when donors can interact with the organisation. Some of these interactions will be moments when the donor simply watches passively. Look for key areas, such as web pages, social media, order forms for materials, phone scripts, brochures materials and leaflets.

The key in the operational building block is to find ways to re-engineer these touch points so that they contain a legacy message or opening. An example of this is where a fundraising leaflet is produced which contains the standard list of ways that a donor can get involved – such as a running or other events or giving a regular gift – alongside tick boxes that supporters can complete to request further information. This tick-box approach is used extensively, but very often organisations do not include an option to find out more about leaving a gift in their will. The argument for this omission is that space is limited and that there is a need for immediate responses to cash-generating activities. However, another way to look at this is to recognise that the tick-box option is advertising, making a clear statement that gifts in wills are needed and wanted. This soft influencing is in line with the way donors consider leaving a gift. While some people may request information directly through this simple offer, promoting legacies is beneficial even if there is no immediate response.

Having clear touch points and agreeing how to position legacies are both important in making the processes behind them operationally effective. For example, what steps are you taking when somebody requests information? How are you monitoring and measuring responses to determine their effectiveness?

Refining and presenting your plan

There are now a range of practical next steps that can be put in place to advance your plan:

1. Make a presentation to your organisation setting out your case for integration. At the heart of this must be a compelling and emotive argument and case, which is best articulated through a story. To support the case, include raw internal and external facts and figures, such as the number of gifts on average received each year and their value. Compare this number to a competitor's or show how only a few extra gifts will make a difference. Most people will not know this, so this information will help to educate and inform them.

2. Write a supporting paper reflecting your position and the feedback received from your conversations at the three levels.

3. Formally present to teams at team meetings. For instance, fundraising departments may have their own departmental meeting. This is the perfect opportunity to raise the subject of legacies and seek further input.

4. At these meetings, ask specifically for a list of barriers and reasons why integrating legacies will be difficult, but also ask for opportunities and ideas to drive an integrated approach. Collect these and turn them into two lists. The first are objections that need to be addressed and met. The second are ideas around which you can gather support.

5. After this round of input, you will be in good position to finalise a plan and approach, and any costs that may be associated with it. It is at this point that you should seek approval, in whatever format is needed, to move ahead with confidence. One option is for the board to review your paper on your legacy fundraising approach and formally approve it. This can help to cement a level of authority and leadership.

Case study: WaterAid

When WaterAid developed a new legacy marketing strategy at the end of 2014, it recognised that, while there had been consistent growth in legacies, to continue this growth it needed to reach a wider audience. The most cost-effective way available was through its existing channels and relationships. It recognised that a step change could take place if it helped to normalise the legacy offer for supporters and staff alike. The charity's key aims were:

• making legacy giving available and accessible for all audiences;

• creating opportunities to engage supporters in a legacy conversation;

• creating a culture at WaterAid where consideration of legacies is a normal part of the supporter journey;

• developing opportunities to reach other audiences.

As part of this strategy, WaterAid set about training its staff in how to have legacy conversations in such a way as to help encourage these conversations to feel normal and natural. Staff were trained to understand what legacies were, how to confront their fears (both professionally and personally), to engage with the strategy and to be able to have a legacy conversation comfortably. At the heart of this approach was the core method of encouraging engagement through conversations.

To support this approach, WaterAid joined the Remember a Charity campaign so as to acquire tools to facilitate the following goals:

• to give staff a relevant reason to talk to all audiences about gifts in wills, by using the content of the Remember a Charity campaign and the awareness week;

• to allow staff who had been trained in legacy conversations to practise what they had learned and to engage supporters with the legacy message;

• to enable staff to focus on talking about gifts in wills and create a consistent message and noise around the legacy message to create more impact;

• to allow WaterAid to test legacy messages and deliver a supporter-friendly campaign;

• to help embed a legacy culture at WaterAid that everyone can get involved in.

Remember a Charity created a will-writing campaign involving volunteers skydiving while writing wills, called Extreme Will Writing. Having two WaterAid volunteers selected for the national campaign meant that WaterAid was able to tailor its stories for each of its audiences to make the legacy ask both relevant and inspiring while overcoming the barriers some fundraising teams had about promoting gifts in wills.

The campaign's new approach engaged supporters and staff:

• All fundraising teams were asked to promote legacies to their key audiences and to practise their legacy conversation skills, which they had been trained in.

• More people engaged through email, with the overall email open rate 10% higher than WaterAid's average open rate; this was achieved because of the engaging content and story.

• A higher conversion rate (23.5% versus the average of 20%) was achieved in WaterAid's telephone activity, because staff were able to begin conversations by referring to a subject that was easy to share, opening the way for better-quality phone conversations.

• The legacy web page normally saw 2% of web traffic; however, this rose to 17.7% during the campaign.

• Account managers for community volunteers and water industry partnerships became more confident in talking about gifts in wills. In the process of these conversations, they uncovered supporters' intentions and realised that their audiences were interested in legacy giving. They continued to talk about legacies throughout and beyond the campaign.

• WaterAid was founded by the UK water industry in 1981 and still works very closely with the industry. Two companies had legacy roadshows that were launched with a new free will service, reaching 1,500 water-industry staff. Other water companies got involved in sharing posters and intranet stories, and Yorkshire Water issued a press release about a retired employee who took part in the Extreme Will Writing challenge and the impact that gifts in wills make to WaterAid.

The first national presentation about gifts in wills took place at the annual WaterAid Supporter's Day, featuring the two skydiving volunteers and reached 500 key supporters. The two volunteers who took part in the campaign made a huge difference through their personal stories, making stories the heart of the campaign.

Overall, the campaign enabled a culture shift to take place where staff became empowered to engage with legacies and supporters were engaged in a positive and uplifting style.

Conclusion

Integration is about:

• understanding the purpose and strategic reasoning behind legacy fundraising;

• how these link to your organisation's overall purpose;

• communicating the purpose and strategic reasoning through good leadership;

• creating a conducive organisational mindset;

• following this all up with a plan, supported by the confidence to act.

At whatever level of integration your organisation is, there are many ways in which you can choose to influence your organisation's staff and volunteers to work together towards ever-increasing integration of legacy fundraising into the wider fundraising strategy. Legacy fundraising works when fear and misunderstanding are replaced with acceptance and confidence and perhaps more importantly, inspiration. When people know how to engage others in legacy conversations, opportunities open. Taking steps to deliver a joined-up approach should always be about influencing and supporting the donor, which is supported by a belief that it is good and right to highlight to them the chance to leave a gift to your charity and it is good for the donor.

Follow these building blocks and integration can open up a huge opportunity to inspire and engage the whole of your organisation in promoting legacy gifts.

Notes

1 'The global and real-time state of employee engagement report' [web page], Officevibe, 2017, www.officevibe.com/state-employee-engagement, accessed 1 December 2017.

2 *Legacy Trends 2017 Update: Discovering potential through data* [PDF], Smee & Ford, London, 2017, http://smeeandford.com/whitepaper/index, p. 2, accessed 1 December 2017.

3 *Legacy Giving 2017*, East Chiltington, Legacy Foresight, 2017; *Legacy Trends: Discovering potential thorough data* [PDF], Smee & Ford, 2017, https://smeeandford.com/whitepaper, p. 2, accessed 30 December 2017.

4 Andrew Nash, *National Population Projections: 2016-based statistical bulletin* [PDF], Office for National Statistics, www.ons.gov.uk/peoplepopulationandcommunity/populationandmigration/populationprojections/bulletins/nationalpopulationprojections/2016basedstatisticalbulletin, 2017, p. 3.

5 Andrew Nash, *National Population Projections: 2014-based projections* [PDF], Office for National Statistics, www.ons.gov.uk/peoplepopulationandcommunity/populationandmigration/populationprojections/compendium/nationalpopulationprojections/2015–10-29, 2017, p. 40.

6 Andrew Nash, *National Population Projections: 2016-based statistical bulletin* [PDF], Office for National Statistics, www.ons.gov.uk/peoplepopulationandcommunity/populationandmigration/populationprojections/bulletins/nationalpopulationprojections/2016basedstatisticalbulletin, 2017, p. 6.

7 *Affluent but forgotten: The demographic opportunity for wealth management in the UK* [PDF], Strategy& (formerly Booz & Company), PricewaterhouseCoopers, originally published by Booz & Company in 2013, www.strategyand.pwc.com/media/file/Strategyand_Affluent-but-Forgotten.pdf, accessed 25 January 2018.

8 Cecil Prescott, *Internet Users in the UK: 2017* [PDF], Office for National Statistics, www.ons.gov.uk/businessindustryandtrade/itandinternetindustry/bulletins/internetusers/2017, p. 2.

9   Chris Prescott, *Internet Access – households and individuals: 2016* [PDF], Office for National Statistics, www.ons.gov.uk/peoplepopulationandcommunity/ householdcharacteristics/homeinternetandsocialmediausage/bulletins/ internetaccesshouseholdsandindividuals/2016, 4 August 2016, accessed 7 December 2017.

10   David Kane, Peter Bass and Joe Heywood, *UK Civil Society Almanac 2014*, London, NCVO, 2014, p. 81. At the time of writing this chapter, NCVO noted that these volunteer figures had not been updated owing to no more recent findings being available: https://data.ncvo.org.uk/a/almanac14/who-volunteers-in-the-uk-3.

11   *Legacy Trends 2017 Update: Discovering potential through data* [PDF], Smee & Ford, 2017, https://smeeandford.com/whitepaper, pp. 2 and 6, accessed 25 January 2018.

12   Alex McDowell, 'NSPCC's supporter care gifts in wills "mind map"' [web page], Showcase of Fundraising Innovation and Inspiration, 2015, http://sofii.org/case-study/nspccs-supporter-care-gifts-in-wills-mind-map, accessed 1 December 2017.

CHAPTER SIX

Improving strategy with research

Claire Routley

Introduction

This chapter discusses the value of research in helping to develop a legacy fundraising strategy. It focuses on formulating a research problem and setting appropriate research objectives, before moving on to consider the specific research tools you might use and the value of working with a research agency.

When the term 'research' is used in this chapter, it means (to paraphrase Alan Wilson): the collection, analysis and communication of information undertaken to assist decision-making in fundraising.[1]

Why research?

Using research to inform your legacy fundraising practice comes at a cost in terms of time, and generally of money. Why then would you choose to invest in this way?

By its very nature, there are a number of risks inherent in legacy fundraising, both reputational and financial: it can be a sensitive subject to talk about, and the true value of legacy fundraising approaches is unlikely to be known for five to ten years or longer. Sargeant and Jay point out that research can help to reduce risk in fundraising decision-making – in the context of legacies, it could help us to reduce risk by understanding how responsive our donors are to a legacy ask and the type of communication they prefer, among other topics.[2]

In addition to addressing the broad concept of reducing risk, legacy research has a broad range of practical implications. For example, research projects in legacy fundraising have been used to:

• understand who, within an engaged audience, is most likely to give legacies;

• understand potential new audiences for legacy fundraising;

• develop a compelling case for support for legacy giving;

• test new ideas with potential audiences;

• test reactions to different channels and modes of ask;

• feed into the development of a stewardship programme.

Given the comparatively high value of the average legacy gift, even small increases in fundraising effectiveness developed via research can have a substantial impact on your organisation's income. More importantly, however, using research to understand your audience can help you to develop a better donor experience, designed to meet donor needs more effectively – and thus, ultimately, should result in increased income for your organisation and its beneficiaries.

The research process

So, if understanding more about your supporters can benefit both those supporters and your charity, how do you go about it? The process of designing and developing a research project is illustrated in figure 6.1, and several of the stages will be discussed below in more detail.

FIGURE 6.1 THE STAGES OF THE RESEARCH PROCESS[3]

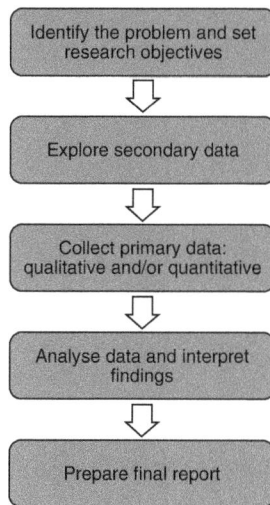

Identifying the research problem and setting objectives

According to Malhotra and colleagues, identifying the research problem or opportunity is the most important step in any research project.[4] Without absolute clarity at this stage, it can be very easy to waste time and money during the research process, and even, ultimately, for the project not to deliver the information that you need. In order to get the most out of your research project, Malhotra and colleagues recommend defining both a marketing decision problem and a marketing research problem. In the context of legacy fundraising, a marketing decision problem might be something like:

• Which of our supporters should we contact with our legacy direct mail appeals?

You can then think about the information you would need to facilitate that decision, to define the marketing research problem. In the case of the example above, your marketing research problem might be:

• To understand the key indicators that suggest donors may be responsive to a direct legacy ask.

Once the problem has been identified and expressed, it can be translated into a set of research objectives that specify precisely what it is that you would like to find out. In the above example, they might include, among others:

• to understand the extent to which gender influences the legacy-giving decision;

• to understand the optimal age(s) or age ranges at which to communicate with donors about legacy giving;

• to understand the relationship between giving frequency and the decision to leave a legacy.

Clear objectives can also help you to choose the most appropriate research method; very broadly, objectives which are concerned with understanding 'how much' or 'how many' point towards a quantitative methodology, while those concerned with understanding 'why' tend to point towards a qualitative methodology.

Secondary research

The best place to start in most research projects is with secondary research – i.e. drawing on data and research that already exists, such as in externally published sources or internal reports or databases. It might be that the research question you're seeking to answer has already been examined elsewhere, and exploring that research could save you considerable time and money. Chapter 2 may be useful in giving you a broad overview of the academic research picture in legacy fundraising at the time of publication; however, new studies are published on a regular basis, so it would be worth conducting your own desk research. Some secondary sources of relevant information on legacies are as follows:

• academic journals including the *International Journal of Nonprofit and Voluntary Marketing*, *Nonprofit and Voluntary Sector Quarterly*, *Nonprofit Management and Leadership* and *Voluntas*;

- sector suppliers including Bluefrog, Legacy Foresight, Listen and nfpSynergy;

- sector bodies such as the Directory of Social Change, the Institute of Fundraising, the Institute of Legacy Management and Remember a Charity, and the councils for voluntary action: NCVO (National Council for Voluntary Organisations), NICVA (Northern Ireland Council for Voluntary Action), SCVO (Scottish Council for Voluntary Organisations) and WCVA (Wales Council for Voluntary Action);

- trade magazines and websites, including *Civil Society*, *The Fundraiser*, Fundraising.co.uk, *Third Sector* and SOFII (the Showcase of Fundraising Innovation and Inspiration);

- university websites including those of the Centre for Philanthropy, Encourage Generosity, the Lilly Family School of Philanthropy, the Marshall Institute, Queensland University of Technology and the University of Plymouth Hartsook Centre for Sustainable Philanthropy;

- searches in Google Scholar.

In addition to published research, you may be able to gain some helpful insights via exploring your own data. The possibilities for exploring your data are discussed in more detail in chapter 9, on data analysis.

Although secondary research is relatively quick and cheap to carry out, Sargeant and Jay point out that it has a number of disadvantages:[5]

- It may be out of date.

- It may have been collected for another purpose and thus its applicability to your organisation might be doubtful.

- It may not always be possible to judge the quality of the research.

In legacy fundraising, the specific combination of the profiles and motives of your donors may well be unique to your organisation, and thus you may wish to undertake primary research – i.e. research where you gather your own, new data to supplement what you can glean from secondary data. Primary research can be grouped into two main types: quantitative and qualitative, which will be explored in the following sections.

Quantitative research

Quantitative research uses a structured research approach, and the findings about a sample of people in the population can be quantified in order to understand their behaviour, motivations or attitudes.[6] Commonly, quantitative data is gathered through structured interviews or surveys. These can be delivered through several channels: online, postal, telephone or face to face. The channel you choose for your legacy research will depend on a number of considerations. For many charities, cost will be a key factor, and therefore the online channel can be a very cost-effective choice, while face to face would normally be the most expensive option. However, you should also consider issues such as reach (for example, how many of your audience for legacy fundraising have an email address), representativeness (for example, do those people with email addresses reflect the audience you're interested in?) and, particularly, in the case of legacy research, accessibility (for example, are your older donors comfortable completing surveys online?).

In order to gather useful data, you will also need to pay particular attention to the design of your survey to ensure that you can generate the data you require. This includes the topics you cover, the types of questions you ask, the wording you use, the order in which your questions appear, and the overall length and design.

The other key issue to be aware of is sampling. It is unlikely that you will have the budget or time to reach all of your potential legacy audience. However, you can use sampling methods to select a smaller group. The power of statistical analysis means that you can then extrapolate from this smaller group to say with a specified degree of accuracy that, for example, 15% of your existing donors would consider adding a legacy for your organisation next time they updated their will.

The downside of quantitative research is that, while it can tell us how many people think something, it is not so effective at understanding *why*, and it can be easy for researchers to impose their views on their audience. For example, in a survey, a researcher might list a range of possible motivations for a legacy gift and then count how many people tick each box; however, in compiling the list, the researcher may not have included a motivation that would have been key for a number of people.

Testing

As human beings, we don't always understand the reasons we behave as we do, and we can't always articulate them clearly – and, sometimes, our actual behaviour differs from how we believe we might behave in any given situation. It could be argued that this is a particular issue in legacy giving, which might be affected by our subconscious reactions to issues such as death and dying. Therefore, rather than applying methods that ask people whether they might do something like leave a legacy or whether they might be influenced by a certain approach, you can test some of your ideas in a real-life situation – for example, testing differences in scripts in legacy telephone campaigns, or differences in copy in legacy fundraising direct marketing.

Testing properly can be a challenge, however. Firstly, it is important to ensure that you are testing in sufficient volumes for the results to be statistically significant. In my experience, that can sometimes be difficult in legacy fundraising, where direct marketing approaches, for example, may often only achieve 1% response rates.

In addition, tests must be designed carefully. If you want to know which of two mailing packs works better, then you can test two quite different packs against each other and measure the difference in response or pledge rates. However, if you want to understand *why* there is a difference in the response rates, then you have to change only one thing at a time – perhaps something as small as changing just a word or two in a letter or script. All other factors (such as timing when a message is sent) should be held constant. Without these disciplines, it can be easy to impute meaning to results which aren't justified given the design of the research or the statistical significance of the results.

Qualitative research

Qualitative research is research undertaken with a small number of individuals that produces deep, but generally non-quantifiable insights into their behaviour, motivations, and attitudes.[7] Qualitative data can be gathered through a number of methods, most commonly focus groups and interviews.

Focus groups are typically made up of six to ten people, meeting for one to two hours to discuss a specific topic, most typically face to face, although it is also possible to facilitate focus groups online. According to Sargeant and Jay, typically, a project might involve six to eight groups in order to hear a range of opinions from a variety of stakeholders.[8] Interviews are often one to one, although they can occasionally involve couples or trios. They can be carried out on the phone, via software (such as Skype) or face to face. In both interviews and focus groups, the researcher tends to have a guide to the topics to be covered, although they can build in flexibility to follow up on interesting themes that emerge through the conversations.

While both focus groups and interviews enable an in-depth understanding, they have their own strengths and weaknesses in relation to legacy research. In-depth interviews can be particularly useful for understanding the experience, journey or views of people on an individual basis. They can also work well where there might be a concern over sensitivity, where people might not want to share their views in a group environment, and/or where the researcher may need to adapt their approach depending on the reaction of the individual. Therefore, for example, they might be an appropriate tool when discussing potential legacy donors' personal experiences of your organisation's work. Focus groups, on the other hand, can work well where the research benefits from the social interaction that occurs – for example, they might be a good forum to discuss new legacy marketing materials, where the discussion can build on the inputs from the various members of the group.

The key benefit of qualitative research is the opportunity to gain an in-depth understanding, particularly around the 'whys' of legacy giving. Its flexible, exploratory nature means that you may discover completely new or unexpected information that you might not find from within a more structured survey. The downside of the flexibility of the method and the smaller number of people involved is that you can't tell with any degree of certainty how widely these opinions are shared among your audience.

Mixed methods

Qualitative and quantitative research can be used together in a single project where the strengths of one method may be used to address the weaknesses of the other. Commonly, qualitative research is used to understand opinions, perceptions or motivations, then quantitative research is used to measure how many people share those ideas.

Working with an agency or a consultant

In charities in general, and smaller charities in particular, budgets available for research can be extremely limited. Many of the research tools discussed above can be applied internally, or through creative approaches such as working with local college students or qualified volunteers. However, where budget is available, your project might well benefit from professional research input. To paraphrase Alan Wilson's description of the benefit of working with agencies:[9]

• Their experience might mean that they can carry out the research more efficiently than less experienced internal staff, which can mean that, when you take into account the cost of staff time, an agency might be the cheaper option.

• They may have access to specific facilities (such as recording equipment) which can be expensive to purchase for limited use.

• They have specific expertise (such as focus group facilitation and data analysis) which might be difficult to replicate internally.

The first, and often the most important, step in working with an outside agency (or in briefing internal staff or volunteers) is to create a research brief, so that the agency and your charity share the same perspectives on the project and particularly what needs to be understood. Typically, this might include:

• background information on the organisation and the project;

• research and fundraising objectives;

• target audience to be researched;

• initial thoughts on methodology, if appropriate;

- budget and timescale;

- details of how the project will be managed.

Once the brief has been developed, you can circulate it to several agencies, which are likely to respond with a detailed research proposal describing how they would address your research brief. There are several types of agencies that address legacy research projects, from individual freelancers to international market research agencies. Your choice is likely to depend on a combination of your available budget, the quality of the proposal, the agency's experience in undertaking legacy research, personal recommendations, and fit between the agency and your organisation.

Conclusion

Investing in legacy fundraising research can help both to inform your fundraising approaches and to allay risk in legacy fundraising decision-making. Most importantly, it can help you to design fundraising that meets the needs of legacy donors, while helping you to raise the money your charity needs to support its beneficiaries.

For your legacy research project to do this, it's vital that you're absolutely clear, and as precise as possible, about what it is that you need to know. Once you've achieved this clarity, you can apply a variety of techniques and approaches to the problem, from reading what others have written to a full-scale project generating new data through a combination of focus groups and surveys.

Notes

1   Alan Wilson, *Marketing Research: An Integrated Approach*, Harlow, Pearson Education, 2003, p. 4.
2   Adrian Sargeant and Elaine Jay, *Fundraising Management: Analysis, Planning and Practice*, London and New York, Routledge, 2014, p. 40.
3   Based on figure 3.1 in Adrian Sargeant and Elaine Jay's *Fundraising Management: Analysis, Planning and Practice*, London and New York, Routledge, 2014, p. 40.
4   Naresh K. Malhotra, David F. Birks and Peter Wills, *Marketing Research: An Applied Approach*, Harlow, Pearson Education Limited, 2007.
5   Adrian Sargeant and Elaine Jay, *Fundraising Management: Analysis, Planning and Practice*, London and New York, Routledge, 2014, p. 44.
6   Definition based on Alan Wilson's in *Marketing Research: An Integrated Approach*, Harlow, Pearson Education, 2003, p. 135.
7   *Ibid.*, p. 37.
8   Adrian Sargeant and Elaine Jay, *Fundraising Management: Analysis, Planning and Practice*, London and New York, Routledge, 2014, p. 45.
9   Alan Wilson, *Marketing Research: An Integrated Approach*, Harlow, Pearson Education, 2003, p. 27.

CHAPTER SEVEN

Budgeting and evaluating

Jonathan Cook

Introduction

This chapter outlines the basic tools and techniques used to budget for and evaluate legacy fundraising campaigns. It looks at some of the areas you will need to consider when you put together your budgets, areas you could think of investing in, and how to measure the success of your legacy fundraising campaigns.

When you start to think about legacy fundraising, you will need to consider the budget you have for the fundraising campaign. Legacy fundraising can have one of the largest returns on investments of any fundraising method, but it can take some time to realise the income, so in the short term other techniques need to be used to assess the performance of your fundraising. Often, because of this lag factor of how long it takes to see the income, legacy fundraising can be neglected and invested in poorly by charities. Being able to demonstrate the success of legacy fundraising campaigns is key to persuading your organisation to invest in this method of fundraising.

Plan your objectives, activity and budget

First, think about what you want to achieve; next, plan what activities will support what you want to achieve and then work up a budget last of all. Developing a budget from the plans will allow you to see whether there are any areas where you can cut costs or areas where you can invest more money.

Think about whether you want to meet prospects face to face, as it is more expensive but has a higher success rate. In contrast, would you prefer to reach a far wider audience through a direct-marketing style of campaign? This will be cheaper per supporter but will be unlikely to have such a large impact.

Think about what you want to offer to supporters who respond to your campaign. You might want to offer a free or discounted will-writing scheme, or you might prefer to send out an information pack. Again, the first of these examples will have higher unit costs but better success rates, while the second will have lower unit costs but lower success rates.

To decide what type of campaign you should embark upon, it is wise first to conduct some research into your supporters and your audience.

This will ensure that you base your campaign on evidence and insight, and will make it much more likely your supporters will respond positively. (The research process is explained in 'Research and insight processes' below and elaborated on further in chapters 6 and 9.)

What should go into your budget?

Think of legacy fundraising as having five key elements (see figure 7.1). Four of these elements can be thought of as part of a cyclical planning process, whereas the fifth (staffing and human resources) underpins all of the other elements. You will need to budget for the required staff to deliver on your plans.

In any given year, you will probably need to invest in some of these elements more than others. If the year is about planning a new legacy marketing campaign, you will probably need to invest more of your time and resources into the research and insight and the creative and product-development elements. If the year is more about running and fulfilling your legacy campaign, the marketing and the fulfilment and evaluation elements will be more important.

FIGURE 7.1 ELEMENTS OF A LEGACY FUNDRAISING BUDGET

Research and insight processes

There have been several negative press stories of charities bombarding people with appeals[1] and so it is natural that considerations about fundraising ethics, particularly in a sphere as sensitive as legacies, are front of mind (see chapter 3 for details on legacy fundraising ethics). Think of research and insight processes as the look-before-you-leap element of your budget and plans that can help your charity avoid any unintended negative consequences. Carrying out these processes effectively can help you to ensure your charity is targeting people who want to know about legacies as opposed to taking a blanket approach. This will also allow you to talk to them in the way they want, about what they want, and when they want, thereby avoiding any perception by the public of unwanted requests.

This might involve analysis of your supporters' behaviour in relation to your charity. You might look at their giving history, other ways they engage with you (are they a volunteer, perhaps?) or their location. If you have their consent, you can also look at external factors, such as their socio-demographics or outside interests. Your analysis could also involve speaking with your supporters directly and conducting focus groups or one-to-one interviews.

Before you budget for this, think about what you want to discover. Do you want a big list of supporters to whom you can send a direct-marketing legacy appeal? If so, the data-analysis approach might be more productive. Or do you want to understand what messages might motivate someone to respond? In that instance it is probably better to use focus groups and one-to-one research.

You should also consider how much a data-analysis project might cost and how long it might take versus the likely output for your fundraising. It is likely to give you a small yet highly engaged pool of prospects. How much might you save by not marketing to everyone but only to those identified through the data analysis?

There are other questions to consider too. For example, how might you hold focus groups and one-to-one interviews? Could you conduct them online using survey tools or using video conferencing platforms such as Zoom, or will you have to meet people in person? If so, where could you host the meetings and who would attend?

Think about the staff resources that you have internally – and not just within your team. Do you have the skills in your charity to conduct this research or will you have to use external providers? (See also 'Working with an agency or a consultant' on page 82.)

Creative and product development stage

The creative stage of the legacy marketing process is the bit that will hopefully motivate people to leave gifts in their wills to your charity. This and the research and insight stage tend to go hand in hand; they are often carried out together and don't have to be repeated every year. However, you should aim to do both every couple of years to keep your appeals looking fresh.

The creative stage could involve some element of idea generation, producing new themes for appeals or campaigns. Next, those ideas need to be turned into a reality, so copy must be written, photography and images taken or sourced, and then all elements brought together as an effective piece of design.

Again, think about your internal staff resources. Are you able to conduct a good creative workshop internally? Can you write the copy yourself and can someone use design software? Or will you need to use external help to come up with the creative ideas, write the fundraising copy and put the two together in a catchy and inspiring design? External help can be expensive, but an outside view of your charity can sometimes be a wise investment.

Marketing

This is the 'doing' part of the budget. This is where you budget for the expenditure for your legacy events; your direct-marketing programmes; printing of your materials, leaflets and booklets; and all of your marketing collateral.

The insight and creative stages will outline your marketing plans, and this is where you should calculate all of the costs associated with these plans. For example, if the strategy is to hold a number of legacy events around the country, think about everything you will need to run and fulfil these events. What will it cost to invite people, will you need to pay for travel expenses, do you need to hire a venue or pay speakers, and will you feed your guests or just provide tea and coffee? Then you will also need to think about materials for the day: do you want pull-up banners, and what materials will your guests take away with them?

If the strategy is to conduct a telephone campaign, you will need to understand the cost per call, determine the set-up costs of the campaign and decide what materials you will send out to the audience after the calls. If your strategy is to use a simple direct-mail approach, you should think about the cost per pack and freepost responses. Additionally, if the volumes are expected to be high, then management of the responses by external suppliers might be required.

You should also think about where you need to invest digitally. You will almost certainly want to have some materials available on your organisation's website and you might want to consider targeted social media advertising or email communications.

Fulfilment and evaluation

The final stage of your legacy fundraising programme will be to fulfil the responses and evaluate the performance of your campaigns. Depending on the products being offered, the fulfilment of your legacy campaigns could be quite expensive. For example, if you decide to have a free or discounted will scheme, this will require a large overhead in the first instance. A simple will might cost only £150 to your charity, but, if your campaign is a success and you have hundreds of respondents, these costs could become quite high. You may want to do a trial to gauge the level of demand you have for this type of legacy product.

Evaluating the success of a legacy fundraising campaign has always been a tough task. Unlike other fundraising mechanisms, which produce almost instant income, it takes many years for the money from legacies to be realised. As such, assessing the results of your campaigns in terms of income is not usually possible in the short term.

To evaluate your degree of success, you therefore need to look at other key performance indicators, not just income. The simple indicator to examine is the pledgers. These are people who have indicated that they have written your organisation into their will. There are many arguments that some pledgers don't actually tell the truth, or intend to put you into their wills but don't get around to doing it. However, regardless of those discussions, having a campaign that doubles the number of pledgers can be judged to have had an impact. If you go from 100 to 200 pledgers, and 50% haven't actually put you into their wills, then you've still gained 50 more pledgers through the campaign than you had before. Finding techniques within your marketing to allow people to pledge is essential to the fulfilment of your legacy fundraising campaigns.

To gauge the truth behind your pledger figures, look back through your pledger file and calculate how many of them have died and left a legacy gift. This will give you your *true* percentage. From this you can begin to assess the success of your pledger recruitment in real terms.

The following case study outlines a legacy fundraising product that had the distinct advantage that it was also an incredibly efficient way to capture whether someone was a legacy pledger.

Case study: Animal charities' caring for pets schemes

A number of animal charities, including the RSPCA, have run schemes whereby a person's pet is looked after by the charity upon their death. These products encourage the pet owner to mention in their will that the animal charity in question will look after their pet upon their death. Many of these charities have used this kind of programme as a way to talk about legacies, and many of the owners do leave legacies as a thank you for looking after their pets.

These schemes require the pet owner to sign up to the scheme (thereby allowing data capture of name, address, age, type of animal and so on). At the point of data capture, the scheme also allows the pet owner to pledge to leave a gift in their will to the charity. This product gives the owner peace of mind and the charity valuable data about the individual, their age, their demographics and whether they have pledged to leave a gift to the charity.

It is then possible to look at the number of pet owners enrolled in this scheme who die and also leave a legacy to gauge the success rate of this product as a legacy-acquisition device. For example, if

50% of the enrolled pet owners go on to leave a gift upon their death, this figure can be used to put a reliable estimated value on the pledgers recruited through this product who are still alive, thereby allowing reasonably accurate figures to be compiled on the success of this campaign at acquiring legacy pledgers.

Demographics of responders

Not only will you wish to inspire people to leave your charity gifts in their wills but also you will need to inspire those supporters who are able to leave the largest sums of money; moreover, if there is a need for the money to be realised quickly, you may also want to inspire gifts from individuals who are likely to be older. You can therefore assess the performance of your legacy campaigns according to the types of people who respond. Data is freely available from the Office for National Statistics (which can be found online at www.ons.gov.uk) and the Land Registry (www.gov.uk/government/organisations/land-registry) on house prices, income levels, wealth data and average age. (Do ensure, however, that appending external data is explicitly covered in your organisation's privacy notice.)

You can look at those supporters who have responded and assess whether they fall into the higher socio-demographic groups, have higher-value properties and are older. Set yourself a target for the demographics of your responders. You could aim to recruit 80% of your responders from higher socio-demographic groups – for example, individuals with house prices in excess of £500,000 – who are over 75 years of age. Even if you received fewer pledges from this group in comparison to other groups, you could be reasonably confident that this group of pledgers will be able to leave relatively high sums of money to your organisation. (For more details on targeting different demographic groups, see chapter 9.)

Table 7.1 shows a way of tracking the age of your pledgers and other legacy responders. This kind of table can be used to assess the success of a drive to recruit older pledgers.

TABLE 7.1 TABLE OF LEGACY RESPONDERS BY AGE

	Average age now	Average age at death	Number within each age bracket						
			<30	30–39	40–49	50–59	60–69	70–79	80+
Pledger	70	82	0	0	0	1	4	5	122
Intender	69	89	0	0	0	0	0	1	5
Considerer	67	74	0	0	0	0	2	2	26
Enquirer	62	81	0	0	1	5	5	21	196

Conclusion

Legacies can have some of the highest returns on the investment of any form of fundraising, but these returns can be increased greatly with some simple research, planning and targeting of supporters most likely to leave legacies and of those who are able to leave the largest sums of money. Supporters of the right age, wealth and connection or commitment to the cause are likely to give more and larger legacies, so spending time understanding and researching these audiences will pay dividends.

Investing more money and time into these groups will make a larger impact in both response rates and income, so ensure that any budget includes money for the research and insight process and for the results of the creative and product development stage to be tested against the identified audiences.

For income budgeting, good analysis of previous legacy marketing responders, including age now, average age at death, the percentage of the deceased legators who were previous responders and the value of their legacy gifts, will allow you to get an idea of the income you can expect from your existing supporter file.

Notes

1   Aimee Meade, 'Everything you need to know about the charity fundraising crisis' [web article], *The Guardian*, www.theguardian.com/voluntary-sector-network/ 2015/jul/10/everything-you-need-to-know-charity-fundraising-crisis, 10 July 2015.

CHAPTER EIGHT

Legacy forecasting

Eifron Hopper

Introduction

Legacies are, or could be, such an important source of income for many charities that reliable forecasting methods are needed to help predict their flow. This chapter covers the basic principles and describes the characteristics of a good model, suitable for evaluating available methods, both for short-term and longer-term forecasting. Technology can be a great help, but there are still many uncertainties that make predicting legacy income a challenge, to say the least. Understanding the broader environment is valuable, and in this regard the chapter introduces you to the resources available from Legacy Foresight (www.legacyforesight.co.uk).

For many years, legacy forecasting seemed to be more like alchemy than science. Certain legacy officers of an arithmetical bent would pore over lists and tables to come up with figures that, the further into the future they stretched, tended to be knocked badly off course by unanticipated fluctuations in the housing and stock markets. However, technology and the skills to use it have now come together to make legacy forecasting a better understood and more exact science – although there are still huge variations in the results achieved.

Legacy income is volatile, some would say capricious, and very difficult to fit into patterns or contain within formulae. The only certainty about any legacy forecast is that it will be wrong, so why bother forecasting at all? The answer to that is simple: legacies are such an important source of income for most charities that a great deal of effort has to be put into trying to predict what the legacy income is going to be.

In the short term, having some idea of projected legacy income is invaluable when engaging in financial planning or risk management. In the longer term, an understanding of the likely bigger picture for legacies and its relevance for your organisation will help to inform decisions about the strategic direction in which you are going.

Definitions

In this chapter, 'short term' means one to three years. It encompasses in-year forecasting and comparisons with what has been budgeted for at the end of this one-year period, as well as the process of looking a bit further ahead to fix budgets for the following couple of years. This form of forecasting usually depends upon different factors from longer-term forecasting.

'Long term' here covers three to twenty years. Such a far-off horizon may seem to be too far away to expect any real accuracy (and it is true that precision is difficult), but a prudent charity will always want to have some idea of the direction in which such a significant source of income is going.

Whatever the term over which forecasting takes place, it is always worth involving in the process colleagues from the finance function and other managers who will make decisions based on what the forecast tells you. There are three reasons for this:

• They will have data and insights that will enable you to construct a more accurate model and deliver a more useful forecast.

• You will be able to share, test and (if necessary) adapt your assumptions about the internal and external factors that will affect legacy income.

• Although it may be tempting to try to maintain some of the mystique that surrounds legacy forecasting (the alchemy rather than the science), no one benefits from this. If forecasts are wrong (as they inevitably will be to some extent), it is better, from the point of view of risk management, that everyone who is affected by them understands how they have been arrived at and is involved – some would say implicated – in what they say.

What information do you need?

It is important to remember that the main variables in predicting the amount of legacy income you are going to receive are the average value of legacies and the number of notifications you receive. Some forecasting methods rely upon little more than these two factors; others look in rather more detail at what is behind these numbers and also take into account the other main component: time.

To enable your forecasting to be as accurate as possible, you will want to record a number of facts, including:

• numbers of notifications, split by legacy type – pecuniary, residuary, reversionary (see 'Conditional and reversionary gifts' on page 223);

• the value of each legacy;

• the time taken for each legacy to be fully paid up.

For the more sophisticated forecasting models, it will also be helpful to know the asset mix making up the estates from which these legacies come. For example, a charity which knows that cash makes up a large proportion of these estates is not going to see its legacy income affected very much by stock market fluctuations or the vagaries of the housing market.

Chapter 20 looks at how to record this sort of information. One point worth emphasising in connection with forecasting is that it is important to keep this information up to date by, for example, ensuring that the recorded estimated value of the legacy (initially often little more than guessed at) is updated as more accurate information is received as part of the legacy administration process.

Short-term forecasting

The forecasting model you choose will depend upon the information you have at your disposal and the resources you have available. Many legacy officers will have built up their own models over the years; what follows is a look at some of the basic principles involved and some of the models used.

Extrapolation

At its simplest, this form of forecasting looks back at past notifications and average values, and projects those figures forward to create a prediction of future income. For example, a charity whose legacy notifications have remained consistent and whose average values have been increasing by 5% a year may want to anticipate those trends continuing over the short term and multiply the resulting figures together to predict future income.

Added accuracy may be achieved if the charity has an idea of the asset mix of estates from which it benefits. If, for example, it knows that these estates are substantially made up of real property (land and buildings), it may want to build into its projections an assumption that takes account of changes in property prices.

This method of forecasting performs at its best when notifications and values are stable over a period or move up or down on a steady progression. Its main disadvantage is that it provides no understanding of the underlying factors that affect legacy income.

Intuition

It is commonplace these days for legacy officers to record 'pipeline' income (i.e. income about which you have been notified but that you have not yet received) so as to be able to report on what income is anticipated. An experienced legacy officer should be able to look at the data and correspondence on a legacy file and give a reasonable estimate of when this income is likely to be received. This may be workable when there are only a few dozen files to consider, but when there are hundreds of open files it is unlikely that there will be the time (or the will!) to examine each individually.

In such a case it is possible, by looking at current data and applying averages for value and payment time, to give an estimate of how much income is in the pipeline and when it is likely to be received. This is all very well for legacies about which you already know, but it doesn't take account of those about which you have not yet been notified.

As long ago as the 1990s, a more detailed approach was developed and used by a small number of charities. This involved dividing legacies up into bands (up to £20,000, £20,000–50,000 and so on) and using historical data to establish average values and payment times that could be applied to notifications in order to ascertain what income could be expected at what time.

The model dealt with the problem of legacies for which no notification had yet been received by examining historical data to see what the trends were for notification numbers in each band, and projecting forward numbers in each of those bands. When this model was being used, many calculations were carried out manually and there was not, for example, the capacity to track individual legacies.

Similar approaches, using the same principles but much more sophisticated, have been developed by a number of charities and agencies in the intervening years.

Bottom-up forecasting

This model recognises from the outset that any period for which a legacy income forecast is attempted must take into account income for which notification has been received and is in the pipeline, as well as income from future notifications. It is based on the following formula:

forecast = pipeline + future notifications

The simplicity of the formula disguises the fact that the most accurate forecasts will be those that take into account a wide range of factors and carry out a large number of calculations. In some models this is done for each individual legacy, which is a great improvement on the cruder method used all those years ago. Whether you have a model as sophisticated as this or something more home-grown, it may be helpful to look at the above formula in a little more detail.

Pipeline

It is useful to categorise legacies by type and by size (within pre-set bands such as up to £20,000, £20,000–50,000 and so on) and then look at average payment times within each band. They will vary greatly, so taking account of these variations will improve the accuracy of the forecast.

It is also important to keep the anticipated value of your gift up to date as more information becomes available. However, if no value is known, the average value for that legacy band should be inserted as a temporary measure.

Crucially, remember not to count the money twice. If payment is received earlier than the average payment time would suggest that it should be, make sure that the legacy is not counted as still being in the pipeline.

Future notifications

While the number of notifications that you will receive is difficult to predict, some indications can be given by factors such as:

• **Trends:** have your notification numbers been going up or down?

• **Death rates:** government statistical rates are a very useful tool. For example, death rates were falling for some years but the general trend has been moving upwards since 2010, with some fluctuations, and rates are projected to continue rising over the next 40 years.[1]

• **Legacy marketing:** if you have records of successful legacy marketing activity, it may be advisable to anticipate that this will lead to an increase in notifications, but beware of the time lag. Currently the average time between the last will and death is around five to six years.[2]

The average values for these future notifications may also be different from those you are currently experiencing; they will depend upon the asset mix of the estates from which you benefit. Are you particularly vulnerable to stock market variations or house prices, or does cash dominate your asset mix? The answers to these and other questions will give you an indication of which macroeconomic forecasts you should be bearing in mind when trying to establish the possible average value of your legacies over the next year or two.

Forecast

If you have a bottom-up forecasting model, it should be updated regularly, so that trends and averages are as accurate as possible. You should also consider running multiple scenarios using a variety of assumptions about notification numbers and average values. This will give an indication of the range within which your future income is likely to fall, whatever happens.

Longer-term forecasting

Once you have an understanding of the factors that affect legacy income, there is a huge amount of information publicly available that can be used to form some sort of picture of the mid- to long-term future. Even though death rates (discussed on page 95) can never be projected with absolute accuracy, when compared with projections about economic factors such as house prices and stock market variations they may be regarded as dead certs (forgive the pun). Nevertheless, there are a lot of projections (provided by banks, building societies and government departments, among others) so, again by running multiple scenarios, it is possible to get a feel for what the future holds.

In addition to these more tangible variables, long-term forecasting should take account of sociological and qualitative factors such as intestacy rates, people's propensity to leave legacies to charity, the tendency to favour pecuniary over residuary legacies, or what types of charity are favoured by particular groups of people (such as the vast number of baby boomers, whose legacies charities will soon start to receive).

Where to get help

A great deal of research has been carried out in all these areas which, if you have the resources, you can tap into and overlay with details about your own charity (such as wealth, gender and age profiles of supporters, as well as legacy and general marketing activity) to get a view of what the future looks like. It is worth keeping an eye open for occasional pieces in the charity press (online and offline), such as *Charity Times*, *Fundraising* magazine and *Third Sector*, and reports from sector bodies such as NCVO (National Council for Voluntary Organisations) and the Directory of Social Change.

A simple Google search for agencies working in the field of legacy forecasting will reveal that the foremost among these is Legacy Foresight, which grew out of a piece of forecasting work carried out for a consortium of charities in the mid-1990s and today works with around 50 charities to map, model and predict the legacy market. Crucially, it also works with individual charities to interpret this intelligence and apply it to their own situation.

Twelve rules for legacy forecasting[3]

1. Forecasting work (even if the horizon seems a long way off) can help to provide a framework for thinking about the future.

2. Forecasts need to be revisited and updated reasonably regularly ...

3. ... but resist the temptation to do this too frequently.

4. Be aware of the need to collect and maintain historical data with the forecasting process in mind.

5. Involve the marketing, finance and admin functions to ensure that the data is collected and interpreted correctly – and to ensure that assumptions are shared, and results are 'owned'.

6. Keep an eye on other charities and the bigger picture.

7. Don't assume that past history on its own is a sufficient predictor of future performance.

8. Remember that values may change quickly, but notification numbers are slow to change.

9. Include exceptionally large and small legacies in your calculations, but remember that they are exceptional.

10. Forecasts are based on a wide variety of assumptions.

11. Multiple scenarios and alternative forecasts (pessimistic, central and optimistic) can help with the management of risk.

12. Accept that forecasts about legacy income (like those about the weather) are probably going to be wrong.

Conclusion

Many people, including Mark Twain and Niels Bohr have been credited with the aphorism 'Forecasting is difficult, especially about the future'. However careful you are, and however complicated your model, a legacy forecast cannot be much more than a best guess.

As legacy professionals, we are doing well if we can always get our finance directors and other managers to understand this.

Notes

1   Andrew Nash, 'Compendium: Summary results' [population projections release], figure 2.2: 'Estimated and projected births and deaths, UK, year ending mid-1971 to year ending mid-2091', Office for National Statistics, www.ons.gov.uk/peoplepopulationandcommunity/populationandmigration/populationprojections/compendium/nationalpopulationprojections/2016basedprojections/summaryresults, 26 October 2017.

2   *Legacy Trends: Discovering potential thorough data* [PDF], Smee & Ford, 2017, https://smeeandford.com/whitepaper, p. 10, accessed 24 January 2018.

3   I am indebted to Legacy Foresight for these rules.

CHAPTER NINE

Applying data analysis to legacy fundraising

Nigel Magson

Introduction

This chapter covers how analysis is applied to legacy fundraising. It is well established that investment in data analysis brings substantial returns to organisations undertaking legacy fundraising. Typically these returns are realised through the data mining of existing supporter relationships (i.e. examining the data to find new information and patterns), and applying the results of these investigations to appropriate stewardship programmes. This can be done both to identify new legacy prospects and to manage communications with those who have already shown an interest in giving a legacy.

Why do data analysis?

The simple answer to the question of why you might want to undertake data analysis is that, as highlighted in the introduction, effective data analysis and insights, such as mining or applying models to target your campaigns to potential legators, will significantly increase your legacy income. There are now numerous examples and case studies from across the sector that show the rewards of long-term investment in analysis and of the effort involved in stewarding potential legators. One such example is Age UK, which has an active stewardship programme for legacies backed by advanced analytics. In 2015/16, legacy income rose to represent over half of all voluntary income received, contributing to a substantial income increase for the organisation.[1]

Understanding who your legacy donors are

Analysis is part of what can be called the 'insight creation process'. It can enable you to understand who – in demographic terms – your legacy donors are, at various points in their relationship with your charity before becoming a legator. It also allows you to quantify and maximise legacy fundraising investment. It helps to answer questions such as:

• When and where does the legacy supporter journey start?

• Where do these supporters live now?

• What is their life stage, i.e. enquirer, considerer, intender, pledger or legator? (See the following section for details on life stages.)

• How old are they, and how old were they when they enquired about leaving a legacy, pledged or made/last changed their will?

• How wealthy are they?

• Where did they live when they considered leaving a gift, make a pledge and become a legator?

• What influences a supporter to be interested in giving a legacy?

When you understand your donors in terms such as these, you can create strategies, tactics and marketing materials with them in mind, making your legacy marketing more effective. For example, this data can be combined to create a legacy pledger profile (comprised of what pledgers have in common), which then allows you to target more people who fit the profile and who are therefore more likely to respond positively to legacy invitations.

Legacy life cycle analysis

Legacy life cycles are a way of classifying individuals according to behavioural stages; typically these life stages are enquirer, considerer, intender, pledger and eventually legator. The results of this analysis of donors at different stages of the legacy life cycle can help inform how you market legacies. Donors at different stages of the life cycle have different characteristics: for example, legacy enquirers and considerers might be younger than legacy pledgers and, as such, would be marketed to differently from older groups. By analysing these stages, you can also reveal the characteristics of the conversion from enquirer to considerer, and so on, including aspects such as which donors are most likely to convert from enquiry to consideration to pledging, and how much time such conversions may take. But the relationship between these behavioural stages and time is not necessarily linear and supporters may enter at a later stage or jump between stages. For instance, someone may already be a pledger but hasn't informed your charity of their pledged gift and so they will be listed on your system as an enquirer.

Increasing numbers of legators

In the UK, as reported by Smee & Ford (shown in figure 9.1), the value of legacies left to charities is increasing, rising from £1.8 billion in 2011/12 to just under £2.5 billion in 2015/16. Furthermore, while there are always fluctuations over the years (with notable drops in the number of charitable estates recorded in 2010 and 2014), the proportion of people who leave a legacy to a charity is also increasing: in 1997, only 4.6% of people left a legacy to a charity, but this number had grown to 6.2% by 2016.[2] This trend may be attributed to the growth of legacy fundraising at individual organisations and the impact of various awareness initiatives, such as Remember a Charity, and will-writing services such as the Free Will Service and Will Aid, where there is evidence that these initiatives are expanding the overall number of intenders and pledgers. (See 'Will-writing analysis' on page 103 for details.)

FIGURE 9.1 AGGREGATE LEGACY INCOME AND THE NUMBER OF ORGANISATIONS RECEIVING LEGACIES OVER TIME (£M)[3]

Reproduced by permission of Smee & Ford.

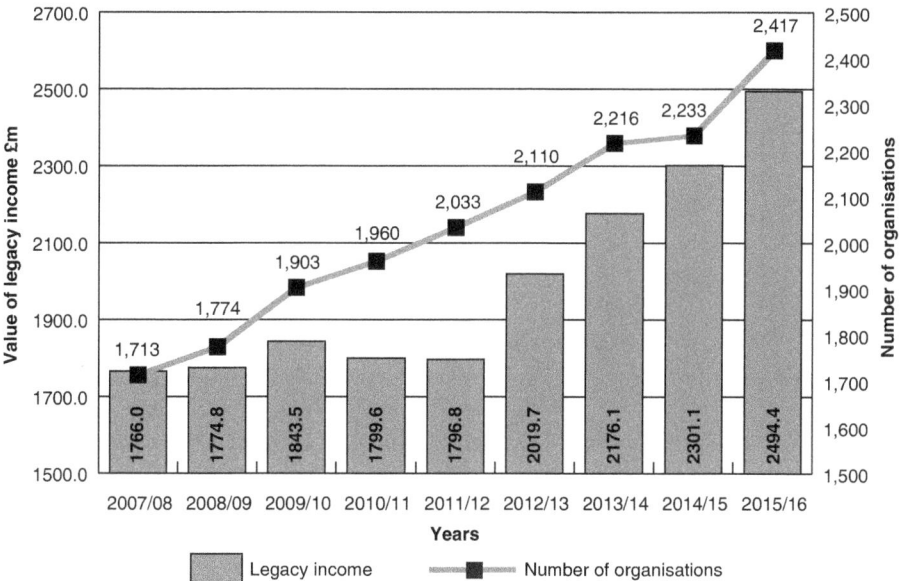

While it remains the case that only a comparatively small percentage of overall supporters will leave a legacy, analysis by Adroit Data and Insight (Adroit) for a variety of organisations shows that once someone makes a pledge they are very likely to become a legator – typically over 90% of pledgers will do so – so it makes financial sense to focus on increasing the numbers of and stewarding these types of supporter.

Legacy metrics and reporting

Your charity can understand the true return on investment of its fundraising activities better by analysing data on legacy donors and income. By measuring certain elements, recording numbers and reporting the data, you can evaluate investments and, as a result, direct where resources should go. The analytical reports you can generate can cover a range of metrics, for example:

• the number of people who have pledged a gift to your charity and the estimated value of those pledges;

• the proportion of people who pledged a gift as a percentage of all the people (in any given campaign) you invited to pledge (i.e. the conversion rate);

• the number of people at each stage of the legacy life cycle (i.e. the number of intenders, pledgers, and so on you have) and how these numbers are changing year by year;

• the levels of your charity's legacy income in terms of residuary versus pecuniary split and the trend by year;

• how much it costs your charity to acquire a new pledger and the trend by year;

• notifications of new pledgers – the number and the trend by year;

• open and closed cases, i.e. the number of pledgers you have versus legators.

If you combine analysis of legators and income, you can create a picture of the true return on investment of legacy fundraising activities. Are pledgers acquired through a particular source, or are those who interact with the charity in a particular way more likely to become pledgers? Furthermore, by analysing both pledger and legacy data you can reveal the true lifetime value of your legacy supporters.

Forecasting

So how much legacy income can your charity expect to receive and when can it expect to realise it? Questions like this are often asked when fundraisers need to justify investing in legacy marketing. In addition to seeing a snapshot of your charity's current legacy income profile, it is possible to examine previous legacies left to your charity to see how the picture is changing and to predict *future* legacy income. Forecasts typically look at trended benchmarks (i.e. key performance indicators or statistics that are looked at over time), including whether income is increasing or decreasing, if you are bringing in a greater number of legacies, and whether the legacies that you receive are increasing or decreasing in value, and combine this information with demographics and market trends, sector studies and consortia studies.[4] You can also apply actuarial techniques on life expectancy – based on known age, gender and region data – to government population statistics. Typically, the larger the population involved, the more accurate these techniques become.

Analysing changes to legacy life cycle stages (enquirers, considerers, intenders and pledgers) is one way of forecasting how long it will take for legacy gifts to be realised. So, if you know how much time elapses on average between a supporter pledging a gift and eventually becoming a legator, you can make a prediction about when your current pledgers' gifts will be realised. If your pledgers are normally in their mid-70s, the amount of time it will take your charity to receive the income from these gifts will obviously be sooner than if your pledgers' average age is in their mid-30s. Similarly, you can look at your life-stage groups to estimate what proportion of people you expect in each group to eventually become legators. For instance, the proportion of pledgers who will become legators will be far higher than the proportion of considerers who will become eventual legators. All forecasting techniques, of course, involve scope for error, but they can provide some empirical evidence for you to take to your finance director when those difficult questions are asked.

Will-writing analysis

In the UK, will-writing services are offered by many organisations and present a legacy fundraising opportunity. Typically offered to existing supporters, they can be promoted more widely and extend your charity's footprint through engaging a solicitor network to prompt or remind will makers that they can donate to a charity.

Consortia analysis of 56 charities in the UK by Adroit in 2013 and 2016 showed that over a ten-year period since 2005 over 70% of people who used these will-writing services pledged a gift. The study also showed that the majority of those pledging do go on to leave legacy gifts (typically over 90% of pledgers do so, as noted earlier). It examined Capacity Marketing's Free Wills Month, which started in 2005 and in the first 10 years ran 39 campaigns (consisting of Free Wills Fortnights and Free Wills Months). Each campaign produced over 500 pledging responders, and overall this initiative generated 38,256 wills, resulting in 21,985 legacy pledges, of which 2,487 were residuary gifts with an estimated £30 million value; the remainder were pecuniary, with an estimated value of £15 million. In total, therefore, £45 million was pledged in donations to the participating charities. Approximately 300 solicitors are involved each year.[5]

The Cancer Research UK scheme has been running in the UK since 1993. Up to 2013, it generated over 91,000 pledges representing £426 million. Of the 5,000 notifications Cancer Research UK receives each year, around 900 come from wills written through the charity's Free Will Service. Analysis of deceased pledgers also showed that 90% of those who pledged went on to give, but at 110% of the value originally indicated (due to the increased value of the residuary element thanks to, for example, the increase in the value of property over time).[6]

In its 2016 study, Adroit noted that, despite the targeting of will-writing services to individuals over the age of 50, there was a high demand among individuals in their thirties and forties: 28% of people who take up will-writing services are under 55, and 26% of people who become pledgers are under 55. Typically the arrival of children prompts people to write their first will. This is reinforced by research from Adrian Sargeant and colleagues which found that the average age of legacy pledgers was 47.[7]

This research shows that there is a long-term opportunity to attract legacy interest at a much earlier life stage than charities commonly do.

Adroit also investigated the financial sophistication of people using will services, and the types of charities and causes that they are likely to support. This varied by charitable organisation, and there was a distinct difference around the motivations and interests of those using will services at an earlier life stage as compared to older individuals. For instance, the research shows that younger people (those in their mid-40s and younger) are far more likely to support humanitarian or environmental charities than those with an older profile (those in their mid-40s and older). And older people have a much greater interest in animal charities than people with a younger profile. No marked difference was noted between those two groups with regard to supporting medical charities.

What data should you collect and store?

This section covers the data your charity needs to collect and how it can be enhanced, stored and managed.

Data needed

Table 9.1 shows the types of information that you can collect, grouped by broad data areas.

TABLE 9.1 SUPPORTER INFORMATION THAT CAN BE RECORDED IN A
DATABASE

Overall data areas	Data detail	Notes and observations
Contact details	Name and address information, both current and historical	Current contact details, including email address, social media handles, etc. As people age, they often change address; by retaining previous addresses on a database, it is possible to analyse where someone lived when they made their will, rather than where they lived when they died (which adds useful information to your legacy pledger profile, allowing future pledgers to be targeted more effectively).
Contact classification	Position of segment at point in time and geodemographic information	Additional information that can be derived from or ascertained about a contact, such as their age, wealth indicators, internal classification (such as 'current active supporter') and life cycle stage.
	Legacy life cycle stage	The person's current status in the legacy life cycle: enquirer, considerer, intender, pledger or legator.
	Age (date of birth)	The person's actual date of birth or, if no date of birth is available but a date band (such as 40–45) is, the year is estimated picking the mid-point of the date band.
Transactional history	Gift and transactional history, such as events, symbolic giving and campaigning.	Information on legacy supporters' giving history. Information on gift details, including payment methods, is commonly recorded and may offer useful indicators when modelling. However, the longitudinal nature of data sets means that certain variables may change over time: for example, Gift Aid has only been around for a limited period.

Other relationships	Such as being a volunteer	What other, non-giving relationships have your supporters had with your charity?
Legacy source and campaign	Legacy communications and response history	Understanding how legacy contacts have been communicated with, particularly those who have gone on to pledge or leave a legacy, is vital in order to evaluate the success of these activities.
Content classification	Campaign and content coding	You can use content taxonomies to classify communications with supporters or enquirers, including how people interact with social and web content (such as a web page, or a piece of social media content). This is often done in a web content or marketing asset management system. Note that communications content and interactions with enquirers are increasingly taking place in digital platforms, such as social media, so feeds from these are becoming ever more important.
Interpersonal links	Relationships	By recording relationships between individuals, you can potentially understand something of their legacy motivation. For example, a legacy donor may be related to a service user or to another legacy donor. Understanding relationships between individuals will help you to understand the complex networks that link legacy donors with your organisation.
Attitudes and questionnaire results	Survey results and coding	It is useful to collect information about people's attitudes to giving and their motivations for giving to your charity, including whether they would consider leaving a legacy gift, and organisations that your contacts also support.

Wills and probate information	Will and third-party data	Smee & Ford reads wills once probate has been granted and notify charities of legacies they have been left. The reports include useful information, including the legator's last address, the type of legacy, the amount or share left to the charity, the date the will was written, the details of the executors and any other charities included in the will.

Data quality and recency

General contact and transactional data that your charity holds on supporters should be of good quality, legally compliant and up to date. It is therefore important that you have robust data management procedures to capture full contact details, including:

• common templates such as standardised forms for collecting data including a name field information template and the Royal Mail Postcode Address File (PAF) format;

• field validation, such as titles and the @ sign within an email address;

• permission centres, which are essentially lists of people who have opted in to receive legacy marketing communications;

• suitable metadata (data that provides information about other data) about when and where the details were collected.

Legacy relationships are long ones. If a donor pledges in their fifties, the relationship is likely to continue for 20 or more years before the legacy is received. During this time, the pledger may move home, downsize and possibly end up in a care home. By retaining previous addresses in a database, it is possible to analyse where someone lived when they made their will, rather than where they lived when they died, allowing future pledgers to be targeted more effectively (by using this information as part of your legacy pledger profile). Given these points, you must take care to store historical as well as current data with dates.

Where to store your data

Typically the main repository for fundraising data is a fundraising database, but this is not necessarily the best place to store information for long-term analysis and is not the place to undertake analysis or campaign activity. Larger organisations will have a data warehouse (a central repository that contains data from various sources) or a datamart (a subset of a data warehouse that holds data serving a specific need or groups of users). You can extract data from a data warehouse or link it to specialist analysis or business intelligence packages. I would recommend a platform such as an SQL (structured query language system) or SAS (statistical analysis system) that supports a relational data structure (for example, one that will relate many gifts or communications to a supporter) and can then be accessed by suitable analysis or business intelligence technologies.

Sources of data

While fundraising database systems are an important source of data on your current supporters, they are generally not the only system your organisation will have that contains valuable information for legacy programmes. Other information collected and stored in various parts of the organisation might relate to audiences such as service users, members, volunteers, employees, ex-employees, pensioners, traders, website users, and event participants and organisers. You can also use a separate administrative system (for example, FirstClass) and/or spreadsheets.

Service user data

Research shows that people's motives for leaving a charitable gift in their will include reciprocity, or a sense of 'paying back' the organisation for services received.[8] Similarly, as outlined in 'Life experience' on page 18, online respondents in Russell James's study showed the highest levels of interest in leaving a gift to charity when reference was made to supporting causes that had been important in their lives.

Given these motivations, having access to data on service users, can clearly be valuable. Someone may, for instance, have decades of memories of spending time in the grounds of a heritage charity, or their relative may have been cared for by a cancer charity. Owing to such experiences, people are likely to feel highly motivated to offer a gift to charities that have touched them.

It is of course crucial to respect legal stipulations regarding who has permission to access information on service users and for what purpose.[9] This is particularly important, for example, with charities that hold sensitive data internally about service users, such as medical charities. Nevertheless, within appropriate boundaries, such data can be useful in helping you to improve your understanding of the relationship of an individual with your charity and can allow you to contact those people who would welcome the opportunity to express their thanks to your charity.

Data via additional services

If your organisation provides additional services, such as funeral plans or an executorship service, these can generate further information on potential pledgers. This information might be recorded within your fundraising database or in a separate system.

Keeping control of multiple data sources

With many potential sources, formats and collection processes, you may need to develop what are known as data management ETL (extract, transform and load) processes to match different data sources with associated business rules. For example, your database might have a 'J. Smith' and a 'John Smith' at the same address and both are male – the business rules could allow these two records to be consolidated into one, or the rules might dictate that further information needs to be gathered to determine whether J. Smith is, in fact, a different person. These data management ETL processes also allow you to enhance and create appropriate metadata, such as information on address history or permissions. Business rules may need to change in your fundraising database and in other systems when data changes: for example, when someone pledges a legacy, their status would change from enquirer to pledger.

Data enhancement

You can supplement internal data with information from external sources to fill in the blanks of a legacy pledger profile – for example, to target legacy messages at particular age groups, you could use date-of-birth data to generate age profiles and subsets of supporters. You can then direct a specific campaign at these subsets of people. I recommend that external information is added at an individual level as opposed to postcode (or census enumeration district) level, as this can easily exclude good prospects.

Variables worth considering include age, number of dependants, gender, marital status, income and wealth. Supporters' levels of wealth can be powerful to determine which of your legacy contacts have higher-value estates, as these individuals may need a different strategy from other legacy prospects.

There are a number of data providers that offer wealth screening and cold legacy prospect databases specifically designed to target legacy prospects, with a variety of depths of data. In the EU, once the GDPR (General Data Protection Regulation) has been introduced in 2018, you will need to ensure that appropriate permissions have been collected and observe prevailing legislation when using third-party data, or prospect research.

As well as buying in external data, you can also develop questionnaires internally to provide more information about individuals' motivations for supporting your charity, their interests (which could be lifestyle interests, or interests in the organisation's services or campaigns) and their requirements from the relationship in the future. Figure 9.2 shows a one-off exercise for a medical charity to produce a file suitable for legacy analysis.

FIGURE 9.2 PRODUCING A FILE SUITABLE FOR LEGACY ANALYSIS

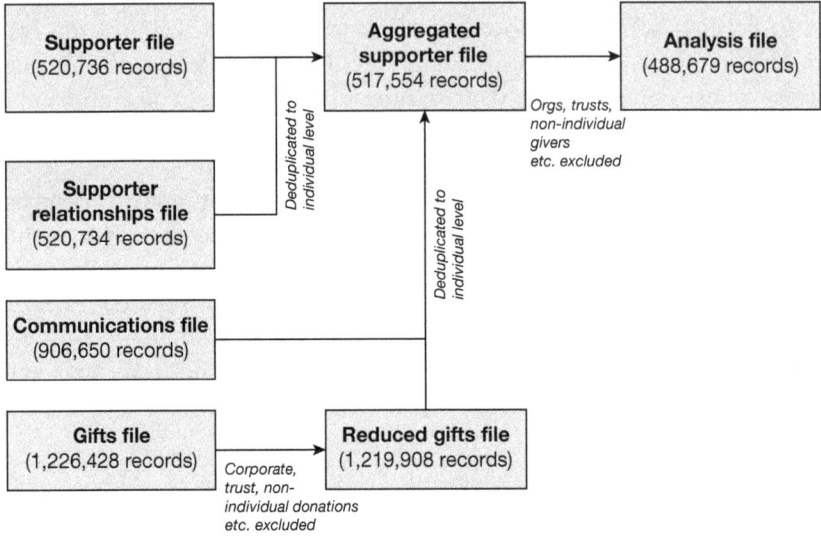

Applications: What can be done with the data?

Once the systems and processes for capturing and storing data are in place, what can you do with them? – Apply the data in different ways to target prospective legacy-givers more effectively and strengthen engagement. This section focuses on descriptive analysis, which can lead to more advanced targeting models that can be used to identify individuals who are more likely to pledge. The section also examines the process of model creation and outlines the notable pitfalls you need to keep an eye out for.

Descriptive analysis: Understanding pledgers and legators

When a set of data is analysed to create brief summaries about the data, these are called descriptive statistics. These simple summaries can be about your legacy finances and audience (outlined in the following sections) and their associated measures such as:

• means (your average pledger age, for instance);

• profiles (including gender, age, employment and location);

• indexes (used to compare the relative change between one population and a base population, for example the age of a pledger population compared to all supporters);

• *z*-scores (these allow you to see how important any given factor, such as gender, is in terms of how likely a group of people are to pledge; note that *z*-scores can be misleading on small population sizes, so I would also recommend using *t*-scores which are more accurate for analysing small populations).

Descriptive analysis typically compares descriptive statistics on one target group, such as pledgers, with a wider base. Your base could be all those who have enquired for a will pack, or it could be all your supporters. Defining the base is important.

There are many types of descriptive analysis that you can do on your known legators, your current pledgers, and/or on individuals who are known to be at an early stage in the legacy life cycle, such as an enquirer or considerer. These can reveal important insights which you can incorporate into your legacy fundraising programme, a few of which are outlined in the following sections.

Income analysis

Income analysis is a type of descriptive analysis which can help you build up a picture of current pledged and legacy income, including:

• the total amount of legacy income received by your organisation in the past;

• the amount currently pledged (both known and an estimate of what is unknown);

• the number and percentage of legacies of each type received – for example, residuary or pecuniary;

• the amount and percentage of income attributable to the different legacy types.

If you look at trends on a year-by-year basis this will show you the most common types of legacy and which types provide the most valuable source of income. In many organisations, the greatest numbers of legacies received are likely to be pecuniary; however, the greatest value is likely to be received from residuary legacies. See figure 9.3 for an example of the results of income analysis.

FIGURE 9.3 INCOME ANALYSIS

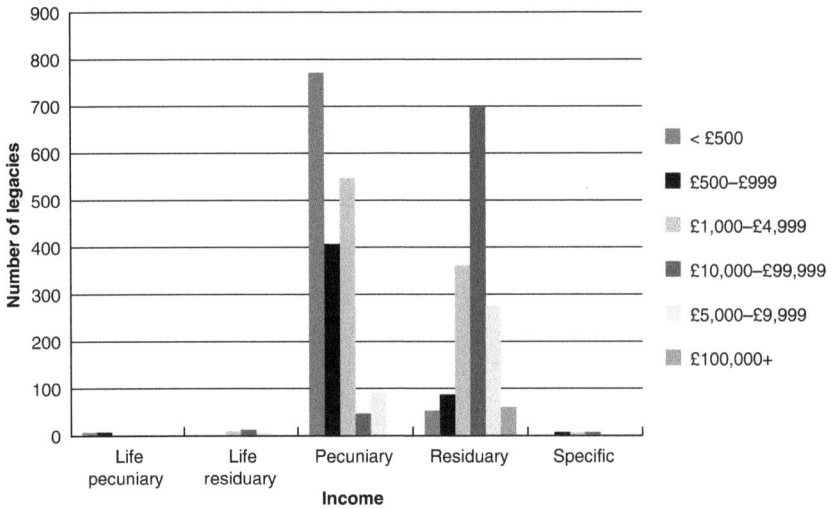

Legend:
- < £500
- £500–£999
- £1,000–£4,999
- £10,000–£99,999
- £5,000–£9,999
- £100,000+

Age and income analysis

Age analysis is another type of descriptive analysis that is widely and perhaps overly used, but is useful in combination with income analysis. As you can see in figure 9.4, legators naturally have an older age profile. This type of analysis can help you to predict how long it will take to realise future legacy income, and the likely split of income type (mainly pecuniary or residuary), by comparing your current pledgers' age with forecast data on your legators' age at death and income split.

FIGURE 9.4 AGE AT DEATH BY LEGACY TYPE

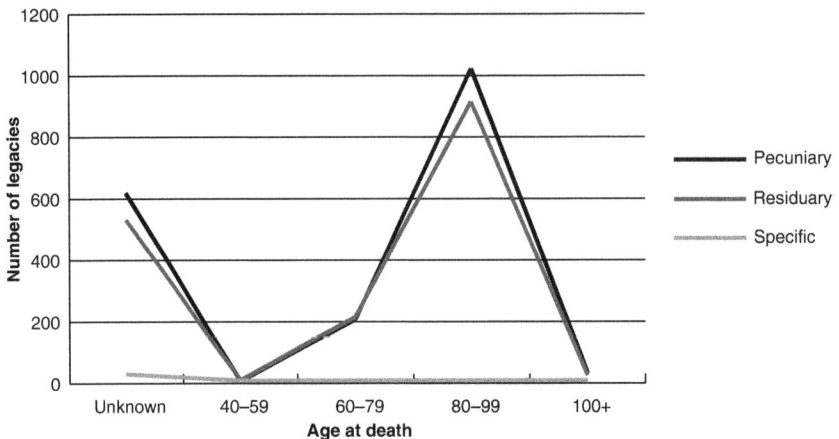

Legend:
- Pecuniary
- Residuary
- Specific

Pledger and legator source analysis

Yet another type of descriptive analysis you can do is to cross-reference pledger and legator data with donor, volunteer, supporter or client databases. This can identify relationships between, for example, pledger data and these other database groups. A pledger may also be a donor or a volunteer, or both, and you can then identify the progression of a pledger's support (i.e. the legacy supporter journey), such as when the person first made a donation to your cause, then when they began volunteering, and so on.

This cross-referencing can also help you find a way to find new legacy prospects. If you don't find evidence of a supporter's other relationships with your charity, this may just mean you don't have any other recorded information about them. In other cases it can also offer a fruitful source of legacy prospects without an existing relationship with your organisation but who are on your system for other purposes, such as solicitors or health professionals.

This cross-referencing can also offer you clues as to what percentage of fundraising effort and budget to devote to approaching people who have shown an interest in your organisation versus approaching those who have had no contact, and which are the most effective channels for spreading legacy messages.

Advanced targeting: Modelling

The information you have gleaned from descriptive analysis techniques can be combined into what's called 'advanced targeting'. Advanced targeting can help you to:

• find people who may be interested in leaving a gift to your charity, from a base of known supporters or within an alternative audience (for example, service users or traders);

• identify those more likely to pledge;

• find higher-value pledgers.

Identifying higher-value pledgers allows you to ensure that you're both maintaining the major-pledger relationships appropriately and applying different strategic approaches in developing new sources of support.

Predictive modelling and propensity scores

Predictive modelling

Predictive modelling uses statistics to create a model that will predict the likelihood of a particular outcome. For example, in a campaign for The Children's Society in 2015/16, Adroit used predictive modelling to identify groups among the charity's existing supporters that would be most likely to pledge legacy gifts. By targeting these groups, the charity substantially improved upon previous pledger conversion rates and estimated as a result to have generated £3 million of pledged legacy income within 12 months.

Predictive modelling software typically allows an analyst to run multiple iterations and apply different analytic techniques. This might, start with the most significant variable, such as number of relationships with an organisation, and progressively adding one variable at a time, for instance gender, then income band, until there is no further uplift, i.e. no further increase in predictive power. When building a model, often the variables used have the same or overlapping power, as essentially some variables are too alike. For instance, a major donor flag and a high-income band might explain the same thing and therefore do not add to the model's predictive power.

Analysts will usually try a variety of modelling techniques and pick the best one, comparing the results and uplift against a test data set where the outcome is known (see 'Discriminant analysis' on page 119). Neural and AI (artificial intelligence) solutions are also among the techniques being deployed, and while these techniques can take longer to set up and 'train', they have the advantage of coping with a wider variety of data and adapting or learning as new outcomes appear.

Propensity scores

An analyst can use statistical techniques to create propensity scores, which indicate how likely any given individual is to be positively influenced if they were contacted with a legacy-giving campaign. The scores are created by combining and using 'hard' factors (i.e. those in the supporter's records) that can be identified which make someone more likely to pledge. Below is a list of many of the common factors found, although it is important to stress that these vary according to the data your organisation has available as well as its fundraising and legacy history:

• the number of relationships a person has held with your organisation over time;

• how long they have supported your organisation (this can itself become a proxy for age);

- their giving behaviour – for example, cash, pledged gift, use of Gift Aid;

- types of previous or existing relationships with the organisation (such as campaigner or volunteer);

- attitudes collected in relation to the causes the person supports, their relationship with your organisation and general life attitudes;

- age of prospect (often excluded from models but can be introduced as a filter);

- title (traditionally Miss, Mrs or Ms for women, though the use of titles is lessening over time, and some charities use military titles);

- dependants (age and number of);

- gender;

- marital status;

- content and web pages accessed (for example, website legacy pages).

Figures 9.5 to 9.7 give examples of how these factors can be compared with a potential base of supporters.

While the initial descriptive analysis might identify a large number of these factors, combining them into a single score may mean only a few factors will be used: those that create the optimum combination to be able to identify potential legators. In many scores these factors are assigned different strengths or weights. For example, those with an active gift aid flag might be weighted more than those who are new regular givers.

With certain techniques, you will need to reassess this weighting periodically to create the optimum score, which is one that represents the true population most accurately. The score can change over time; for example, as population and response behaviour changes – millennials versus baby boomers.

Length of relationship

Figure 9.5 shows the importance of the length of a supporter's relationship with a charity and the need to build up a picture of a supporter's history. In this example, the longer the length of support for an organisation the more likely they are to be a pledger or legator than the overall supporter base.

FIGURE 9.5 LENGTH OF RELATIONSHIP: PLEDGERS/LEGATORS V. BASE

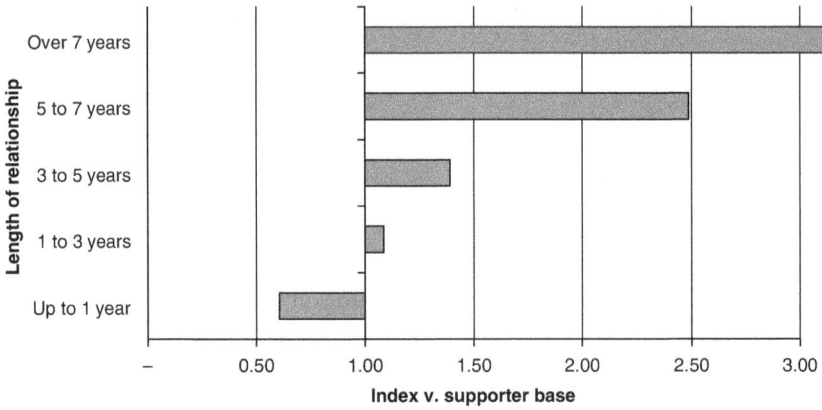

Titles

Figure 9.6 shows how title can be used as a proxy for whether someone has children and therefore that person's likelihood of pledging a legacy (childless people are significantly more likely to leave a gift to charity than those with children).[10] However, given that titles are becoming a less reliable indicator of family status, their predictive power is lessening over time.

FIGURE 9.6 PLEDGER/LEGATOR TITLE PROFILE

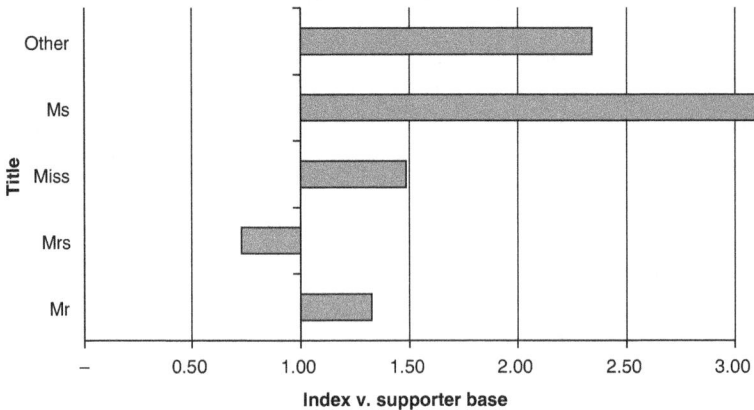

Multiple relationships

Figure 9.7 illustrates the importance of a supporter having multiple relationships with a charity: the more relationships a person has the more likely they are to be a pledger or legator.

FIGURE 9.7 NUMBER OF RELATIONSHIPS WITH A CHARITY: PLEDGERS/ LEGATORS V. BASE

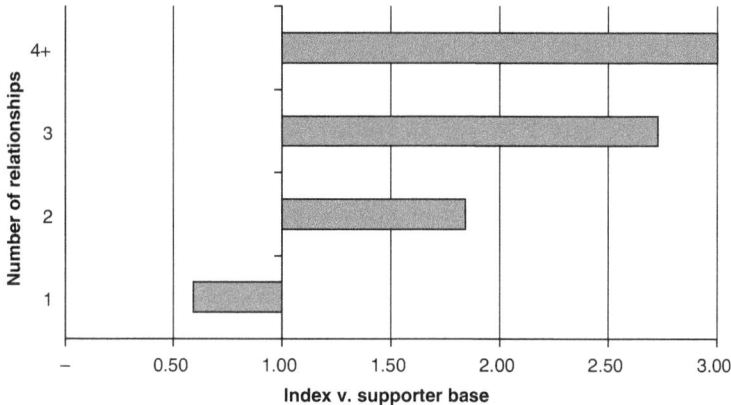

Testing the model

Once these factors have been combined into a score, the analyst can gauge the strength of the model by testing it on a new set of data. You can see an example in figure 9.8, where the responses from pledgers are higher using the new model than they are using the previous model.

If you use a model such as this your charity will have far more success than mailing a standard selection of people. In figure 9.8, the diagonal line shows that if you were to send a mailing to 20% of individuals you could expect on average 20% of the people mailed to become pledgers. In this example the new model is built using binary logistic regression (which is more powerful than the previous modelling technique), and in fact 47% of pledgers can be identified within the first percentile of the entire supporter file, so it is highly predictive.

The upshot is that by using such a model, a charity can identify the 20% of supporters most likely to respond to a legacy pledge message, contact them and find that around 90% of the people it contacts in that group will make a pledge.

FIGURE 9.8 MODEL GAINS: NEW MODEL V. OLD MODEL

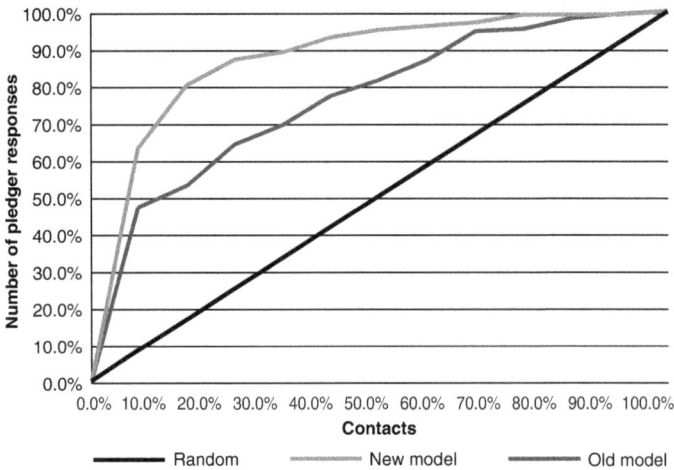

Applying scores

Figure 9.9 shows the volume of all individual supporter records who were pledgers, as scored as part of a legacy pledger model process. It shows that those supporters who pledged and had the best legacy prospect scores had the highest 'penetration' level, which means that they were indeed the most likely to become legacy pledgers. This shows the accuracy of scores when applied to a full base of known pledgers on the organisation's database, including those not used in the model creation.

FIGURE 9.9 PENETRATION OF KNOWN PLEDGERS V. SCORE

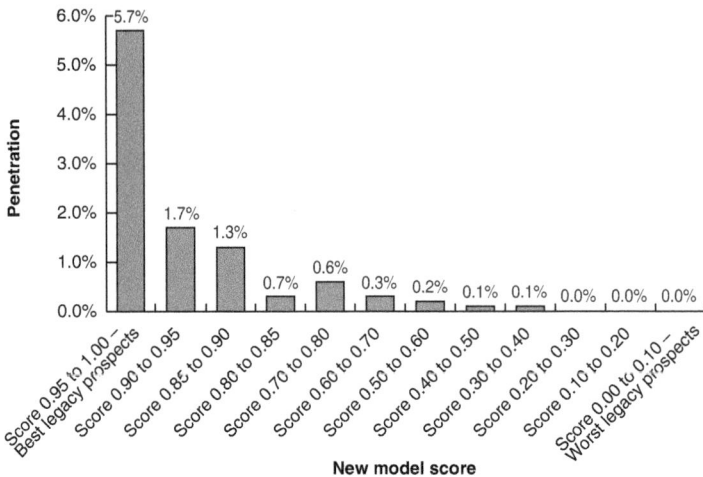

Discriminant analysis

Discriminant analysis is a technique which can help evaluate how good a model is at both predicting a yes/no outcome. When building a model, the analyst splits their data set so that they can have a 'train' and 'test' population. In figure 9.10 we can see that 70% of the overall population was used for training the model, and the remaining 30% of the data for testing. Discriminant analysis shows how many people are correctly classified, in this instance:

1. how many people are pledgers;

2. how many people are *not* pledgers.

In the test data set, because the outcomes are already known, you can then conclude how many of the predictions were correct, and how many were wrong. This allows you to determine how good your model is at correctly classifying outcomes. It is important that a model can both predict those people who aren't going to do something, as much as those who will go on to do something. The balance of prediction is important.

So in figure 9.10, you can see that the accuracy levels of both the training and the testing data sets of the model are high. This is important because there should be a good balance between the two: between who is going to become something and who is *not* going to become something (in this case, a pledger). If the percentages were imbalanced, it would be a less strong model. For example, you could use a model that's good at predicting who is going to become a pledger but one that is not very good at predicting who *isn't* going to become a pledger.

FIGURE 9.10 MODEL ACCURACY: TRAINING V. TEST

	Training of model (on 70% of known data)		Testing of model (on 30% of known data)	
Pledger	**No**	**Yes**	**No**	**Yes**
Predictions	4,875	631	2,125	271
	708	4,878	272	2,041
Correct prediction	87.3%	88.5%	88.7%	88.3%
Overall	87.9%		88.5%	

☐ Correct prediction   ▨ Wrong prediction

Modelling pitfalls

Applying advanced modelling techniques can have pitfalls. Models can become overused or misapplied. For instance, a model could be applied to different areas of fundraising yet lead to a similar set of supporters being selected in each area. A legacy pledger model can favour supporters who have had longer and multiple relationships with a charity, which would mean that opportunities to get younger, recently recruited donors to pledge would be ignored. In this way, when supporters have just started giving, they can be deemed ineligible for a supporter model due to not having had time to build up the required relationship.

To avoid this particular pitfall, using a new supporter model would allow these prospects to be targeted more efficiently. But, because the usual factors that rank prospects higher – i.e. factors that make them more likely to pledge, such those of having a long relationship or multiple relationships with your charity – cannot be factored in, you would need to add external data, such as income data, to otherwise discriminate which prospects may score more highly.

Advanced targeting: Campaign planning and success

By using campaign planning spreadsheets, you can run test scenarios for the rolling out of your campaigns. These scenarios can be based on changes in average cost per contact, expected overall response rate and the average legacy value of respondents. Given the nature and size of legacy bequests, even very low response rates can be worthwhile. Thanks to legacy marketing campaigns becoming increasingly multichannel (including using more digital media) and reaching out to new audiences, you will need to apply different techniques to track and monitor how much people read about and are interested in/respond to your legacy materials.

The future of legacy analysis

Since the previous edition of this book (in 2010), the collection and use of digital and behavioural web data has become considerably more developed in the sector. Charities are increasingly using linking techniques between digital media to collect information on those who are browsing sites, responding in social media and expressing an interest in legacy giving. A charity can collect information (where this is legally permissible) on a visitor to its website who visits legacy pages and link this behaviour to the visitor's supporter record. The charity can now act on this information – for example, by inviting the visitor to an upcoming seminar, sending a triggered communication or flagging the visitor to receive the next offline legacy pack.

Looking ahead, AI technologies able to classify unstructured data, such as audio, video, web pages, presentations and social media content, are set to become part of IT and customer relationship management infrastructures. Using this content to understand your supporters' reactions to legacy marketing will help charities to develop stronger engagement and tracking capabilities.

To be effective, charities will no longer be able to take a one-size-fits-all approach to channels and communications, given the underlying differences between potential legacy donors. It will be more important than ever to take multichannel approaches, including having the underlying infrastructure to store and work with unstructured data. Finally, technology and the expectations people now have around responsiveness itself are creating pressure on organisations to be quick to act. In due course, consumers will expect the sophistication from charities that will come with the use of machine-learning algorithms.

Conclusion

The effective use of data is a key component in a successful legacy fundraising programme: it allows fundraisers to communicate with the most promising legacy prospects in the way most appropriate to them. Analysis of your supporter base and indeed your own legacy programme is an ongoing prerequisite for legacy marketing campaigns.

It is perhaps worth reiterating that, like most areas of legacy fundraising, analysis and modelling should not necessarily be viewed as a quick win (although it can be!); they require a long-term attitude to investment. So, in a sector where fundraisers are likely to move between roles every couple of years, an organisation must take a long-term attitude not just to legacy fundraising but also to the collection and use of data, and robust procedures must be adhered to, despite changes in staffing.

Data analysis is an ongoing activity. The profiles of your charity's pledgers, legators and income will change over time – for example, members of Generation X have very different profiles from the baby boomer generation that preceded them, as will the millennials and Generation Z in due course. It will be vital to continue to test, learn from and rebuild models, and to approach different groups of supporters with different messages.

In order to grow their long-term legacy income, charities need to invest in their data collection, management and analysis capabilities. The next generations who will give the legacy gifts of the future are making their wills now.

Notes

1   *Report of Trustees and Annual Accounts 2015/16* [PDF], Age UK,
     www.ageuk.org.uk/globalassets/age-uk/documents/annual-reports-and-reviews/
     report_of_trustees_and_annual_accounts_2015_2016.pdf, p. 23, accessed
     26 January 2018.

2   *Legacy Trends 2017 Update: Discovering potential through data* [PDF], Smee &
     Ford, 2017, https://smeeandford.com/whitepaper, pp. 2 and 6, accessed
     8 December 2017.

3   *Ibid.*, p. 3, figure 1.

4   See, for example, studies conducted by Legacy Foresight – a UK-based legacy
     marketing benchmarking consortia: www.legacyforesight.co.uk/benchmarking.

5   Consortia analysis conducted by Adroit in 2013 and 2016. Available from
     www.adroitinsight.com/free-wills-service-insights for members only.

6   Figures stated in a presentation given by Pauline Meyer and Jack Visser from the
     Cancer Research UK legacy team at the 2013 Institute of Fundraising conference.

7   Adrian Sargeant, Walter Wymer and Toni Hilton, 'Marketing Bequest Club
     Membership: An exploratory study of legacy pledgers', *Nonprofit and Voluntary
     Sector Quarterly*, vol. 35, no. 3, 2006, pp. 384–404.

8   Adrian Sargeant and Toni Hilton, 'The Final Gift: Targeting the potential charity
     legator', *International Journal of Nonprofit and Voluntary Sector Marketing*,
     vol. 10, no. 1, 2005, pp. 3–16.

9   Note that the introduction in 2018 of the EU's General Data Protection
     Regulation will have an impact on the collection and use of personal data across
     European countries.

10   See, for example, Russell James's *Causes and Correlates of Charitable Giving in
     Estate Planning: A cross-sectional and longitudinal examination of older adults*,
     Association of Fundraising Professionals, 2008, p. 28.

CHAPTER TEN

Crafting the vision: the legacy case for support

Richard Radcliffe

Introduction

The objectives of this chapter are simple. It aims to show you how to craft:

- a macro legacy vision (or more than one) to show you have an ambitious future;

- micro visions (short ones) which can be dropped into everyday communications;

- regular supporting statements (based on the stories of each stakeholder);

- information on wills and legacies in simple everyday language to show that wills are easy to do and that legacies are simple to include and are now a social norm.

What is a legacy case for support?

The legacy case for support is the legacy vision – your charity's overall vision brought to life through gifts and wills. It's what makes your charity unique, and is the simple answer to the question 'Why should I leave your charity a gift in my will?'. The legacy vision should be written once internal and external research has been conducted to establish current perceptions of your charity. This will enable you to address perceived weaknesses and to play to your strengths, which is crucial to do given that legacy pledgers are known to be more concerned about organisational performance than other types of donor (see 'Organisational factors' on page 21).

The legacy vision will form the heart of all your legacy communications. This statement (or statements), which can comprise both macro and micro visions, can be used across all channels and at every event and talk. It forms a link between the motivations for giving now (through one-off or ongoing support) and giving later (through a gift in a will).

The vision should express the need that the prospect is going to want to buy into, and it should be adaptable to various communication methods and various target audiences (current donors, the general public, volunteers, staff, service users, beneficiaries and so on). The legacy vision should dovetail with the overall vision of your charity. It should also be tangible so as to engage prospects despite the fact the gift might not be received for many decades.

There can be more than one vision. A potential starting point is to take your organisation's charitable objectives and convert each one into a legacy vision. For example, a cancer research charity can have one vision (a world without cancer) but also legacy visions relevant to children's cancers, breast cancer and testicular cancer. A hospice can have an overall vision of providing superb care for the local community but also have legacy visions for its in-patient unit, hospice-at-home services and bereavement support. An arts charity, such as a museum, can have a vision of a world where people embrace diversity through the understanding of other communities, and also have legacy visions for the growth of its collections, curatorial specialisms, conservation and education.

A legacy vision can be of any length, depending on how it is used. It can be helpful to think in terms of micro visions, which can be dropped into everyday communications, and one (or more than one) main macro vision, which forms the heart of your legacy communications programme.

Legacy visions, unlike organisational visions, are not always permanent. Organisational visions are normally permanent as they are your ultimate picture of what the completion of your ambition for your organisation's beneficiaries would look like. (The exact wording may change but the charity's original founding objects usually stay the same.) Legacy visions are not permanent because, like your organisational mission (that is how you reach your organisational vision), they should change according to altering circumstances and as progress is made possibly over a 50-year period. Because legacy visions age and you might be reading this book in 2020 or beyond, it is recommended that you visit the legacy webpages of competitor charities and leading legacy charities to get a snapshot of how they are envisaging the future in their legacy vision and mission statements. It is also sensible to become a legacy enquirer (or just contact charities) and obtain examples of legacy brochures, letters and so on.

Strengthening your case for support

When considering the heart of your vision, there are two key questions to ask yourself. Firstly, what is the motivation for supporting your charity? If it is a personal experience, then your charity is at a huge advantage in terms of attracting legacies. A personal experience means every prospect has a reason to say thank you for what your charity has done for them and/or their family. (See also 'Life experience' on page 18 for details on why this is such an advantage.) In contrast, if supporters of your charity are motivated more by a sense of duty, then legacy giving will be driven more by a sense of 'there but for the grace of God go I'. This kind of motivation is less tangible and applies to many causes, such as homelessness, mental health and support of individuals with learning difficulties. Duty-motivated legacies to religious causes can often have an element of personal experience if the charity carries out work only in the UK.

Secondly, do your best prospects know and understand how your charity is funded? A legacy is a less spontaneous gift than a donation and will generally be thought about more. A legacy usually (but not always) needs to be put into a will, which is a legal document that often involves others, such as family members, a professional will writer and an executor. It can take years, if not decades, from thinking about it to doing it. This means that the more knowledge a potential donor has about your sources of funds the better: most people prefer to make major decisions of this kind based not just on their heart but their head too.

There is also a third element which can raise its head, and that is trust and confidence. Above, I alluded to UK-based charities and how they can attract a strong level of trust from their supporters. But a religious charity working overseas has a different dimension that may lead potential donors to wonder whether their gift will get to the intended beneficiaries. So, trust will be higher for missions run by a supporter's own church than for many international development agencies. The greatest legacy visions dovetail not only with the cause but also with trust and confidence in the cause. Consider that people who are sitting at their kitchen table scribbling their thoughts down on paper before they go to their solicitor will not scribble the name of your charity if they do not have trust and confidence in your organisation. The major current prospects for legacy gifts are the first baby boomers, who are bright, rational and 'thinking donors'. They want facts and they want to know your charity is not going to fail. Negative media stories and high administration and/or fundraising costs can lead potential donors to consider your charity a risk as an investment.

When this book was first published in 1998, the best prospects were relatively unconcerned about which charity or charities they might put in their will. They tended not to be inquisitive and communications were almost exclusively paper driven. Now, sitting in focus groups two or three days a week, I hear the best prospects saying that they go to websites (in particular the Charity Commission's website) in order to view charities' accounts. If they visit your charity's website directly to view your accounts and the information they need is not there (or, indeed, if your accounts have been posted late), they may wonder whether you are trying to hide something.

So, when you prepare your vision, there are simple add-ons which will strengthen your case for support and will increase the size of the gifts you receive. In summary, these add-ons are focused on accountability, transparency and honesty:

• where your charity's funds come from;

• how well, and where, funds are spent;

• proof of great governance and administration.

Keeping these principles in mind will help you to craft a great legacy vision.

The legacy vision framework

The framework for the legacy vision is simple:

• It needs to be unique, so it can answer the fundamental question 'Why should I leave your charity a gift in my will?'.

• It must be tangible, so that everyone can easily relate to it and buy into the impact a gift in a will can make.

• It must be achievable, to help ensure prospects are inspired to fulfil your dream (and theirs).

• It needs to be fundable, so that there is a balance between vision ambitions and financial reality: if the sum is too large – in other words £billions – then prospects will feel it is not achievable by them.

• It should be inspirational, so that it strikes right at the heart of every prospect.

• It must make action easy, to ensure prospects take action – which is the cognitive or brain-led element.

In addition, there should be at least one 'legacy voice', though there can be many legacy voices who can communicate the story of your vision. For example, this could be the fundraiser responsible for legacies, a trustee, a pledger or the next of kin of a legator (see also 'Storytellers and storytelling' on page 130). Legacy visions which have no author or speaker tend to fail.

Legacy vision language

Language must be used carefully. From my own experience working with approximately 27,000 people in focus groups, I recommend banning the following words in all legacy visions: 'bequest', 'bequeath', 'pecuniary' and 'residuary'. This is supported by the work of Professor Russell James at

Texas Tech University, which shows that the word 'bequest' is not liked or even understood.[1] 'Bequests' are considered to be unusually large legacy gifts, often pieces of land or property – a perception that might work for the National Trust but not for a local charity looking after vulnerable people. The word 'legacy' is also disliked and considered to be 'large' and 'deathly', although it is a much better and more meaningful word for high-net-worth individuals as it has a sense of living on beyond death.

As for 'pecuniary', this Latinate word is too far outside most people's day-to-day vocabulary and should be avoided. Instead, mention a 'cash sum' and then continue with 'of any size' to ensure prospects understand they can each make a difference regardless of wealth or even lack of it.

Finally, the word 'residuary' refers to a gift consisting of a percentage of the residue of a person's estate once all cash and other gifts of fixed amounts have been accounted for. However, almost everyone I meet in focus groups assumes that a residuary legacy can only be 100% of the residue. Nearly everyone, when they get to the word 'residuary', stops reading or listening, thinking the charity takes everything.

Using language carefully to clarify people's perceptions can make a big difference. For example, of the last 5,000 donors, volunteers and service users I have met, 38–52% were seriously considering leaving a gift in their will once they found out how easy and affordable it is to do. Legacy numbers will rocket if we use simple and effective language.

When you have finished writing the first drafts of your vision statement(s), remember to test each statement internally – it is crucial to have all trustees, staff and volunteers behind each statement. Once the statement(s) have been agreed, the next stage is to create a booklet of key legacy messages. This booklet forms a crucial part in a legacy toolkit, which must be kept incredibly simple if it is to be used by volunteers.

Putting your visions to use

Macro visions give people a sense of the wider effect of their gift – or, indeed, the effect of *not* receiving their gift. It is possible (although, depending on the complexity of your organisation's overall vision, not necessarily easy) to sum up a macro legacy vision in one sentence. For example, 'By leaving a gift to ABC Charity, you can help future generations to…' or 'By leaving us a gift, you can make your mark on the world by…'. Or you can take the reverse approach: 'Without your support, we couldn't help future generations to…' or 'Imagine a world without [the positive impact your charity makes]'.

In addition, the best legacy programmes integrate simple phrases – micro visions – into almost every supporter communication. It is only necessary for a couple of people to see a simple statement, just before they start planning their will or going to see their solicitor, and it can have just the right effect at just the right time.

Indeed, it is the micro visions which often produce legacy miracles. Micro visions make people aware of the day-to-day outcomes of legacies. These micro visions will either be positive, such as 'In a typical year gifts in wills help us to achieve *this*', or negative, such as 'Without gifts in wills we would not be able to do *that*' – this can be specific to each service or activity. You can also do both, varying the positive with the negative. These simple micro visions can also appear on social media, in carousels on your website, on bookmarks, in your shops (if you have them), on posters at events and in reception areas, and (for some charities) in leaflets about your services.

The macro vision should form the heart of your legacy webpages and legacy brochure (if you need one). This vision should also make up the last part of every talk you give to an adult audience. Remember that you can have a macro vision for each of your charitable objectives. If you have multiple macro visions, you can either use all of them (if doing so is relevant to the activity you're undertaking) or select one for the relevant target audience.

Micro visions are different because you can drop them into a variety of places: thank you letters, compliment slips, email signatures, posters, bookmarks and so on. In other words, micro visions serve as gentle reminders and can catch prospects at exactly the right time – when they are thinking about making or changing their will.

Visions versus wills: Getting the legacy into the will

It is great to have a vision. But the trouble is that visions do not get prospects running to their professional will writers. They may fully appreciate that leaving a gift in their will would be a good thing to do, but then do nothing about it.

Moreover, we should not assume that prospects have knowledge of the world of wills. Unlike all other ways of giving, a gift in a will is just a few words on a page. It is just a line in a legal document but the process of leaving a gift in a will can be a source of great confusion – for example, in focus groups, I am frequently asked what the difference is between a will and a legacy. There are also other types of time-of-death giving which are becoming more popular: gifts from pensions, death-in-service schemes (an employee benefit where if you die while employed, the company pays out a tax-free lump sum to your chosen beneficiary), part of a life insurance policy and so on, but 95% of gifts are still made via a will.

People tend to take action regarding their will when they understand they should have a will, or should change or update their existing will. This can be at times of life changes such as marriage, deciding to be child-free, having children, divorce, retirement, inheritance from a parent, or a child or grandchild getting divorced and needing financial help. These changes can often trigger people to make or change their will and when they make the change they may think 'Lets include charity x' or possibly 'sadly, we will have to take charity x out of the will because of family changes'. This is, in effect, a selfish motivation, in contrast to the proactive philanthropic motivation for a legacy.

On average, taking a sample of around 5,000 donors and volunteers I have met in focus groups, over 80% have a will but about 65% of wills need to be updated because the will no longer reflects the person's current wishes. But people commonly take 15 years or even more to get around to making these changes because people are busy, and it is human nature to prefer, say, booking a holiday than to changing a will. Because of this yawning gap between inspiration and action, it is essential to make action incredibly easy. Prospects do not think it is easy, but it is easy at any stage of life. Existing wills are usually stored on a computer, so all that is needed is the wording to be added to the will and so these days does not even require a codicil (a separate legal document to modify a will).

You can make this process easy for your donors by providing a simple document containing the wording for a cash gift and a residuary gift. This can be supported by the inclusion of a straightforward explanation of what to do:

> You can leave us a small cash sum or a small percentage in your will – every gift makes a difference. All you have to do is phone your will writer and it can happen in minutes.

Focus on the ease of making and changing a will. State that it might cost little or even nothing for a donor to add their favourite charity to their will.

There is one other issue: families. Many people disregard the whole idea of leaving a gift to a charity in their will because they have a family and so they only think of family beneficiaries. Anybody can leave a modest gift. But perhaps, depending on your cause, you ought to express in some way the fact that charities come after 'your family'. Other ways of wording this are to say that 'loved ones', 'those closest to you' or 'those you care about most' come first. This is a sensitive issue because your best prospects might not have a family. It's your call, but remember that 'loved ones' can include companion animals.

Make contact easy

Imagine what it is like for an older person to contact you about a private legal document and a private future gift (which might change). It is crucial to provide them with personal contact details to make the process as easy as possible. Particularly, do not have a 'legacies@...' email address. The best prospects need to contact a real person, not a death department. I also recommend not including your job title, because all legacy-related job titles (and other job titles which are not related to legacy roles but do discourage contact from prospects, such as: major donor fundraiser, direct mail officer to name a few) are not liked. In 2014, Radcliffe Consulting carried out research into job titles (Professor Russell James has done similar research)[2] and the following job titles and positions were either hated or laughed at: 'donor relations manager', 'supporter development', 'direct mail officer', 'direct marketing team', 'high-value-giving assistant', 'major donor fundraiser', 'legacy and in-mem officer' and 'legacy administrator'. Generally speaking, 'fundraising team' will suffice.

Storytellers and storytelling

Great fundraising is driven by great stories. Generally speaking, though, the mix of stories must include the following:

• The vision, possibly related by the chief executive or a person doing the work of the charity (the trouble with a chief executive is that they can come across as highly paid or too businesslike).

• How legacies have been used in the past (ideally expressed by the fundraiser responsible for legacies to encourage ease of contact).

• How well the charity uses its money (which is, of course, the money from your donors who might also leave you a gift in their will), communicated by a trustee or the finance director. For instance, this might include your return on investment for fundraising and the amount that is spent on governance (which the public think is administration). It is also important to clarify performance figures (which can be different for each charity depending on where it gets its money from) and why return on investment changes over time, as these are topics that commonly confuse donors.

• How well you do your work now, as this will increase trust and confidence in your charity's future. This is best communicated by a charity service provider, such as a nurse in a hospice or a field worker for an international development agency.

• An explanation from the next of kin of a legator to explain why their relative's legacy was left to your charity. This shows that families accept (or are even thrilled about) gifts left by their relatives.

• Milestones to show your charity has been a success in the past and can be a success in the future with the help of gifts in wills. These also trigger nostalgia, which (according to research by Professor Wing Yee Cheung and colleagues at the University of Southampton[3]) enhances the level of happiness in older people.

• Answers to frequently asked questions about wills and legacies, ideally expressed by a solicitor. This information about the ease of making or changing a will and the importance of wills overall, together with information on inheritance tax benefits, can serve as a simple call to action.

The other kind of storyteller that can be used is a legacy pledger. Professor Russell James has studied this in detail in the USA, where it is the preferred story because it shows that leaving a legacy is a social norm.[4] American donors are very different from UK donors. Americans tend to be proud donors and like to talk about their philanthropy. My experience is that the UK population is different – more subtle and private. The best pledger to ask to be a storyteller in the UK is someone who has directly or indirectly benefitted from your charity. For example, in a hospital or hospice, this could be a patient or the relative of a patient. In such cases, the pledger will be perceived as someone who has received an amazing service. The same would apply to somebody who has received a bursary from an educational charity. It is also important to ensure the pledger does not come across as rich and pompous, as this could lead less-well-off individuals to believe pledges are not left by people like themselves; for the same reason, it is vital to indicate that the legacy being left is modest and therefore affordable for everyone. The words of the pledger's story must be carefully crafted to make sure it is not considered to be boastful or egotistical.

Conclusion

Developing inspiring legacy visions is the most important action you can take. They form the heart of all of your legacy communications. But it is equally important to change attitudes to making and updating a will. The call to action must prove, beyond doubt, that that action is easy and affordable. And, when the action is taken, your charity must be absolutely at the forefront of the mind of the donor in terms of needing a gift in their will. The donor's final decision will be led by a mix of personal engagement and experience, understanding your charity's need and knowing your charity is a great investment for their gift in the future.

Notes

1   Russell James, 'Talking Planned Giving: Words that Work', 2014, presentation available at www.slideshare.net/rnja8c/talking-planned-giving-words-that-work, accessed 4 December 2017.
2   Russell James, 'Testing the Effectiveness of Fundraiser Job Titles in Charitable Bequest and Complex Gift Planning', *Nonprofit Management & Leadership*, vol. 27, no. 2, 2016, pp. 165–79.

3   Wing Yee Cheung, Tim Wildschut, Constantine Sedikes, Erica G. Hepper, Jamie Arndt and J. J. M. Vingerhoets, 'Back to the Future: Nostalgia increases optimism', *Personality and Social Psychology Bulletin*, vol. 39, no. 11, pp. 1484–1496.

4   Russell James and Claire Routley, 'We The Living: The effect of living and deceased donor stories on charitable bequest giving intentions', *International Journal of Nonprofit and Voluntary Sector Marketing*, vol. 21, no. 2, 2016, pp. 109–117.

CHAPTER ELEVEN

Engaging legacy prospects via intermediaries and events

Ashley Rowthorn

Introduction

A continual challenge you are likely to face is how to reach and engage potential legacy donors. Changes to fundraising and data protection regulations are making it harder than ever to communicate with donors through traditional direct-marketing techniques. Not to mention the fact that around half of all legacy donors are not known to charities in their lifetime.[1] So it is important to consider who else could communicate your legacy message on your behalf, reaching well beyond your current pool of donors. From engaging your community fundraisers and volunteer base to working with solicitors and partnering with other charities, this chapter explores the use of intermediaries to widen your fundraising reach and raise more money from legacy gifts. It also explores the benefits of using events to engage supporters on a personal level and gives practical guidance to help you make your legacy events a success.

Internal engagement

As emphasised in chapter 5, legacy fundraising works best when it is integrated across the whole organisation. Fundraising should not be the sole responsibility of the legacy team, although they will need to lead the effort; instead, the legacy conversation should be a collective responsibility. Getting the whole organisation on board and making more noise about the importance of legacy gifts will increase the level of awareness and consideration among charity supporters and ultimately encourage more people to leave charitable gifts in their wills.

But to do this well requires leadership, co-operation and support, from the trustees at the top to the staff and volunteers at the grassroots. The legacy team can and should play a vital role in giving a lead and supporting others, but they will not achieve their goal without bringing the rest of the organisation along with them.

And herein lies the challenge, because there are a number of barriers relating to legacy giving that are just as true for you, the fundraiser, as they are for the donor. Legacy giving, whether we like it or not, is linked to death, and our natural reaction when faced with this subject is to avoid it. In fact, social psychologists theorise that this behaviour has evolved to help us manage the fear that comes with knowledge of our own mortality.[2] So, in order to engage those within our organisations to promote legacies on our behalf, we need to reframe the conversation away from death and onto the drivers of legacy giving – namely life experience and values. And this is not even to mention the number of internal barriers that can get in our way, such as conflicting priorities, competing targets and silo working, to name but a few.

So your goal as a legacy fundraiser should be to create an environment and culture where everyone in the organisation has the knowledge, tools and confidence to integrate legacies into their day-to-day conversation. This will require time, effort and resources, but the fruits of your success will be in the ability to reach a much wider audience, in a sustained, cost-effective way.

So, how do we go about creating a culture where legacy conversations can thrive?

Trustees and senior management

It is worth starting at the top – not because trustees and senior managers will necessarily be holding legacy conversations themselves, but because they will give you the permission to integrate legacies into other teams' activity, which will be critical to your success. Furthermore, you will need your senior staff and trustees on board if you need to secure budget investment.

There is something to be said for leading by example, and, if you can find a trustee who has decided to leave a gift in their will and is willing to tell their story, that can drive legacies up the agenda. But, you also need to be considered in your use of senior people to front your campaigns, as this can sometimes be off-putting to potential donors, particularly if it detracts from the social-norming process. Donors want to see 'people like me' leaving a legacy, and a suited senior executive may present the wrong image.

Fundraising staff

A number of charities include legacy promotion within the role of regional fundraisers, which can work well where there is good training and monitoring. Of course, most regional fundraisers have 'real' income targets to achieve – 'real' in the sense of hard income that has to be achieved *this* year. They may truly support the need for increased legacy income, but their priority is getting money in today, not in five years' time.

Some charities have therefore set up schemes where the fundraiser is credited with, say, a proportion of the current year's legacy income or a notional credit of some kind. These schemes are not always easy to operate but they can help to ensure that legacy promotion work is valued.

Volunteers

A charity's volunteers can be its greatest allies: who better to sell the cause than someone who actively supports it in their own time? An appropriately skilled volunteer (preferably one who has already included your charity in their will) can be a very successful legacy fundraiser. Volunteers may also be strong prospects for considering a legacy donation, but care should be taken before directly soliciting legacy gifts from volunteers. A better strategy is to engage them as ambassadors and allow them to be exposed to the legacy message more indirectly.

If you are considering recruiting legacy-specific volunteers, you need to be confident that each volunteer has the relevant experience, qualities and attributes to take on the role. There should also be clear supervision and support available for the volunteer and the relevant resources and training for them to perform the role effectively.

Non-fundraising staff

Don't overlook other members of staff just because they aren't directly involved in fundraising. You will benefit from considering everyone as a potential route to your target market. The further removed somebody is from fundraising, the more time and care you may need to spend getting them on board, but don't let the added effort deter you.

For example, staff involved in direct service delivery may be able to subtly and sensitively raise awareness of legacies by sharing stories of past gifts when the time is right. But they will need to see the benefit, know the right time to raise the topic and have the right language to use – which again highlights the importance of investing in training and support.

Case study: NSPCC[3]

The NSPCC's legacy team created a tool to help colleagues in the supporter care team feel more comfortable and confident when promoting gifts in wills and to make more supporters aware of this option. This was based on insights from a 2013 behavioural economic study carried out by the Cabinet Office, the Charities Aid Foundation and Bristol University, in partnership with Remember a Charity.

After listening to the supporter care team's concerns and barriers when promoting gifts in wills, the solution was the development of a co-created 'mind map'. This visual solution was designed to help the team see the challenge from the perspective of the supporter and to remind the team of some helpful phrases or offers to use when promoting gifts in wills. The mind map was influenced by the aforementioned behavioural economic study, which highlighted the importance of 'social-norming' statements and a 'passionate' ask. To this end, the mind map featured two characters – 'Norm' and 'Pasha' – who spoke about how the conversation could reflect both the supporter's and the charity's passion for helping children when promoting gifts in wills.

When the team started using the mind map, there was a significant increase in the number of supporters whom they felt able to talk to about gifts in wills. The supporter care team reported generating between 50 and 100 legacy leads (or enquirers) per month, the equivalent of 600–1,200 prospects a year, or a telemarketing or direct-mail campaign, at no extra cost to the NSPCC.

Not only has this work saved the NSPCC money but also it has ensured that more supporters have been offered a relevant alternative way of donating to a cause they care about.

Events

One tried-and-tested way of talking about legacy giving with supporters is through events. They will allow you to personally connect with your charity's supporters, bring them closer to the cause and give them a positive experience and association of gifts in wills that should stay with them long after the day.

As a legacy fundraiser, I have personally planned, delivered and attended well over 100 legacy events of all shapes and sizes and for various charity causes. Of course, the look and feel of each event will differ from charity to charity, but I believe most charities can hold a legacy event of some kind and integrate it into their legacy strategy.

Setting your objectives

Right at the outset, it is important that you think through the objectives of your legacy event – namely, what are you aiming to achieve? There are a few ways you could approach the event, and deciding on what is right for you will naturally lead to a certain type of event, perhaps one that is very different from anything another charity would consider. Are you aiming to generally raise awareness of legacy giving as well as other ways to support your charity? Is the event aimed at encouraging consideration and action among people you feel are good legacy prospects? Or is it aimed at nurturing the relationships of existing legacy supporters (pledgers)?

The following sections are based around a prospecting event – one focused on encouraging consideration and action among your best legacy prospects.

Measuring success

Again, at the outset, you need to set some measurable goals that you can evaluate after the event. I suggest using a range of metrics, including:

- number of attendees;
- drop-out rate;
- number of conversations on the day;
- number of legacy enquiries.

Whom to invite

Once you've set your objectives, you need to think about the best people to invite. In the example used here – a prospecting event – you're looking to speak to good legacy prospects, so you need to narrow down the type of supporters you'd like to invite. Legacy giving is linked to life stage, so it makes sense to look to invite people approaching or into retirement, as they are more likely to be open to a legacy conversation. Also look for a good level of engagement with your charity, as you will want to speak to people who are already giving and who may be open to extending that support through a gift in their will.

As it is a physical event, the proximity of supporters to the venue will obviously affect whom you can invite. In my experience, a driving time of 30 minutes is usually the limit people will travel to an event, so you need a concentration of supporters within an area in order to get critical mass and make an event viable.

The venue

One of the strengths of legacy events is the ability to bring your supporters closer to your cause. So, if you are fortunate enough to have facilities or venues owned by your charity, then I recommend you consider using these. We're not all as lucky as the National Trust, but it has successfully given its supporters access to venues at legacy events that other people aren't normally able to see. This kind of approach provides a unique offer and will be very attractive to supporters of your charity, and it should therefore encourage attendance.

Having an exclusive venue, or an activity after the legacy event, can encourage attendance, but make sure your attendees are also coming because they are open-minded about legacy giving and supporting your charity. In addition, when choosing a suitable venue, you also need to think practically. Does it have good parking or public transport links? Is it accessible for people with restricted mobility? Is it cost-effective?

On the day, make sure you have good, clear signage so people can find you, and ask a friendly volunteer to welcome people.

The invitation

Once you have a list of people to invite, you need to give thought to the best way of inviting them. Write a clear letter, thanking them for their past support and inviting them to a special supporter event to hear about the work of the charity and future plans and ambitions. Make it clear that you will be talking about the future and how people can continue to support the charity, including through gifts in wills. Here you need to strike a balance by not putting people off through use of the wrong language (see Russell James' work on the right language to use)[4] and ensuring that people know why you are inviting them and that you will be talking about legacy giving on the day.

The clearer and more upfront you are in your invitation, the more you will be able to talk about the subject on the day without compromise, and the better engagement and consideration you will get.

How to maximise attendance

One of the biggest challenges to holding a successful legacy event is the drop-out rate. Plans change, the weather gets in the way, people forget – and, if you are not careful, all your hard work could go to waste.

While some things are beyond your control, there are things you can do to maximise attendance on the day. Firstly, allow people to bring a guest – if they have any reservations about attending, they will feel more comfortable if they know they can bring someone with them. Send a reminder nearer the time, with a personalised invitation card that can sit on the mantelpiece. And, of course, make sure you include detailed directions and give your contact details so people can let you know if plans change. Think about the time of year and the time of day. People are less likely to come if it means travelling in the dark or through rush hour. And remember, your best prospects are likely to be retired, so a mid-week event starting at 11am could be a good option.

The structure and content

On the day, you will have a captive audience, so it is down to you to make the most of the opportunity and deliver a really compelling reason why your attendees should consider leaving a gift to your cause in their will. I like to think of this in terms of telling a story. Break the content down into multiple parts, and make sure each element has its own objectives and works with all the others to get your message across in the most engaging way possible.

Having held many events, I have found that around an hour of talking is probably the optimum level. It allows you to deliver depth of content, but without losing interest. I would usually break the talk down into a number of stages:

• **The big picture.** This concerns your vision and key achievements towards this. Make this inspirational and ambitious, and ideally have it delivered by someone senior, such as a trustee. Having a trustee or your chief executive present shows your supporters they are important to you and that you are taking gifts in wills seriously.

• **Get local.** If you are a national charity, then this is your chance to make your work relevant to the local area. Local is a strong motivation in legacy giving – people want to benefit their communities.

• **Make it interesting.** You may have a part of your work that really gets people's attention. Maybe you invest in medical research and can get a researcher to talk about the latest breakthroughs, or perhaps you work overseas and can get someone recently back from the field to share their experiences.

• **Make it personal.** The best speakers are often those who directly benefit from your charity. When at a national health charity, I would always make sure we had a beneficiary or close relative to share their personal stories. This will resonate much more than words from a member of staff.

• **Make it fun.** You can get creative and engaging with the subject too. Guide Dogs often gives its supporters the chance to do a blindfolded walk, and RNLI supporters sometimes have the opportunity to go on a lifeboat. Use your imagination and think of ways you can bring your event to life.

• **Be varied.** Don't just have a speaker for the whole hour; mix it up and keep people engaged. Show some video, demonstrate a project, incorporate a quiz – there are lots of ways to deliver your message.

• **Be inspirational.** Above all, you should use this opportunity to engage with your supporters on an emotional level and show them the difference their legacy gift will make.

• **Be direct.** Don't be afraid to ask. I would always finish an event by asking those present to go away to the privacy of their own homes and consider whether leaving a gift in their will was right for them. Use your tact and sensitivity, but don't miss the opportunity to ask people to consider a gift.

Whatever your content, make sure that it is well planned. Make sure your speakers are well briefed and know how and when to incorporate the legacy story. They should all talk about legacy giving, but each bringing a slightly different angle so it all works together to put your message across in the most engaging way possible.

Overall, face-to-face events can be a very successful way of connecting personally with your supporters and showing them the difference legacy gifts can make.

Will-making professionals

Will-making is very much driven by major life events – births, marriages, retirements and deaths. And, when the time comes to make a will, there is now a plethora of choice – from visiting a solicitor to using a will writer (either in your own home or at their offices) to using a telephone-based or online service. One survey found, as figure 12.1 shows, that a similar number of people surveyed chose either a will writer or a DIY route (around 20% of people for each will-writing route) while around half of people chose a solicitor.

FIGURE 12.1 HOW WILLS ARE WRITTEN[5]

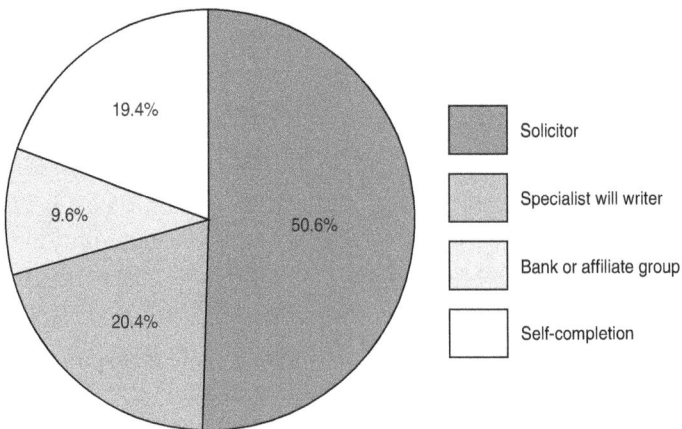

Research carried out by Remember a Charity and the Behavioural Insights Team in 2013 and 2016 shows that professional will writers are hugely influential in encouraging people to include a gift to charity when making their will. Therefore, they should be considered an important part of a legacy fundraising strategy.[6]

The following case study explores who gives, what they give and how they give.

Case study: Trials by Remember a Charity and the Behavioural Insights Team

This 2013 trial aimed to test different legacy-giving prompts, to explore whether subtle changes in language would encourage more people to give to charity. The trial had three groups:

- a control group who received no prompt;

- a group who received a plain ask: 'Would you like to leave any money to charity in your will?';

- a group who received a social norming ask: 'Many of our customers choose to leave a gift to charity in their will; are there any causes you are passionate about?'.

In the control group, 5% of people left a gift to charity, with an average gift of £3,300. In the plain ask group, 10% of people left a gift to charity, with a similar average gift value of £3,100. Therefore, just a simple ask almost doubled the amount of money that was given to charity.

In the final group (social norming), 15% of people left a gift in their will. But, even more significantly, not only did more people donate but they also donated twice as much money – an average of £6,661. The message received by this final group tripled the numbers of people leaving a legacy and overall raised more than five times the amount of money as when people received no message. This is possible as a result of the magic formula of combining a social-norming message with a passionate ask.

Solicitors

Solicitors remain dominant in the will-writing marketplace. While there may well be a gradual shift towards telephone and online providers, the traditional solicitor will always have an important role. Many charities try to raise their profile with the will-writing profession by advertising in charity directories or law journals, by mailing probate solicitors or by sending local volunteers round to solicitors' offices.

In fact, for many charities starting out in legacy fundraising, advertising in legal journals seems to be an easy way to begin. But there are several problems with this. Firstly, solicitors will not suggest a specific charity to their client as it goes against their ethical practices. Secondly, people want to leave gifts to causes that have mattered to them in life, not one that they have randomly pulled out of a magazine. And, even if they did choose a charity in this way, what are the chances your charity will stand out from the endless adverts? Finally, there is evidence to suggest that many solicitors do not refer to such journals any more. Today the world is online, and it is possible to look up a charity in minutes.

So, rather than trying to utilise solicitors as a means to promote your charity, the greater prize is simply to encourage solicitors to routinely prompt the concept of giving to charity during the will-making process. Following the trials with the Behavioural Insights Team in 2013 (see the case study on page 141), Remember a Charity has focused its efforts on encouraging professional will writers to actively prompt their clients to consider leaving a gift to charity, and Remember a Charity's own research suggests that 64% of solicitors and will writers 'always or sometimes' make the prompt,[7] which is positive news.

Will writers and DIY wills

Most charities currently take the view that only professionally qualified will drafters (solicitors) should be recommended to supporters as it is the only way for the legator to be certain that their wishes will be carried out. With will writers, there are anxieties about lack of training, supervision and accountability, and, particularly, lack of professional indemnity cover. DIY wills are never to be recommended when a supporter is considering making a gift to charity, as mistakes are easily made which can have serious negative consequences for any surviving family and for beneficiaries. But are these long-held opinions valid?

Due to growing concerns over the negative consequences of poorly written wills, in 2010 the Legal Services Board (LSB) proposed to make will-writing a reserved activity.[8] During the consultation, it gathered evidence regarding the impact on the consumer of poorly written wills, and this evidence interestingly showed that errors were made by both solicitors and will writers, as well as in DIY wills.[9] But the LSB argued that only wills made by solicitors are covered by a clear course of redress, including mandatory professional indemnity insurance. However, the UK government rejected the proposal to make will-writing a reserved activity despite accepting that the LSB had identified 'consumer detriment in the will-writing market'.[10]

A study has found that 68% of individuals using a will writer were unaware that will writers aren't regulated or insured (59% were unaware of the lack of regulation), and 74% would not have used a will writer if they'd known.[11] It is therefore down to individual charities to determine the risk of working with non-regulated will writers.

You must always bear in mind that the majority of the adult population do not have a valid will, and will-making schemes to encourage action should play a part of your legacy fundraising. But you also need to balance the perceived risks involved, such as invalid wills or challenges due to undue influence, which would lead to negative consequences to your charity and other beneficiaries down the line.

Remember a Charity actively works with both solicitor firms and independent will writers through its Campaign Supporter Scheme. However, it has committed to only work with will writers that are part of the Institute of Professional Willwriters, which sets standards among its members through a code of conduct.

Will-making products

Initially pioneered by the two major cancer charities in the UK, free wills schemes are now a mainstay of charity legacy fundraising. 'Free will' is an umbrella term for a wide variety of partnerships and activities, including discounted wills, donations in lieu of fees, wills paid for by charities, and pro bono wills that are completely free to the charity and donor. But at the root of all schemes is the stipulation that the consumer is under no obligation to leave a legacy gift or make a donation to the participating charity. Instead, the scheme is offered with a soft ask or suggested donation amount to encourage the gift.

Evidence released by Cancer Research UK in 2012 showed that, after 20 years of running its Free Will Service, the scheme had made a cumulative net contribution of £50 million and benefitted from a return on investment of around 2.5:1.[12] The charity also released strong evidence that the majority of users do leave a gift to Cancer Research UK in their will, despite having no obligation to do so. Of the gifts that are left, around 90% ultimately bear fruit (the other 10% are people that removed the gift in a later version of their will).[13]

Similar evidence has been reported by Capacity Marketing, which operates a Free Wills Month and a Free Wills Network, suggesting that between 65% and 75% of people who make a will choose to leave a legacy to charity.[14] There is good evidence, therefore, that free will schemes do indeed drive legacy gifts; however, your charity should ensure its investment is carefully considered to ensure the return on investment justifies the use of charitable resources.

Paying for wills

The Charity Commission guidance 'Raising Funds Through Wills and Charitable Legacies' is available on its website and is essential reading for anyone contemplating a will-making scheme.[15] The Charity Commission especially warns charities involved in offering to meet the cost of will preparation to take great care to avoid inadvertently creating any contractual relationship between them and the solicitors that actually prepare the will. There are two main risks:

• The charity might be regarded as having taken responsibility for the will, even though it was prepared by the solicitor. This could expose the charity to financial liability if the solicitor's conduct of the business proves to be negligent.

• If the charity, rather than the solicitor, is regarded as having taken responsibility for the will, there may be a greater risk that any legacy in the will to the charity will be invalid on the grounds of undue influence or want of knowledge and approval.

The same arguments apply where a charity is considering offering its own will-writing service.

Will Aid

Will Aid is a closed consortium of nine UK overseas development charities working together to promote professionally made wills. Its major campaign runs every November and currently has approximately 1,000 participating solicitors who draw up straightforward wills for no fee. The person making the will is asked to give a suggested minimum donation, which is passed to the consortium. Over 300,000 wills have been made through Will Aid since 1988, raising some £19 million for the consortium in donations.[16] The Will Aid charities expect many times that figure in eventual legacies, though hard evidence for this is difficult to track down.

The National Free Wills Network

The National Free Wills Network consists of 900 UK law firms that write wills for donors referred to them by member charities. The charities provide access to the network by publicising it to selected donors, usually through direct mail or articles in newsletters or magazines. Around 70% of donors who use the network decide to leave something to their charity in their will – though there is no obligation to do so.[17] By the end of 2016, 70 national charities were using the network, raising an estimated £15 million in future legacy gifts for each charity.[18]

Communications after death

Charities tend to handle legacy promotion and legacy administration as two distinct and separate activities, to their detriment. Prior to a legacy donor's death, a charity may be in touch frequently, inviting them to events, with Christmas cards and other messages, designed to build and nurture a relationship with them. But the moment a charity hears of the death, they seem to go into purely administration gear, writing formal letters to solicitors and banks to deal with the legal ramifications of the gift.

Charities may initially ask the solicitor to convey their condolences and appreciation to the next of kin. When the gift has been received and all matters tidied up, the charity may then ask the solicitor to convey its appreciation. But they are rarely directly in touch with the family to express their thanks and, potentially, to build a relationship with them. Charities also might forget to communicate with their internal teams, with their regional fundraisers about legacies that have come in from their patch, or with the volunteer groups to which the donor belonged.

However, bear in mind that, if one member of a family leaves a gift to a particular cause, or charity in general, then others will be more inclined to consider that charity for a lifetime gift or a legacy, particularly if they feel that their late relative's gift has been used effectively. The additional work is not great: for example, a letter written to the next of kin following the death of your legacy donor; a thank you leaflet to go with a letter when the gift has been received, together with feedback for the solicitor on the possible impact that the gift might have; one further letter prior to the anniversary of the death; or a regular report (monthly or quarterly) on legacies by region, sent out to regional fundraising directors and/ or local branches and groups.

Collaborating with other charities

Anyone working for a charity in a legacy role will know how collaborative the sector is. The average legacy donor leaves gifts to three charities in their will,[19] so there usually isn't a conflict of interest when charities share best practice and support each other.

Remember a Charity

Founded in 2000 and now with 200 UK charities involved, Remember a Charity pioneered the idea of charities working together to grow the market.[20] Remember a Charity works on a membership basis, charging charities an annual fee based on the size of its eligible voluntary income. Member charities enjoy the benefit of attending forums to share best practice and shape the wider consumer campaign. They also tap into the annual awareness week, which presents an excellent opportunity to engage staff internally and promote legacies to donors and the wider public.

But, more than a marketing campaign, Remember a Charity has been hugely influential in changing consumer behaviour, by focusing its strategy not just on the donor but also on partners that can effect change – from central government to the local professional will writer.

Other collaborations

There are now many similar legacy-promotion campaigns across the world, in countries such as Australia, Austria, Belgium, the Czech Republic, Germany, Ireland, Italy, the Netherlands, Norway and Spain. In the UK, there are also several smaller legacy-promotion campaigns focused on a locality or cause area. Faith-based partnerships include Catholic Legacy, Christian Legacy and Jewish Legacy. Locality-based partnerships include Leave a Gift to Cornwall and Legacy Liverpool.

Conclusion

To reach and engage the highest possible number of potential legacy donors you need to communicate beyond your current pool of donors and communicate in a way that focuses on the motivations for leaving a gift in wills, i.e. life experience and values. To help achieve this goal of maximal reach, it is also crucial to create an environment and culture within your organisation where everybody has the knowledge, tools and confidence to integrate legacies into their day-to-day conversation.

Whichever route you decide to use to engage more people, the essential thing is to sell your cause – specifically, to clearly communicate *why* someone should consider leaving a gift to your charity in their will and the long-lasting impact it will have. Create opportunities for people to express an interest, and finally, follow this activity up, really well.

Notes

1   Meg Abdy, 'Confessions of an Invisible Legator' [web article], Legacy Foresight, 16 August 2017, www.legacyforesight.co.uk/viewpoint/3620843-confessions-of-an-invisible-legator, reporting on the Legacy Marketing Benchmarks study conducted by Legacy Foresight in 2016, accessed 5 January 2018.

2   See, for example, Robert W. Firestone's article 'Individual Defenses Against Death Anxiety' in *Death Studies*, vol. 17, no. 6, 1993, published online 14 Aug 2007 and Ernest Becker's *The Denial of Death*, New York, The Free Press, 1973.

3   For more details see Alex McDowell, 'NSPCC's supporter care gifts in wills "mind map"' [web page], Showcase of Fundraising Innovation and Inspiration, 2015, http://sofii.org/case-study/nspccs-supporter-care-gifts-in-wills-mind-map, accessed 1 December 2017.

4   See Russell James, 'Talking Planned Giving: Words that work' [web-based slide show], 2014, www.slideshare.net/rnja8c/talking-planned-giving-words-that-work, accessed 8 December 2017; Russell James, 'Phrasing the Charitable Bequest Inquiry', *Voluntas: International Journal of Voluntary and Nonprofit Organizations*, vol. 27, no. 2, pp. 998–1011.

5   Table 10.7, 'Consumer retrospective interviews broken down by channel of purchase and mode of will-writing' in *Understanding the Consumer Experience of Will-Writing Services* [PDF], IFF Research prepared for Legal Services Board, Legal Services Consumer Panel, Office of Fair Trading and Solicitors Regulation Authority, 2011, www.sra.org.uk/sra/how-we-work/consumer-research/summaries/the-consumers-experience-of-will-writing.page, p. 66, accessed 4 January 2018.

6   Michael Sanders and Sarah Smith, 'Can Simple Prompts Increase Bequest Giving? Field evidence from a legal call centre', *Journal of Economic Behavior and Organization*, vol. 125, 2013, pp. 179–191; Michael Sanders, Sarah Smith, Bibi Groot and David Nolan, *Legacy Giving and Behavioural Insights* [PDF], The Behavioural Insights Team, University of Bristol and Remember a Charity, www.behaviouralinsights.co.uk/publications/legacy-giving-and-behavioural-insights, 2016, accessed 11 December 2017.

7   'Impact report 2016' [web page], Remember a Charity, 2016, www.rememberacharity.org.uk/wp-content/uploads/Impact-Report-2016.pdf, accessed 8 December 2017.

8   *Regulating Will-writing*, London, Legal Services Consumer Panel, 2011, p. 5.

9   'Will-writing and estate administration' [web page], LSB, 2017, www.legalservicesboard.org.uk/projects/reviewing_the_scope_of_regulation/will_writing_and_estate_administration.htm, accessed 11 December 2017.

10   Catherine Fairbairn, *Regulation of Will Writers* [PDF; Briefing Paper no. 05683], London, House of Commons Library, 2017.

11   Stephen Hill, 'Stephen Hill Comments on Confusion Over Will Writing' [web page], Bolt Burdon Kemp, 2017, www.boltburdonkemp.co.uk/articles/confusion-over-will-writing, accessed 8 December 2017.

12   Jack Visser and Pauline Mayer, 'Free Wills: What's the catch?' [web slide show], Cancer Research UK, www.slideshare.net/iof_events/free-wills-whats-the-catch-pauline-mayer-jack-visser-cancer-research-uk, 3 October 2012, slide 5.

13   Figures stated in a presentation given by Pauline Meyer and Jack Visser from the Cancer Research UK legacy team at the 2013 Institute of Fundraising conference.

14   'Legacy marketing for charities' [home page], Capacity Marketing, 2017, https://capacity-marketing.com, accessed 4 January 2018.

15   'Raising Funds Through Wills and Charitable Legacies' [web page], Charity Commission, 2013, www.gov.uk/guidance/wills-and-charitable-legacies, accessed 11 December 2017.

16   'Introducing Will Aid' [web page], Will Aid, 2017, www.willaid.org.uk/about, accessed 11 December 2017.

17   'Free Wills Network' [web page], Capacity Marketing, 2017, https://capacity-marketing.com/services/free-wills-network, accessed 11 December 2017.

18   Capacity Marketing, 'Free wills work!' [web article], The Law Society Gazette, http://directories.lawgazette.co.uk/directories/charity-explorer/free-wills-work/5059977.article, 2 December 2016.

19   *Legacy Trends: Discovering potential thorough data* [PDF], Smee & Ford, 2017, https://smeeandford.com/whitepaper, p. 7, accessed 4 January 2018.

20   'Remember a Charity welcomes 200th member' [web article], Remember a Charity, 26 October 2017.

CHAPTER TWELVE

Having legacy conversations with supporters

Fiona Riley

Introduction: The legacy toolkit

Every good legacy fundraiser needs a set of tools to help them have successful legacy conversations with potential pledgers. This chapter provides an introduction to having legacy conversations yourself in your capacity as a fundraiser, and tips on equipping your colleagues and volunteers with the skills to have legacy conversations on your behalf.

Relationship fundraising is one of the key elements of any strong legacy programme, and the ability to have positive and engaging conversations as a legacy fundraiser will go a long way towards helping your legacy marketing to be a success. Ever since the introduction of Ken Burnett's seminal textbook *Relationship Fundraising*,[1] legacy fundraisers have been adopting the relationship fundraising approach to their legacy marketing, using the skills and approaches of building relationships to broach this most sensitive of subjects with their supporters.

Moreover, legacy messaging is strongest when it is adopted by multiple stakeholders in your organisation, not just by legacy fundraisers, as anyone can be in the market for considering a gift in their will and may wish to discuss this in any interaction, not just in conversation with your legacy team. Therefore, it is important not only to have legacy conversations yourself but also to empower colleagues and volunteers within your organisation to have their own conversations to promote legacy giving.

Finally, a note of caution. Although much is to be gained from having a positive legacy conversation with a key donor, legacy giving is an area that can hold a degree of risk, given the legalities involved in writing a will. This chapter should be read in conjunction with chapter 18 (on legal pitfalls), which highlights some ways to protect yourself from risk and ensure you limit the potential liability to your organisation in case a contentious issue is raised in the future.

Key points covered in the chapter

This chapter outlines the various factors you need to have a grasp of in order to have successful legacy conversations, and to help your colleagues to do so also. It includes:

• what makes a good face-to-face legacy fundraiser;

• how to prepare for and conduct a face-to-face meeting, in terms of ascertaining what the prospect knows already and/or is likely to think, what they want to know and what the objectives of the meeting are;

• what puts people off from giving a legacy gift or, indeed, motivates them to give;

• how to understand social cues and body language (yours and the prospect's);

• what language to use in legacy conversations;

• the legal implications of legacy conversations, including undue influence;

• how to record information from the conversation;

• how to ensure your own safety during, and travelling to and from, meetings;

• what deters people from making a will, such as lack of knowledge or motivation;

• having telephone conversations about legacies, including the type of campaign, pre-call contact, timing, scripting, recording data from the call and fulfilling any requests.

Face-to-face conversations with supporters

This section includes a number of key considerations for anyone beginning to have face-to-face conversations about legacy giving, to ensure that you are well prepared and have thought through the issues that you are likely to encounter.

What makes someone a good face-to-face legacy fundraiser?

Although most people can, with support, be encouraged to have legacy conversations, someone whose primary role is in this area is likely to have a particular set of skills. Integrity, believability and trustworthiness are crucial, as is empathy. Face-to-face fundraisers hear some very sad and personal stories of woe, and receive confidences: you must care about people, be able to keep confidences and be interested in what makes

149

people tick. A sense of humour and quick wit, judiciously used, are very helpful.

Having deep knowledge about your charity's work, and being able to paint a picture in words is valuable, in order to convey (ideally in your prospect's terms) the essence of what it is your charity exists to do. Paint a picture of achievement, of hope and of the future – a picture your prospect is going to want to buy into – and how legacy gifts to your charity will make this happen.

Sometimes you will need to have particular diplomacy and discretion. Fundraisers will talk, for example, about witnessing marital and family tensions, or about being told of a serious tax evasion in language that invites them to endorse the activity. One fundraiser met a potential legacy pledger who had been sacked by the fundraiser's relation (though luckily the prospect didn't realise it, despite the identical, and somewhat unusual, surname). Sometimes, in your conversations with people, you may just have to be accepting of their frailties, as illustrated in cases like these.

As well as developing good listening skills, you will need an understanding of body language and know how to ensure that yours is open and encouraging. ('Understanding social clues' below offers some detail on how to do this.)

A crucial final point: you must have enough knowledge of the basics of how to make and change a will and other basics of the will-making process to be able to guide people through it, and to remove the inertia that is often engendered by the unfamiliar. (See chapter 21 for details on will-writing and choosing an executor.)

Preparing for and conducting a meeting

Before accepting a face-to-face meeting or approaching a prospect for one, it is important to ensure you have understood your audience. Aside from the obvious demographic differences between having conversations with baby boomers and having conversations with 'Dorothy Donors',[2] there are other things to consider.

Firstly, what does your prospect already know about the subject?

• Is this someone who is new to the idea of legacy giving or do you think they would like to convert to become a pledger?

• Are they new to your organisation or do they have a connection, such as being a long-established volunteer?

• From their demographic status, what can you already surmise about their views on legacy giving? Are they likely to be someone who supports charities because of a traditional belief in the power of charitable institutions to do good? Or have they grown up savvy to charities and their marketing and therefore are looking for more tangible reasons to support charities with a gift in their will?

Secondly, what does your prospect need to know?

• It is your job to curate the information that your supporter would want to know. If they are a legacy intender (i.e. someone who has made it clear that they plan to leave a legacy in the future), then you may wish to discuss free and discounted will-making schemes. If they are an existing donor with an interest in a certain project, you may wish to open the conversation with stories of success on that project.

• Are they looking for practical information on the steps for updating a will or do they wish to be inspired as to why they could support your cause with a future gift?

Lastly, what do you want your prospect to do as a result of the conversation?

• Is this a conversation just to inform or to elicit an action?

• Do you need to agree a follow-up action or date with them? Ensure expectations are managed clearly on both sides once the conversation has ended and you have both agreed what the next steps are going to be.

• Schedule a follow-up call at an agreed time and see how their thought process is progressing. Do they require anything further from you at this stage? Can you suggest a conversation with a volunteer in their area or a bespoke visit to a key service? Maybe a phone call with a senior staff member or an opportunity to meet a beneficiary would be helpful.

• What can you glean that will take this supporter from considering a gift in their will to committing to this action, and how can you be instrumental in this movement?

The barriers and motivators to legacy giving

The ground-breaking research commissioned by the Remember a Charity consortium and delivered by TNS in 2008 to discover the motivators and barriers to legacy giving is embedded in the key approaches of a number of current legacy-giving strategies. The qualitative phase of the research gave legacy fundraisers some insights which underpin approaches to legacy fundraising. The major takeaways included:[3]

• Supporters will be receptive to the legacy message once they have been prompted to think about leaving a gift to charity and it seems like a normal thing to do.

• Legacy fundraisers must reposition legacies as something that 'everyday' people – i.e. anybody – can leave and highlight that the gift left to charity can be small.

• Legacy fundraisers must ensure their communications make clear that they recognise that family comes first.

• The legacy marketing strategy should focus on people who are already in the process of changing their will.

These points were based on the barriers to giving, which are that people:[4]

• don't think about leaving a gift in their will and so most will not do so unless they are prompted;

• think that only unusual people who are unlike themselves – perhaps the very rich – leave legacies and that the amount given has to be large;

• worry about leaving money to their families and so don't think they can leave a gift to charity as well;

• are reluctant to make a will, which they see as unwarranted in their case or expensive, or fear making a commitment to giving a fixed amount to a particular charity in case circumstances change: they don't want to change their will solely to add a gift to charity.

What had motivated those in the study who had already pledged a gift to charity was:[5]

• having had an experience of other people leaving a legacy such as parents and grandparents;

• feeling a connection with a charity because of knowing others who had benefitted from its services;

• the expectation that the legacy would have a large impact, for instance the effect of their gift would have a bigger impact for a small, local charity than for a large, national charity;

• knowing that a particular charity relies heavily on income from legacies, such as the research of a cancer charity being dependent on legacy funds.

One of the most significant findings of the research was that 35% of the charity supporters surveyed stated that they would be happy to leave a small gift in their will to charity (after having included their family).[6] In contrast, only 7% at the time of being surveyed had already included a gift to charity in their will.[7]

These findings highlight not only the huge potential for legacy giving when it is approached in the right manner but also the massive opportunity conversations with supporters on legacy giving could offer, simply by bringing to their attention that this is something that they can do.

Understanding social cues and body language

Everyone gives off social cues in conversations. It's important to be aware of these in all conversations, but when dealing with a sensitive subject, such as legacy giving, they can be a great asset. In legacy conversations, what you say is not always as important as how you say it. Your tone of voice when conversing on such a sensitive topic has to be calm and considerate and you need to speak with authority and confidence to instil confidence in your audience. Any face-to-face fundraising conversation also needs warmth and sincerity. You are the figurehead for your organisation in this donor's eyes and they will associate the organisation and its values with you and the conversation you have. Your tone of voice needs not only to convey trust and authority but also to ensure your passion and enthusiasm for legacy giving comes through.

Legacy conversations are where the business and personal worlds meet: this is not asking for a donation or for someone's time. You are asking them to make a place for your organisation in their last testament – one that will be carried out after they have died.

If your body language is nervous, or if you are shielding your body (folding your arms, perhaps, or hunching your shoulders), this conveys to your audience that you are not comfortable having this conversation. You should adopt an open stance, one that encourages trust and a flow of conversation. By demonstrating with your body language that you are comfortable and confident having this conversation, you will put your prospect at ease and encourage in return relaxed body language from them. If, however, your prospect's body language is suggesting a lack of real interest, fatigue or failing concentration and a change in your stance doesn't help, you may need to reschedule the conversation or, indeed, decide if it's best just to call it a day.

Choosing your language

The language you use when discussing something as sensitive as legacy giving can have a huge impact on the conversation. This is where it's useful to have considered in advance who your audience is. Focus group research has shown that, for everyday conversations about legacy giving, the terms 'legacy' and 'bequest' themselves can be a barrier (see 'Legacy language' on page 23). One supporter once told me in a focus group that they perceived that a legacy was what Tony Blair left in the Middle East – which carries significant negative connotations. A legacy can be felt to mean something serious and substantial and can reinforce the notion that you can only leave one if you are able to leave something significant.

Just a small tweak to language can change perceptions of this type of giving and can side-step this misconception: using the terms 'gift', 'gift in will' or 'donation' softens the idea and make it seem more accessible for all levels of wealth. It can also draw away from the association of legacies with death. A gift is something you give in your life – the term makes writing a gift into their will something positive and proactive a supporter can do now. In contrast, other language may make them consider their own mortality and highlight that, when they leave something to charity, it will happen after their own lifetime.

However, if you are conversing with a more affluent audience – for instance, a major donor or individuals who are considering giving to an arts or university cause – 'legacy' and 'bequest' are terms that will be perfectly at home in your conversations. These will be supporters with a greater awareness of their net value and who will probably be on first-name terms with a financial advisor. Using these more direct and legal terms will be a better approach with this audience, and will help underline your credibility and ensure your access to this group of people. A legacy is also something associated with recognition, and major donors are in my experience more likely than regular supporters to be motivated by the level of recognition that comes of leaving a legacy.

Understanding legal implications

One of the key areas to be aware of when holding a legacy conversation is undue influence. Charities have to be aware of the legalities around mental capacity (i.e. testamentary capacity) and influence and ensure that legacy conversations do not cross a line that may draw them into contentious issues when the gift comes to be realised. Testamentary capacity and awareness of your responsibilities to vulnerable people must be front of mind in any legacy conversation.

There is much more detail on the legal pitfalls in the field of legacy giving in chapter 18, and it is worth reading this chapter before having any face-to-face conversation about legacy giving. The potential ramifications of not being mindful of the legal pitfalls are covered in detail in the chapter.

In all of this, your moral duties as a fundraiser should not be forgotten. If you are concerned about a conversation you are having, even if you feel legally that you are covered, consider the ethical implications of continuing it and whether it is right. (See also chapter 3 on ethics.)

Recording information from your conversations

It is imperative you document your meetings with donors and save your records in your supporter database. This acts as a record of the conversation and captures donor intentions with regard to considering or choosing to leave a gift in their will to your organisation. Although not legally binding, it can be useful to capture anything that states intentions to pledge. It is also good practice to have a paper trail of the conversations you have with your supporters on legacy giving.

Recording conversations can offer peace of mind for your supporters: once someone has made the decision to support you with a gift in their will, that this has been recorded informally, until it can be formalised in a will, can reassure them. At one charity I worked in, a supporter was very anxious to update his will to support us because the charity he had formerly contained in his will had changed its strategic aims and he felt it was no longer aligned with his personal values. After a face-to-face meeting with me, he felt assured that leaving a gift to the organisation I represented would fulfil his values. Before meeting with his solicitor to update his will, he informed his solicitor by letter of his intentions and sent a copy to me for me to put on file, to ensure we were aware of his plans until he was able to update his will. This gave him huge peace of mind.

Ensuring your own safety

Lastly, it is important when you are embarking on a legacy conversation away from your place of work that you have followed any precautions necessary to put your personal safety first. Most organisations have a policy on lone working and visits to donors, so familiarise yourself with these ahead of setting up face-to-face meetings. If you can, try to attend a meeting with a colleague and try to arrange meeting your prospective legacy contact in a public place. It can also be helpful to encourage your prospect to bring along a friend or family member for their own comfort.

If it is necessary for you to attend alone and/or you find yourself visiting the home of your prospect, then there are a few tips to ensure your safety:

• Always tell your line manager or a trusted colleague the address or venue you are visiting, and the key timings agreed for your visit.

• Send your manager or colleague a message before you begin your visit to let them know you are entering the property, and let them know the time you will message again.

• Agree in advance that, if your manager or colleague has not heard from you by the scheduled time, they will call and use a pre-agreed conversation to check you are ok without rousing suspicion if you are in a difficult situation. For instance, you may agree that, if you are in danger, you will tell them something like, 'I forgot to print the month-end report for tomorrow's meeting', but this will really mean you are signalling a need for support.

• Once your visit is safely completed, send your manager or colleague a text or call them to advise them you have finished and left the prospect's house.

Having telephone conversations with supporters

The telephone can be a useful tool when building personal relationships with supporters – for example, when individually stewarding a legacy donor. (See also 'Supporting colleagues who take calls' on page 160). Over the past decade or so, it has also increasingly been used in mass legacy fundraising (for example, approaching donors, often via an external call centre, to ask whether a legacy might be something they would consider). However, there has been considerable debate within the sector between those who believe the telephone is a valuable tool to make personal contact with supporters and those who see it as intrusive and argue that it is disliked by supporters. (See, for example, Stephen Pidgeon's thoughts on this in chapter 14.) In the UK, a tightening of the rules around contacting donors who are registered with the Telephone Preference Service[8] has restricted the numbers of people who can now be contacted via the telephone, and, with the rules around opt-in set to change in 2018, it may well be that the use of the telephone in legacy fundraising will decline considerably.

At the time of writing, the channel is still in use by a number of charities. The following sections offer some brief suggestions below for anyone contemplating a telephone campaign. You are advised, however, to think carefully about the appropriateness of the approach for your audience, and to ensure that your practice in this area is undertaken in line with the appropriate section or sections of the Fundraising Regulator's Code of Fundraising Practice.

Many of the core principles of having legacy conversations – such as understanding the audience, preparation and use of appropriate language – equally apply when using the telephone.

Deciding on the type of campaign – and who will call

The decision about who should call often depends on internal skills and capacity. Relatively large telephone campaigns may need to be outsourced to an external agency, while smaller calling campaigns (for example, around stewardship or event invitations) may be carried out in-house. However calls are undertaken, callers should always be appropriately trained and briefed, and you always need to ensure you have the correct permissions to call each donor.

Pre-call contact

Pre-call contact (for example, a letter) may be helpful in giving supporters who don't want to talk about legacies an option to decline to be called.

Timing of calls

Calls should be timed to fit in with the needs of the audience, rather than when is most convenient for the fundraiser. The most appropriate call times are likely to vary by audience – for example, while a slightly younger audience may not appreciate being called during daytime working hours, this may be an ideal time to contact retired legacy prospects.

Scripting and call guides

Often legacy calls are conversational, and therefore they may not stick to a pre-written script. Nonetheless, it can be helpful for callers to have a guide, setting out key messages to include in the conversation, and perhaps key phrases to use for particular questions. Finally, it should go without saying, but – given how crucial it is to thank a person who decides to give a gift to your charity – it can do no harm to have a reminder of the importance of this in any call guide.

Data capture and fulfilment

Before starting any calling activity, it is wise to think through what you might need to do in terms of:

• capturing information, such as recording a gift;

• fulfilling information requests, such as sending out legacy brochures;

• giving receipts;

• handling any on-the-spot donations (ensuring that the Code of Fundraising Practice is complied with).

Ideally, you will have systems in place that allow any information requested by the person you call to be sent on quickly and efficiently.

Equipping your colleagues and volunteers to have legacy conversations

One, or even several, legacy fundraisers working alone will never be able to achieve the reach that is possible by involving the wider organisation. Encouraging and equipping your colleagues and volunteers to have legacy conversations as part of their work with your organisation can magnify your impact significantly.

As a legacy marketer, you should be comfortable having conversations with your professional peers about the importance of gifts in wills. You should always be looking for opportunities to 'sell' legacies to those internal contacts you feel need to spread the message on your behalf.

Note that it is important to establish your priorities when deciding who to influence with the legacy message. Although any legacy fundraiser will recognise that drip-feeding the legacy message through all staff is the best way to market legacies, if this method is not yet established in your charity, you will need to look at who to give precedence to.

Case study: Identifying wider stakeholder groups

The Chair of Trustees, in a bar, with a mince pie. Sounds like a strange game of Cluedo, but this was what a break-out group I worked with at a sector event came up with as an approach to including legacies in a conversation with key internal stakeholders.

Amid rumblings of fundraisers constantly faced with a senior-level focus on short-term gains, the members of our group on 'talking legacies' with a focus on influencing internally identified three key internal audiences (fundraising networks, senior management and trustees, and volunteers) who we thought needed to take the legacy message to heart. Working with assembled legacy fundraisers, we identified the key approaches to influencing within an organisation to get legacies on everyone's agenda.

This was where the Cluedo element came into play. We identified the details of the specific barriers that each of the three audiences had and then we made suggestions for the best approach for each audience. But looking deeper, we deduced that underlying these specific barriers the issues all came from the same source: all audiences found the subject complicated, or too low profile, or too morbid to engage in legacy conversations. We then worked out where we could make our mark and how we could help these audiences to feel confident in, and feel it was worth, approaching the subject of legacies.

The solutions we came up with stemmed from the principles of relationship fundraising: we decided to have face-to-face conversations to address any barriers and then naturally find openings to promote the idea of legacies. We also decided to provide evidence of the huge benefits legacy income brings to our charity, and to demonstrate how easy and normal it can be to introduce legacies into everyday conversations.

Breaking down barriers to holding legacy conversations

While it is important to be able to hold your own legacy conversations and feel confident doing so, it is equally important to equip your organisation's staff and volunteers with the skills to help spread your legacy message. The idea of legacy giving needs to be drip-fed through all your messaging, and if the legacy team in your organisation is the only team equipped to have legacy conversations then this will be hard to achieve. But how do you empower staff to have legacy conversations on your behalf? Before you can do this, you first need to address the perceived barriers with them.

Fear of not having enough specialist knowledge

Often there is an opinion that you need specialist knowledge to be able to hold a legacy conversation. While this may be true of a legacy income colleague dealing with the intricacies of an estate administration, this does not need to cross over to legacy marketing conversations. In fact, it is important to steer clear of technical, specialist conversations when discussing someone's future wishes so as not to veer into the grey area of offering legal advice.

By establishing this framework of a light-touch conversation, it can be easier to inspire colleagues to consider spreading the legacy message in their networks. Knowing that they are not required to understand estates administration, technical legal language or even the best way to update a will reduces colleagues' perceptions of barriers regarding introducing legacy giving in their conversations.

Fear that the legacy aspect will dominate a conversation

Often staff can be nervous if they feel the legacy element of a conversation needs to dominate, and as a result they may leave it out altogether. A better way to position legacy giving is as just *one* of the ways a potential donor can offer support – the whole list of options might include running a marathon, volunteering, leaving a legacy, setting up a direct debit or giving to an appeal.

The association of legacy giving and death

The biggest barrier in training staff to have legacy conversations, however, is the association that legacy giving has with death. It cannot be escaped and it is very important to ensure you have covered this with any of the networks you are hoping will be having legacy conversations on behalf of your organisation. Legacies are about life – and the possibilities we can provide for the future. Someone will write your charity into their will during their life; that is the point at which they are leaving you a gift and that is the point at which you thank them. For most people the term 'gift in will', not 'legacy', should be used because of the off-putting implications of the word (as outlined earlier) and also because gifts are something a person gives in their lifetime.

Making it easy for them

One of the most successful approaches to starting conversations when you're aiming to empower colleagues and volunteers is to create opportunities for potential prospects to come to *them*, rather than give your colleagues and volunteers the remit of approaching donors and bringing up what they perceive to be an awkward topic. Instead give them the tools to answer queries, and create opportunities for these queries to come in.

An interesting campaign, an unusual take on legacy giving, can be highly effective for this. One year I ran a legacy campaign focusing on people's most prized possessions, with the link being a conversation around who they would like to pass them on to. This led to campaigns internally and through the charity's shops where people brought in their prized possessions and shared their stories peer to peer, staff to customer, beginning a very simple but personal legacy conversation.

Supporting colleagues who take calls

Your supporter care colleagues – or whoever is primarily responsible for taking calls and messages from supporters – are often the first contact that potential legacy prospects will have with your organisation. More often than not, their legacy communications with supporters will be conducted through the telephone. Using the telephone for legacy conversations can be tricky, as without being able to see the donor you are unable to pick up on any visual clues they may be giving you.

There is a huge opportunity with supporter care colleagues if they are confident in sharing the legacy message. When it comes to cross-selling, having legacy giving as one of the options could engage supporters to request more information on legacies or ask for a callback to talk about how they could support your charity with a gift in their will. For this to happen, it is important to look at a 'nudge' messaging strategy and work with supporter care teams on looking for those points in conversations when they might nudge a supporter to consider legacy giving.

The idea of nudging someone to consider legacy giving is in line with a sector-wide approach, spearheaded by Remember a Charity, to normalise legacy giving. By nudging a legacy ask into a conversation alongside other messages, you will encourage supporters to consider it as a perfectly normal way to support, as they would setting up a regular gift, donating to a cash appeal or holding a community event. Including it in a conversation with a supporter care team member means the idea of legacy giving will be brought up when it is relevant, making the ask personal and presented as an option to give, alongside the others mentioned.

Supporting colleagues in charity shops

If your organisation has a network of shops, retail is an excellent opportunity to connect with your audience for legacy fundraising through a focal point in your community. An integrated campaign (the coordinated use of different promotional methods that are intended to reinforce each other) gives shops a focal point to get behind and the opportunity for a visual display to let customers know this is an area of interest. It is important your shop staff and volunteers are prepared for the campaign and understand the role they can play in its success. One of the biggest complaints from shop staff delivering legacy campaigns is that the collateral lands on their shop floor without any prior explanation and so they put the posters up without necessarily having been informed of the wider reach of the campaign and how they might be able to answer any customer queries.

Instead it is imperative you take the time to engage your retail networks and utilise them as champions for your legacy message. Before your integrated campaign goes live, ensure they have been advised of the theme of the campaign. Where possible, organise staff workshops to equip retail staff and volunteers to be able to answer questions on legacy giving that may come from the campaign.

Here it is helpful to give staff and volunteers tools:

• If you use retail point-of-sale materials, can they feature a message inviting customers to approach staff with their questions?

• Could you run staff through a legacy frequently-asked-questions sheet in training and leave a laminated copy at the till for them to refer to?

• Can volunteers co-produce the materials for you? Involving your key stakeholders can be vital to gaining their support. If volunteers have helped you to craft messages on legacy giving that they are confident to use, those messages can have a stronger reach than messages they perceive to have been imposed upon them.

Case study: Cancer Research UK

'Oh no, here comes the Angel of Death' is a common greeting as I travel my region talking to supporters about the importance of gifts in wills and Cancer Research UK's Free Will Service. This is quickly followed by mimed actions of forced pen-holding or assurances that 'I've made mine, leave me alone!' Being the local 'Legacy Lady' does not always make me popular when I visit one of the 30 Cancer

Research UK shops in the South West. Our amazing shop volunteers are always excited to meet a heroic cancer research scientist or nurse, but some are distinctly uncomfortable talking to a legacy fundraiser, despite the fact I help to attract the annual £160 million in legacy donations which helps to pay for those scientists, nurses and researchers. To make that connection be understood, I started to visit our shops dressed in a lab coat. I look like a scientist and I perform engaging, fun science games that illustrate key concepts around genetics, chemotherapy or clinical trials. It feels odd performing with ping-pong balls in a shop window or crammed in the back room of a shop. But now our volunteers listen, they ask questions and, most importantly, they use our Free Will Service or talk to their friends, relatives and shoppers about making a will and leaving a gift to charity.

When I started in this role, I was nervous about talking about wills because, of course, they are linked to death. Now I love talking about a 'product' which I see as helping people and offering the perfect way for them to make a big difference. It's a really easy conversation – easier in many ways than asking people to fundraise or donate in the here and now. And there are plenty of great stories I can share with people about strange gifts, celebrity wills and complex legacies (see the next section for a few examples). Dickens had many a good story around wills and so do we – the members of the legacy fundraising team. Crucially, the stories always come back to how a third of all the progress made in beating cancer has occurred because someone like the person I'm speaking to left a gift in their will previously. Big numbers, little ask.

The lab coat outfit appeared to be a radical move three years ago but has now been adopted by many fundraising colleagues. The drawback of the white lab coat for me, working in a rural region, is that it gets mistaken for the white coat that farmers wear when leading prize cattle or sheep in agricultural shows! The stand-out value of this costume is lost among a sea of similar white-coat-wearing folk. So my next step will be to create a new outfit which is easy to transport and slip on and can represent legacy giving and cancer research. Watch this space.

Supporting face-to-face colleagues

Face-to-face colleagues can include teams in your communities, third-party fundraisers working on private sites, or teams within your organisation whose role it is to build relationships with supporters on a face-to-face basis, including major donors and high-value donors. As it is these colleagues who have the relationships with their donors, it is important that they are the ones to deliver the message on legacy giving as, to those supporters, they will be the face of the organisation. To 'wheel in' a legacy colleague to make an ask about gifts in wills can seem contrived and staged, and, as the legacy team will not have an existing relationship with these supporters, it will not always lead to the most productive conversations.

The best approach is to train these face-to-face colleagues to take on the legacy message and look for opportunities where they would be able to raise the subject of legacy giving. If at that point the supporter would like to be introduced to a legacy fundraiser to have a more in-depth discussion, this is fine, but the initial person to raise the subject should be their key organisational contact. Here, again, nudge messaging can be key. Introducing legacy giving as *one* of the ways to deepen support and as something that other supporters *like you* do can be a soft way of broaching this type of giving with a supporter.

Supporting community representatives

Community giving is the grassroots of many charitable organisations and peer talks to community groups are often the bread and butter of many community fundraising programmes. An integrated legacy campaign can offer these groups a focal point for talking about legacies. Remember a Charity's annual legacy awareness week, for example, is a fantastic opportunity for members to engage with their community groups and to have legacy conversations.

Many community giving approaches work with volunteers or community staff based in regions to deliver presentations and speeches to local groups. This is a prime area for including a legacy ask, and the opportunity to reach communities through a trusted regional representative is one that will pay dividends in sharing the legacy message more widely.

If possible, your goal should be to work with community groups to present solely on legacies. Integrated campaigns, such as Remember a Charity Week, give this opportunity and a focal point for the presentation. In previous years, Remember a Charity has covered the subject of gifts in wills with humorous, exciting and thought-provoking campaigns such as Extreme Will Writing (including feats such as a will writer, solicitor and witness signing a last will and testament while skydiving) and Living Legends (including 94-year-old Tom Lackey wing-walking on a biplane to raise both money for charities and awareness for Remember a Charity).[9] Attention-grabbing campaigns disrupt the norm and can make an audience sit up and pay attention. This can be a great way to open a talk to community groups and then introduce the subject of legacy giving, having warmed the audience up to the concept through the wider campaign.

Where you aren't running an integrated campaign or perhaps don't have the opportunity to take over the entire presentation with a legacy ask, it can still be an opportunity to reach networks if you can add one or two legacy-related slides to standard community talk templates. A set of legacy leaflets to accompany these slides will give attendees the opportunity to find out more at their leisure, and can fit the approach mentioned earlier in this chapter of normalising legacy giving by mentioning it as one of a number of ways to support your organisation.

Examples of unusual gifts in wills

Examples of unusual gifts received by your organisation or others can be a helpful talking point to get conversations started. Some particularly unusual gifts are described below:

• Dr F. W. Cumming left £600 to the Royal Infirmary Edinburgh to give poor patients snuff and tobacco. In the light of later medical evidence, this was probably not the healthiest of bequests![10]

• A donor left £500,000 to the UK in 1928. The gift was worth £350 million in 2013, but it can only be spent once it's enough to clear the national debt (which was £1.5 trillion at the time of the article reporting the story).[11]

• A man left £26,000 to Jesus Christ in 1976, but only if, during a period of 80 years after the man's death, the Second Coming were to occur *and* if the Public Trustee was satisfied of Jesus' identity.[12]

• A cancer charity received a bequest of 12 tractors, horse-drawn ploughs and five sheets of corrugated iron.[13]

• James Gregory left $1,000, the income from which was to be divided up each year between the parents of twins born in Marblehead, Massachusetts, as an expression of sympathy for the 'extra burden and care entailed on loving mothers, poor in the things of earth, who have brought twins into the world'.[14]

Conclusion

Legacy conversations are a wonderful way to connect with your donors as a legacy fundraiser and talk through an extremely valuable way of continuing their support to your charity. If you use the tools available to you as a relationship fundraiser, manage the sensitivities, converse openly and warmly, and watch for social cues in conversation, you can help to move your legacy prospects through to a pledge to benefit your organisation in the long term. Sharing these skills with your internal networks can help them, and by extension you, to reach deeper into the supporters of your organisation – be they volunteers, retail customers, major donors or community groups – and passionately share the legacy message more widely to normalise and encourage legacy giving.

Notes

1   Ken Burnett, *Relationship Fundraising: A Donor-Based Approach to the Business of Raising Money*, New Jersey, Jossey-Bass (Wiley), 2002.

2   Dorothy Donors are defined by Smee & Ford as people who fit the typical charity giver profile: women who are 77 years old on average (or most commonly 88 years old), live in the south of England and leave three legacy gifts to charity; see *Legacy Trends: Discovering potential thorough data* [PDF], Smee & Ford, 2017, https://smeeandford.com/whitepaper, p. 7, accessed 4 January 2018.

3   *Legacy Giving Research Commissioned by Remember a Charity: Final report October 2008* [PDF], 2008, TNS Social, pp. 4–5; report accessible to Remember a Charity members only.

4   *Ibid.*, pp. 14–18.

5   *Ibid.*, pp. 19–21.

6   *Ibid.*, p. 47.

7   *Ibid.*, p. 41.

8   For more information see www.tpsonline.org.uk.

9   'Remember a Charity Week launches today', Remember a Charity, 7 September 2015, www.rememberacharity.org.uk/news/remember-a-charity-week-returns, accessed 2 January 2018; Howard Lake, 'Remember a Charity Week focuses on living legends', *UK Fundraising*, 8 September 2014.

10 Virgil M. Harris, *Ancient, Curious, and Famous Wills*, Boston MA, Little Brown and Co., 1911.

11 'Anonymous £350m fund stuck in legal limbo' [web article], *BBC News*, 2013, www.bbc.co.uk/news/uk-23739598, accessed 2 January 2018.

12 Robert Megarry, *A New Miscellany-at-Law: Yet another diversion for lawyers and others*, Oxford, Hart Publishing, 2005, p. 309; originally reported on 21 January 1977 by *The Times*.

13 Tara Mcinnes, 'Unusual gifts this Christmas' [web article], Third Sector, 2013, http://guest.thirdsector.co.uk/2013/12/18/unusual-gifts-this-christmas, 18 December 2013.

14 Virgil M. Harris, *Ancient, Curious, and Famous Wills*, Boston MA, Little Brown and Co., 1911, p. 109.

CHAPTER THIRTEEN

Using traditional media in legacy asks

Stephen Pidgeon

Introduction

This chapter will cover the four 'm's: method, message, means and media. First of all, the method, then your message, then the means (or platforms) on which you'll hang it and finally the media you will have available for great marketing. The chapter will not deal with all media, just the traditional ones of mail and print, television, radio and telephone – the media favoured by older people. Digital media are covered in chapter 15.

But first, let me describe an experience few of you will know. An experience you cannot imagine until you live it. It is the experience of getting old, and specifically two life changes that, for most people, come with that: retiring from work and having the children leave home. Both of these are intimately connected with the decision to leave a gift to a charity in a will. For many, leaving a legacy can make a small contribution to filling these two holes in their life.

For me, retirement is a real pleasure and brings a freedom from responsibility that is almost exotic. But it also brings fewer opportunities to influence others than I had in the workplace. Donating to a charity restores that influence, just a little, and the deep pleasure of planning a legacy and actually changing your will restores it positively. There is an added bonus: the profoundly satisfying feeling that you'll go on influencing for good, long after your death.

When the kids not only have left home but also have well-established homes of their own, that too brings a new experience. Your responsibility for them becomes less onerous and this brings a freedom of thought and a sense of liberation that you'll not have had for 30, even 40, years.

Many people who are about to retire (or who are well and truly settled into their lives of leisure) will already be receptive to your potential traditional marketing approaches. All you have to do is choose the right vehicle for your particular audience and deliver your message appropriately.

Method

An understanding of these two truths of old age – the extra freedom but less influence, and the absence of responsibility for children – is at the heart of legacy marketing. It affects:

- who you choose to lead your campaign;
- when you ask;
- who you ask.

Who should you choose to lead your campaign?

Take, for instance, the question of who does the ask. Many charities default to the chief executive because this is an important invitation and it feels like it should come from someone senior. The chief executive, though, is usually an administrator. And sadly, many donors still think all chief executives are overpaid. With the one exception of an older chief executive (possibly a founder who is towards the end of their career), a chief executive is unlikely to be a good person to ask donors for a legacy gift.

A good choice to champion the push for legacy gifts might be a senior volunteer, perhaps someone on the trustee board. A board chair might be a perfect choice, but there are two important provisos. Firstly, they must be older not younger – at least 60, although 70 would be better. And, secondly, they must be able to say something like, 'I have left a gift in my will, and I invite you to do the same.' A beneficiary of the charity could also make the ask, though the same two criteria still apply. I have also seen beautiful letters from donors asking others to consider this very different form of support.

If all those suggestions fail, it is possible for a member of the service staff to make the ask, but only if they have long experience with the charity's work. They, uniquely in this group of potential legacy champions, can say, 'I have seen the enormous impact a legacy gift can bring.'

When should you ask?

A major charity in Canada had a legacy strategy that required donors to give 20 cash donations before they qualified to receive a legacy invitation. This is madness. I would ask after three or four donations – that's enough indication of a real interest in your charity. And if you have treated them honourably, then donors will be pleased to be invited to help in this special way. A legacy gift offers people real joy; nobody would leave a legacy if it did not.

167

Who should you ask?

In my view, you are more likely to get commitment for a legacy from those over 60, and I believe that charities should try to avoid asking anyone under 50. There's too much happening in their lives that make such a thought appropriate or acceptable, and by the time they die in 40 or 50 years' time, you will yourself have retired long since.

Message

My approach to the message is based on the same raw emotion as any successful ask for a donation or other support. People give to people, so asking for a legacy gift for your charity, rather than for the outcome of your charity's work, is just daft. Don't do it, don't talk about your charity or your charity's work, talk about what happens when the work is done. As a legacy fundraiser it is your task, and your delight, to tell the donor the sort of progress a legacy gift can achieve.

How asking for legacies is different

You must tell stories of course – stories of change achieved by gifts – but here are three key differences between the ask for a donation and a legacy ask:

1. As well as emotion, the legacy ask must also contain a degree of rationality. The donor is investing a great deal of both thought and emotion into this process. So the stories told must include proof that the happy outcome has resulted from the long experience of your charity in delivering good outcomes.

2. Any gifts resulting from a legacy invitation will not be fulfilled for many years, so there is little point in talking about the need for immediate funds. The stories you use must paint a dream, a vision of what can be achieved in the long term. Yet the need for support must still be compelling. That is a significant copywriting challenge.

3. Professors Adrian Sargeant and Jen Shang argue that, because of the long gap between the promise and the fulfilment of the gift, the donor must be encouraged to match their own values with those of the charity.[1] Your copy must speak of outcomes, of course, but in a legacy ask, these outcomes must be of major visionary change and improvement. They must concern how you are correcting wrong-doing, what goodness you are bringing to the world, the care you are giving, the equality you're fighting for, the kindness you're offering, and so on – not simply the physical change achieved by a donation.

Using direct, clear language and answering objections

A pivotal change in the language of legacy marketing in the UK came in 1986 when WWF ran a highly successful advertising campaign created by my long-term friend and business partner, Nick Thomas. One read, 'More men are guilty of intestacy than adultery' and another 'More women are victims of intestacy than divorce.'[2] These advertisements led a move to legacy asks that were direct and clear. Leaving a legacy became something anyone could do. Other charities quickly followed that lead.

Based on research (see 'Legacy language' on page 23) and over 30 years of direct experience, my thinking has been honed with two key points now firmly established. The first is that you should never use the word 'legacy' in the ask. Do not use a sentence like, 'Please leave a legacy in your will'. Instead say, 'Please leave a gift in your will.' Similarly, avoid other formal terminology such as 'bequests'.

The second key issue concerns the four major objections people cite when considering leaving a legacy to a charity:

1. Their family and friends must come first (this is by far the most important objection).

2. They believe a 'legacy' is a large sum (a very good reason why you should not use that word in the ask).

3. They will have no money when they die.

4. They think changing a will is expensive (when in fact it isn't).

A mailing to donors by the NSPCC in 2008 addresses with incredible neatness three of the four objections to leaving a will:

> We understand that, when you make your will, your own loved ones will probably come first. We wouldn't want it any other way. But you might consider including a small percentage of whatever is left to the NSPCC – after you've made provision for family and friends. The value of such a gift won't lessen over time, and even if you don't think you have much to leave, you would be surprised how little it takes to transform a child's future.

In one short paragraph, three objections are addressed with a clear vision of the good that can be achieved with the gift ('transform a child's future'). This is incredibly effective copy.

And this mailing was smart for another reason. It didn't push for a response. It actually stated elsewhere in the copy that there is no need for the donor to tell the NSPCC if they have committed themselves to a legacy. 'We'd love to know, if only to thank you,' it said, but it was clear that a 'pledge' was unnecessary. Of course, if you ask an elderly person to tell you about something that is deeply personal, they are likely to prevaricate. However, if you say you'd love to know but they don't need to tell you, they will often be happy to tell you.

Means

The following sections outline the means, the 'connection platforms', which you can use with your media options to spread your legacy message.

First a note about what *not* to do: I recall some research conducted in the mid-1980s which showed that no more than 5% of the population had wills. Rationally, then, you would expect that if will-making were generally encouraged, then legacies would increase. As a result of this sort of thinking, the trend was to offer donors – as a blanket approach – a free booklet on 'How to Make Your Will'. But the research showing such low levels of will-making was asking a 'representative sample of the UK population'. Later, in 2004, when Adrian Sargeant and Richard Radcliffe surveyed charity donors with a recent exposure to a legacy message, it turned out that 87.6% of them already had a will.[3] Therefore, a letter offering a 'How to Make Your Will' booklet would only interest 12.4% of this audience.

The strategy, then, although fine in itself (particularly in many European countries, where will-writing is less widespread), is no longer something I'd recommend for a UK donor audience.

Connection platform 1: Via free legal advice

The first connection platform you can use to increase numbers of legacy pledgers centres on free legal advice. In 1993, Cancer Research UK began to invest in free will weeks around the country. Figures given by Cancer Research UK showed that the legacies left through that scheme accounted in 2014 for over 20% of the charity's substantial legacy income.[4] Yet it took 10 years of investment before the income from legacies resulting from the scheme, even matched the considerable running costs. But now, 14 years on, the income is rising exponentially. Who knows? In another 10 years the resulting immense wealth may finally cure cancer. That is proper long-term thinking.

This connection platform also works well for locally based charities, as the following case study demonstrates.

Case study: Tenovus Cancer Care

A superb campaign was run by the Welsh charity Tenovus Cancer Care. Supporters received a letter asking whether they would like to take advantage of a free wills month. Local lawyers had signed up to write simple wills for no fee and the charity's letter simply directed the supporters towards the lawyers.

Copy for the campaign was a mix of the practical – get your will written for free – and the deeply emotional. Stories were told of people who had survived cancer because of the outstanding research work of the charity. That is an easy campaign to put together, though it was made all the more effective with one simple addition. Tenovus Cancer Care, though a relatively small charity, has 37 shops in Wales. So the letter encouraged supporters to pick up more information in any of the shops.

Who works in charity shops? Volunteers, a charity's most committed supporters, who are often elderly. And most of them, when asked in the right way, would consider leaving Tenovus Cancer Care a gift in their will. So legacy colleagues in the charity met with every volunteer, in groups in every shop in the network. It took a long time but it was vital, as it meant all the volunteers knew about the campaign, were part of it and felt they had a job to do. This work also meant that, as well as being able to help supporters coming into the shops for information, many of those volunteers would consider leaving a legacy themselves.

Connection platform 2: Via events

The second connection platform for a legacy ask is technically a two-stage ask and is a simple invitation to attend an event. The National Trust, for instance, runs these all the time and introduces committed supporters to parts of their properties that are not open to the public. These events are always oversubscribed. Other charities hire existing places of interest, combining their meeting with an opportunity to see the exhibits and hear from experts. But it is clear, right from the start, that those attending will hear about the work of the charity and the vital role gifts in wills have in achieving those results.

Connection platform 3: Via a straight ask

Most people you will contact in your legacy campaign are donors who support you with cash or monthly donations, weekly lottery tickets, or goods donated to your shops. They are used to responding to straight asks so, if you want to connect, then just tell them (kindly) what you want them to do.

Connection platform 4: Via memberships

The invitation here is to join a special group of supporters and is highly effective. Membership offers benefits, such as the opportunity to attend exclusive events or to receive special briefings from key experts. But, as outlined in the next case study, membership must be 'earned' by the commitment to leave a gift in their will.

Case study: Special memberships

In a very successful campaign some years ago, the retiring chair of a charity invited supporters to join him as an honorary fellow. He outlined the benefits of fellowship: close connection with the charity's experts, visits to key locations and an annual dinner. And quite casually, he added that, to qualify for honorary fellowship, the supporter must have added a legacy to the charity in their will. The response device then simply confirmed that supporters had fulfilled all the obligations of fellowship.

The idea of an honorary fellowship is an example of a 'pledger society': a grouping of like-minded supporters linked by their commitment to leaving a gift in their will. It is a device that is used widely in the USA, less so in the UK and virtually not at all in Europe. It is one that has considerable scope for development.

Media

Now you have four potential platforms to connect with your supporters, but what media do you have at your disposal? This section will consider five forms of traditional media: letters, telephone, print advertising, TV and radio.

First, however, let's look at some essential steps you must take before your campaign is launched.

Where to start talking about legacies

You can't suddenly write to donors asking for a gift in their will. Well, you can, but it is a crude approach, and in this sensitive area it is pretty crass. Instead, I'd suggest starting to talk about legacies in other communications. An obvious one is an article in a supporter newsletter.

There are two ways to approach this, and I would recommend using both:

1. **In the voice of a legacy-giver's relative:** For example, a daughter, in an article about her mother's recent legacy to your charity, can explain how important the work was to her mother in her lifetime. She can describe how proud she is of her mother's gift. In doing so, of course, she is dealing with the real concern of any elderly parent: 'What will the children think when they discover I've left money to a charity in my will?'

2. **Via a current supporter:** In another article, a current supporter can explain the feeling of deep satisfaction at changing their will in favour of your charity. They can explain their long-term support for the charity's work, why they've changed their will and what their feelings are. The copy can introduce the idea of the supporter telling their children about their gift and achieving support for it.

Many legacy fundraisers claim they cannot source these types of intimate stories. But it is vital to persevere in the search. It is your job to get close to the wonderful people (and their loved ones) who choose to support your charity in this way.

At the same time, though this will be dealt with more thoroughly in chapter 15, your website must address the same issues, ideally using similar images and concepts to those used in your planned print legacy campaign. And, because it is likely that supporters will make contact with your charity asking for more information, you must have simple information available that explains the enormous impact of a legacy gift on people's lives. The following sections consider the traditional media you can use once you've raised the subject of a legacy gift in the ways just outlined.

Letters to your supporters

By a considerable distance, letters are the most important medium when asking for a legacy. A letter is intimate, so it deals well with a subject that is sensitive. Most of your target audience will have been receiving and responding to appeal letters for years. The legacy ask is simply an extension of normal correspondence, so, in this way, it is the perfect medium.

In any copy that asks for a gift in a will, the business of lawyer visits, listing assets and next of kin, and all the paraphernalia of the will-making process have no place at all. They are functional, rational and the realm of people who do not understand real donors. Your message is simple: a gift in your will changes lives, so get your lawyer to change your will.

The letter should have a response mechanism where you invite the donor to tell you whether they have given you a legacy or will consider it in the future. But it must be clear that you want them to get in touch in this way only because you'd like to thank them for their kindness. There was a period some ten years ago in the UK when I observed many charities unwisely using a phrase that went something like, 'Please tell us you've left a legacy, so we can plan ahead.' How they could plan on the basis of the donor's death was never explained.

Telephone

A number of charities, particularly in the USA, have used the telephone to make a legacy ask. Most talk of its success and I heard one speaker at a conference who opined that a positive response to a fifth telephone call (on the subject of legacies) still made the technique 'viable'. I would strongly disagree. If it takes five calls to achieve a positive outcome, I call that harassment.

Personally, I would never use the telephone without having some sort of previous correspondence that indicated that a conversation would be appropriate. Even then, the script would have to be incredibly sensitive to the supporter's feelings, and should allow multiple opportunities to move sweetly out of the conversation if that was required.

Just calling out of the blue is unfair, even unkind, and could upset a great many people. Supporters will only be receptive to a legacy message when they are receptive to a legacy message! And no charity can predict that moment. So, if you upset someone with the harshness of a cold telephone call, you run the risk of ruining any chance of future support, let alone legacy support.

I suspect that advocates of unannounced telephone calls to ask for a legacy have never analysed the subsequent support of those who did not respond positively. I would hazard that it will have taken a nose-dive. So all the effort spent welcoming the donor, sending appeals and thanks for donations and running the donor through a careful stewardship strategy, is blown apart by an inappropriate phone campaign. Such a waste!

Print advertising

This medium delivers mass legacy marketing. Many charities, particularly those with strong brands, have used advertisements in printed media with great success.[5]

The rules are simple, and those who follow them see great results. In one example, an advertisement by the UK animal charity Blue Cross shows a sweet picture of a kitten, a headline ('Remember Me in Your Will'), minimal copy, a coupon and a multiplicity of response mechanisms – freepost, phone, email or online. That's all you need. All propositions in small ads have to be simple. Even Cancer Research UK managed to reduce its complex proposition to a single image in an excellent ad that graphically linked the pen (and the donor's signature on their revised will) with research, symbolised by a syringe. Pen and syringe were morphed and the copy was minimal.

When you write directly to your own supporters, the trick is to make them feel warm to the idea of a legacy. Only a few will be receptive to that message at that moment, and others will return to it later. By contrast, in a mass medium, only those who are at that moment receptive to the message will even read your ad. So your task is relatively easy. You simply have to catch their emotion and provide a simple mechanism for their response.

There are two recurrent stupidities in ads looking for people to leave legacies. The first is caused by overly techie designers who cannot conceive that a respondent wouldn't go straight to the website provided to find out more, so the sole response mechanism they offer is to go online. Most older people will not do this for such a sensitive subject. This is a huge wasted opportunity. The second is caused by designers who think 'clever' delivers a response. 'Clever' has never beaten 'straightforward and simple' in any direct marketing context. A Greenpeace ad has the headline 'Be coldhearted' and the copy 'Remember Greenpeace in your Will and help keep the Arctic as it should be. Cold.' Too complex, too clever and a headline that is off-putting.

Interestingly, Alzheimer's Society has used two ads featuring UK national treasure Tony Robinson. Under a picture of Tony, they used one appealing headline ('Watch my most important broadcast ever' – a reference to a video that was available) and one 'clever' headline ('I don't need a cunning plan to defeat dementia'). My bet is that the first will win every time because an ad in the press has to be very simple to achieve success.

TV and radio

This brings me to the UK's big opportunity for charities seeking legacy support: TV and its older brother, radio. TV is the most underused medium for legacy asks and the one with the most potential to bring in new support. For years I have encouraged charities to invest in TV legacy asks, but no more than a handful of the bigger charities have done it. I personally believe any good legacy TV ad will pay for itself five times over. No ad asking for donations could achieve that on UK television.

If I am promising a return on investment of at least 5:1, why are charities not doing it? Because the response, that is the legacies resulting directly from the ads, will be spread over the next 20 or 25 years. Sadly, trustees are reluctant to think that far ahead.

Furthermore, good legacy TV ads not only generate long-term income, they also make for brilliant brand advertising. These are proper brand ads telling the story of the charity's work *and* describing the charitable support needed to achieve that work. Both are needed in describing the brand.

Making a TV or a radio ad is a specialist art form for which all charities should use professional services. Both media require raw emotion, laid on thickly, as well as simple response mechanisms that are old-age friendly, such as a phone number.

Conclusion

There you have it: method, message, means and media, all applied to traditional audiences. For the next 20 years or so these audiences could provide charities with wealth – in fact immense wealth – that eclipses all other income. And you'll achieve that income by using traditional media: direct mail, TV and radio, advertising, articles in donor magazines and meetings with loyal supporters. Your approach to these good people must be rooted in kindness and sensitivity. But don't hold back, they want to make this ultimate gift and they will do it with joy.

Asking for a gift in someone's will, must surely be one of the best jobs in the world. Truly, you are connecting with wonderful supporters and you are showing them how they can change the world. That is such a privilege.

Notes

1 Adrian Sargeant and Jen Shang, *Identification, Death and Bequest Giving* [PDF], AFP/Legacy Leaders, 2008, www.afpnet.org/files/contentdocuments/ Sargeant_Final_Report.pdf, accessed 8 December 2017, p. 28.

2 Gemma Quainton, 'Change makers: WWF-UK' [web article], www.thirdsector.co.uk/change-makers-wwf-uk/communications/article/1223168, Third Sector, 2 December 2013.

3 Figures stated in the presentation, 'Successful legacy fundraising – just what do donors think is appropriate?', by Adrian Sargeant and Richard Radcliffe at the 24th International Fundraising Congress, Noordijkerhout in the Netherlands, 2004.

4 Figures stated in a presentation given by Pauline Meyer and Jack Visser from the Cancer Research UK legacy team at the Institute of Fundraising conference, 2015.

5 I am indebted to Andrew Papworth's pithy review of these legacy ads in his monthly newsletters. If you would like to receive these newsletters you can sign up at andrewpapworth@btinternet.com. There is also a wealth of practical examples on the Showcase of Fundraising Innovation and Inspiration: http://sofii.org.

CHAPTER FOURTEEN

Using digital communications in legacy marketing

Dan Carter

Introduction

This chapter gives an overview of digital legacy marketing, looking at where it has evolved from, current trends and its potential future direction. The chapter provides a broad outline as to your audience and which channels you should consider, as well as how to integrate digital into your overall legacy marketing strategy.

A vital element to have established before embarking on your digital legacy journey is to have your proposition and key messages in place. This will make it much easier to decide which digital media and which combination of digital tools at your disposal will be most effective for your charity.

Web pages
Legacy web pages

It was not that long ago that digital promotion of legacies was as rudimentary as just having a legacy web page on your main charity site. Many were (and in some cases still are) buried within the deep recesses of the site.[1] But having easily accessible information on gifts in wills on your website in a way that inspires people to take action is still a very shrewd move and very simple to achieve. The combination of a compelling website and excellent follow-up through legacy supporter stewardship (see chapter 15) will help to support the donor from making that initial enquiry to leaving a gift to your charity.

The most important consideration for your legacy web pages is of course the end user. People are not going to be visiting charity legacy web pages due to a lack of anything else interesting in their lives; they are going to be coming with a purpose, and that is most likely to be to gain information about why and how to leave a gift. So it was not long into their development that web pages started to contain digital downloads for people to take away (such as legacy information booklets); they also began to include wording on how to leave a gift and generally focused on a shift to mixing inspiration about why a gift should be left with the practicalities of how that could happen.

Some of the larger charities with bigger budgets then developed legacy microsites to give people a wider range of information. However, no matter how large or small your budget, having a digital presence for legacies is an important part of your legacy marketing mix.

Ten steps to an appealing website

There are ten things to focus on when developing your website:

1. **Ensure your web pages are mobile- and tablet-friendly.** This is now a must for any website. With mobiles becoming the device of choice to browse the internet, it is vital that anyone can access your pages anywhere and at any time.

2. **Accessibility.** With older audiences accessing the internet more and more and with the key legacy target market being aged 65 and older, it is important to ensure your website is accessible. You will need to consider access for the visually impaired in particular. There are simple steps to take to enable your pages to be viewed in different levels of zoom or background colours. This is important if you want to keep your audience engaged.[2]

3. **Limit those clicks.** It's important to ensure that your legacy pages are not hidden within the depths of your website. If there is not a clear path to access your pages, supporters will give up and maybe never come back. The majority will be coming to find information about why and how to leave a gift to your cause. If they can't get to it, all the other digital work you're doing to promote legacies will surely be a waste of time.

4. **Link your pages within your website.** Ensure that there are relevant links to your legacy web pages around your website. For example, if there is a section on fundraising events and you hold legacy events, you will want to ensure there is link to legacy events in the main fundraising section. Similarly, if there is a section on ways to support your charity, legacies need to be in the mix.

5. **Build your pages with insight.** Your supporters should be at the heart of your web pages. It is really beneficial to run some user experience testing sessions to find out exactly what your supporters think about your pages and to help guide what you really need and what is superfluous.

6. **Inspire through great interactive content.** The use of video and imagery is a brilliant way to bring your legacy vision and cause to

life. Remember to really connect your supporters with your impact as a charity, as that will inspire people to take the step of remembering you in their will. You could even be really creative and use an animated video to talk people through the simple steps of leaving a gift in their will to your charity.

7. **Remember KISS (keep it simple, stupid).** This is not telling you to think of your supporters as stupid; it is just about remembering to keep things simple. Far too often, legacy web pages are crammed full of legal jargon and complex paths to follow in order to get the most basic of information. Remember attention spans online are short – you need to be precise and quick to the point.

8. **Downloads.** Remember to have the basic information for people to download and take away and read at their leisure. Supporters will come looking for information. Key downloads include wording for legacies, detailing the type of gift supporters can leave, a codicil form, and a question-and-answer fact sheet to help dispel myths and point supporters in the right direction.

9. **Keep it fresh.** Use analytics to keep monitoring flow through your legacy web pages to continuously enhance what you do.

10. **Follow up quickly and accurately.** The enquiry or the interaction is just the first step. Wow your supporters with the speed and accuracy of your follow-ups and exceed their expectations.

Most importantly, however, to create an excellent legacy website, you need to understand the audience for whom you are creating content – and it's to the digital audience that the next section turns.

Digital audience

The pace of digital advancement has been huge in the past 10 to 15 years, which is a tiny amount of time in the legacy world. At the time of writing, Facebook is a teenager and Twitter, according to some sources, is in decline and giving way to more video-friendly services such as Snapchat. The way your supporters and your audience for legacy fundraising consume digital media has changed an astronomical amount in a very short space of time. Having a digital aspect to your legacy marketing strategy is vital. Social media, digital advertising and websites are all part of the tapestry of telling your charity's legacy story online.

Internet take-up for adults in the UK rose to 86% in 2015, with the use of smartphones overtaking the use of laptops for the first time.[3] According to Ofcom, the smartphone was also considered to be the most important device for internet access by 36% of UK internet users.[4] The number of people who are aged 65 or more now accessing the internet has dramatically increased, from 67% in 2014 to 77% in 2016.[5] This is contrary to the belief that the internet is just being used by the young, and these are useful statistics to cite when talking to digital teams and finance directors to secure budget to conduct digital legacy activities.

With baby boomers taking to the internet in their droves, you will need to consider the approach to this audience in your digital legacy work. It is widely understood that the baby boomer generation demonstrates very different characteristics from preceding generations of supporters.[6] There is more of a requirement with this audience to be able to demonstrate the need for your organisation, what impact your cause has, and thus what impact a legacy will have. The use of the internet and available media at your disposal is ideal for engaging with this audience: you really can, by directly demonstrating the impact of your work, connect the supporter to your cause in a way that could never be achieved with just the written word. The use of video and imagery can help to capture this audience and really inspire them to take action. Videos and imagery can punctuate your legacy web pages, be the main piece of content for a Facebook post or be the basis for a whole online campaign.

Case study: Marie Curie

Marie Curie had been working on a legacy campaign to generate more awareness around legacies for four to five years and was getting mixed results. One of the trickiest elements of its campaign was the development of a hook that could work for both internal audiences and external audiences, making the best use of resources for the organisation. In 2013, Marie Curie joined the Remember a Charity campaign.

The Remember a Charity campaign runs an awareness week in September every year, and Marie Curie decided to use this platform for its month-long awareness-raising work. The campaign used the theme of 'Living Legends', focusing on the fact that lots of people do legendary things for charity, such as skydiving, but something really simple and equally as legendary is leaving a gift in your will to Marie Curie. Marie Curie searched for its own legends: supporters who had pledged a gift in their will to the organisation and whose stories the charity could tell on a variety of different platforms. The charity produced a short video featuring two donors who spoke to camera about two selected donor case studies focusing on the simplicity of leaving a gift in a will to Marie Curie and the reasons why they had done so. The objective of the video was to show that everyday supporters can do this and there is nothing complex about it. This video was then shortened and broken up into small soundbites to be used on Facebook throughout the Remember a Charity Week. During the week, Marie Curie shared Remember a Charity's articles on Facebook about the work going on nationally and then followed up very quickly with its own stories in the video about supporters doing this legendary act. The call to action was about committing to the legendary act of leaving a gift in a will. The ambition was to demonstrate the simplicity of putting Marie Curie in a will and to help make giving a legacy to charity seem like a social norm.

The campaign was a success, with the digital results showing that on Facebook the video posts reached 360,000 users: 20% up on the previous year's campaign, which didn't have video. The number of engaged users (people who took action on the page or with the content) grew from 1,242 in the previous year to 8,998, which was huge growth for the digital legacy work in the charity.

Although Marie Curie is a large organisation, the methods used for developing the material for this campaign were simple and very cost-effective. A talking-heads video can be captured on any smartphone and then uploaded to Facebook, and there are very simple and cheap editing programmes that can be used to develop video if required. The main focus around simplicity and showing real people taking the steps to leave a gift in their will really helped to shape this campaign. The opportunities are there and at a relatively low cost to your organisation.

Channel approach

There are a number of different channels that you can use to promote legacy giving. This section explores each of the options.

Paid-for digital marketing

The best advice here is to make the most of Google AdWords' charity grants. This is a great way to start advertising a legacy message or campaign for free and it is only available for charities. A few things to keep in mind are that the ads can only be text-based, so they cannot contain videos or images. They appear on Google's search results pages below paid-for advertisements and you will need to develop keywords to target your ads to the right audience. It is an excellent way for a charity of any size to establish digital marketing and make legacies the call to action.

Case study: Remember a Charity (experiences of Louise Pavoni, digital communications manager)

Which digital marketing channels (paid-for digital channels) have you used to help promote the work of Remember a Charity and why did you choose those methods?

My colleagues and I began experimenting with paid-for digital marketing in the form of Facebook boosted posts, as they provide good reach for a relatively small cost. Boosted posts are effective for promoting our blog posts and legacy pledger case studies, and they encourage more people to share emotionally engaging stories. To reach the will-writing public and ensure legacy giving is a part of the will-making process, we invest in pay-per-click advertising. Google AdWords allows us to enhance the visibility of our member charities and campaign supporters. It's also a highly measurable channel, making it easy to fine-tune our campaigns.

During Remember a Charity Week, we have seen a huge increase in traffic to our website thanks to video advertising. Through seeding our short teaser campaign films and placing these alongside relevant editorial content, we have brought more people of the right demographic closer to our campaign and generated intrigue during the week. Video advertising was particularly successful for driving website traffic but clearly this relied on having great film content.

We have also used display advertising to promote Remember a Charity Week, by taking over the homepage of consumer websites such as Gransnet, enabling us to reach our target audience. This is an important channel for helping us influence perceptions of legacy giving. Having this presence during the week boosted awareness through both impressions and click-throughs.

Can you give any examples of how you have tested these channels for a Remember a Charity campaign and a short overview of the things you discovered and successes or failures you had?

We have tested the effectiveness of various Facebook boosted posts by altering the copy to tap into people's emotions. The posts which are most successful at prompting users to like, comment and share are those which tell a story and celebrate how legacies make a difference to real people. We discovered that simply promoting a cause and the work it carries out achieves fewer interactions, whereas personal stories are hugely well received.

A post highlighting a family who had pledged a gift to a charity after supporting it for several generations reached 63% more people and had 31% more engagements than a post about a legacy pledger which didn't demonstrate his personal connection to the cause so well, for the same budget. It's important to spend time perfecting the copy so the human element shines through, removing the charity from the picture.

Testing with Google AdWords is really important for us. Our ads previously targeted the whole of the UK as a location for those searching for solicitors, and after tailoring the ad groups by region we saw our click-through rate increase significantly.

What has been the most effective form of digital marketing that you have used and why?

Facebook advertising is really effective for us. The platform is hugely popular with our target audience and it's very easy to reach a large volume of people for a small cost. Providing the content is relevant to them and emotive, the interaction we get from Facebook is very positive. It's helpful that you can target an audience based on factors such as age, gender and interests.

We've also seen a big increase in website traffic thanks to investing in pay-per-click advertising. This channel enables us to have a presence in each step of the online planning process of writing a will, and be front of mind when people are researching legacy giving.

What do you think the future developments of online legacy marketing hold?

Changing online demographics are prompting charities to develop their legacy strategies to focus more on digital marketing. Around one in seven people over the age of 65 now use social networking sites, according to Ofcom,[7] so it's important to make gifts in wills a part of the online conversation.

It's clear that will-making and legacy giving are seen as challenging topics to promote; however, online and particularly social media allow charities to be more humorous and informal to promote legacies, ultimately breaking down barriers.

By 2021, 82% of all consumer internet traffic will be from video traffic,[8] so it makes sense that charities will increasingly turn to film to tell their legacy stories. More baby boomers are online, so we must be a prominent part of the will-writing conversation if we are to change perceptions and influence behaviour.

Pay-per-click advertising is good for transactional approaches to legacies. For instance, you could use this to help promote legacy events focusing on audiences within the locality of your venue. It is important to give a sense of urgency and to get the advert to encourage people to take action to join the event or at least show them the perceived benefit of attending.

Paid-for Facebook advertising is very powerful and relatively straight-forward to action. In order to make the most of using this channel, you need a clear grasp of your target audience. The targeting tools on Face-book are excellent and can really help to narrow down your approach, getting more impact for your investment. You can use geo-targeting techni-ques to even further refine your approach by region, and again this is really useful for events advertising or focusing on certain areas of affluence (for example). The use of Facebook's targeting tools means you can also reach people who are not currently following you on Facebook, which is an excellent way of encouraging new people to support your cause.

Organic social media

The use of organic (i.e. free) promotion of legacies through sites such as Facebook and Twitter is excellent for developing content-led approaches. The focus here is on driving stories to help engage supporters in your work and educate them about leaving a legacy to your charity. If you can engage your active audience (who are in regular contact with you) by using inter-esting stories about the impact of your work and show them people who are supporting your charity through a gift in their will, the impact will be far greater that if you just put out an advertising piece, which people will see through and not engage with. If you can inform, educate and share with your supporters through great stories, your posts will have better longevity. As mentioned before, you have the opportunity through these digital channels to use excellent media, such as short video and pictures, to create engaging legacy stories and at a relatively low cost. Remember to keep your stories succinct, as people soon switch off online and you want them to go away feeling warm and fuzzy, and take action. That is not going to happen after a 20-minute video on how to make your will.

Online versus offline writing

Due to the amount of information online and the way in which it is consumed, there is a very real difference between writing for the online audience and writing for printed materials. Unlike the typical offline reader, the online audience is more of a viewer, and a different approach is required to grab or hold their attention.

A traditional print reader will have more time to read through your letter or leaflet and perhaps return to it. An online viewer will not have time: they will be looking for clear, concise information that is useful and they will not want to come back for it. Online viewers also have many other adverts, letters and emails vying for their time, and often they will have got to your site through a Google search, so it is vital that your online copy stands out and grabs and holds their attention.

Offline writing often has longer paragraphs to suit readers with more time on their hands; online, you need to break up your paragraphs into short, sharp sentences as supporters will be skim-reading your site. Think about how you structure the information. Grab attention right from the start with an introduction that gives an interesting heading or statistic to start your supporters on their journey. This is a good way to show the impact of legacies on your organisation in a quick and simple way that will engage them and make them want to read on. Remember to use imagery, short sentences, bullet points and anything else that can help to chop up your web page, email or article. It is really important to not only write your content but also craft it to bring your supporter with you, because, if you don't, your competitors will.

A conclusion you should have drawn from this discussion is that writing for the web requires a completely different approach from writing for print, and you need to find out more about it before beginning to do so.

What does the future hold?

Integration – i.e. sharing your core message across a variety of online and offline channels – is key. While this may not sound particularly futuristic, it is where legacy campaigns need to be moving to. Integration across all digital platforms is going to be essential to ensuring your legacy message is shared even further among your potential audiences. Campaigns which successfully link offline activity (such as direct mail) to online sources (such as web pages or Facebook) to allow people to interact further are going to be the best way in which you can share your legacy message further and further in an increasingly engaging way.

Online video advertising could also become more prevalent in the future. While direct response television (i.e. television advertising that asks the consumer to respond directly to the organisation usually via a phone number or web address) is often prohibitive due to its cost, online campaigns using excellent and engaging video to encourage people to take action can help organisations to develop their digital legacy marketing capabilities for a relatively modest cost. Tracking and monitoring the success of your campaign is much easier online than offline, which can help you to both improve your offerings and make the internal case for additional investment.

Conclusion

The use of digital communications in legacy marketing is on the increase and is now an essential part of any legacy strategy. It allows you to reach supporters in a more personal way than the more traditional methods, using tailored social media posts or video content which you know will be of interest to them thanks to the careful targeting that you can do through online channels like Facebook.

It is important to remember, however, that your website is still vital to your digital communications mix, as this may well be the landing point for which most of the other digital communication channels point your supporters to. A key take-away point from the 'Ten steps to an appealing website', outlined earlier in the chapter, is to keep your content inspiring: supporters aren't there because they like the organisation, they are there because they're inspired by what impact you have, so show them that impact.

It is worth reiterating that there are key differences between writing online versus offline and that this must be considered if you want to inspire people about your work using digital communication channels. Remember an online audience is more likely to be a viewer with less time than the traditional offline reader, so being short and snappy and grabbing the attention will be essential.

In order to continue to grow this valuable income stream for the future, charities need to invest more now in blended digital communications ensuring a mix of website, social media and digital advertising is used to help attract people to this wonderful form of support. The digital revolution is here to stay.

Notes

1   Emma Rigby, 'Charity websites 'lacking in information on legacies'' [web article], Third Sector, www.thirdsector.co.uk/charity-websites-lacking-information-legacies/fundraising/article/769630, 28 November 2007.

2   On accessibility, see 'Web Content Accessibility Guidelines (WCAG) Overview' [web page], Wc3, 2017, www.w3.org/WAI/intro/wcag, accessed 8 December 2017.

3   'Statistical bulletin: Internet Users 2014' [web page], Office for National Statistics, 2015, www.ons.gov.uk/businessindustryandtrade/itandinternetindustry/bulletins/internetusers/2015, accessed 8 December 2017.

4   *Communications Market Report 2016* [PDF], Ofcom, 2016, www.ofcom.org.uk/__data/assets/pdf_file/0024/26826/cmr_uk_2016.pdf, p. 177, accessed 8 December 2017.

5   See figure 5.9, p. 187, in the same Ofcom report.

6   *Living Forever: Baby Boomers and Posterity* [PDF], Legacy Foresight, 2007 (report available to In-Memory Insight Consortium members).

7   'Rise of the Social Seniors Revealed' [press release], Ofcom, www.ofcom.org.uk/about-ofcom/latest/media/media-releases/2017/rise-social-seniors, 14 June 2017.

8   *Cisco Visual Networking Index: Forecast and Methodology, 2016–2021* [PDF], Cisco, www.cisco.com/c/en/us/solutions/collateral/service-provider/visual-networking-index-vni/complete-white-paper-c11–481360.pdf, 2017, p. 3, accessed 8 January 2018.

Stewarding your supporters through the legacy journey

Katy Williamson

Introduction

A colleague of mine once described writing your will as like writing your last letter to your loved ones. It therefore follows that choosing to include a charity in your will is a big decision and one of great importance. It takes a lot of time and consideration to write such an important document. As a legacy fundraiser, it is your privilege to steward your supporters through the journey of writing this document and after.

The legacy journey

Different terms can be used to refer to supporters who embark on the legacy journey with your charity, and which words people choose can depend on the context. On the one hand, the traditional terms of enquirer, considerer, intender and pledger are used by most charities, especially in the context of their databases. On the other hand, as outlined in chapter 4, another lens through which to view the journey is a supporter starting at a pre-contemplative stage, moving to contemplation, then preparation and eventually action.

Whichever words your charity tends to use, if it has an approach that centres on its supporters (the promotion of which was the intention of employing these new terms), rather than determining activities by pure metrics, that is what matters.

I personally find the term 'pledger' to be a fitting way to describe a person who has made the decision to include a gift in their will to a charity: it reflects the significance of the decision, of similar import to pledging one's love or allegiance to someone or something. For this reason, and for the purposes of simplicity, I use the standard terms in this chapter, but they can be viewed equivalently as pre-contemplators, contemplators, preparers and action-takers.

Enquirers

Enquirers are at the beginning of their legacy journey. It may take them quite a long time to decide whether they want pledge a gift to your charity. Few people enquire having already made an appointment with their solicitor to write their will. They are still thinking about potential charities to include. Actually making an appointment and following through on their intentions takes most people quite a long time.

It therefore pays to make the process as easy as possible for your enquirers. Many charities offer will-planning templates to help their supporters sort out their thoughts. For smaller charities that do not have the funds to create a wide range of materials, being a member of the consortium Remember a Charity is helpful as it has template planners you can use.

Some charities offer will-writing schemes for their enquirers – either for a reduced fee or with the charity covering the bill. They can offer to put their supporters in touch with solicitors signed up to their scheme. An example of a consortium scheme is Will Aid, which runs every November with nine member charities (at the time of writing). Participants in the scheme pay a reduced will-writing fee to their solicitor, who donates this fee to Will Aid. Will Aid then splits the donations among the member charities.

It is important to bear in mind that, compared to the mid-2000s, people are including more charities in their wills.[1] Enquirers are likely to contact several charities for similar information, and so it is vital to try to stay at the forefront of your supporters' minds. By finding out what attracted them to your organisation, offering advice and painting a picture of what a gift in their will could achieve, you can make the difference between them choosing your charity or them choosing another one. Case studies of pledgers who have made that important decision and case studies of projects funded by legacies are great for showcasing how easy it is to leave a legacy and how important it is to your work.

Considerers

Most considerers I have met have been at events. They are people who feel warmly towards your charity and have thought through who they will include in their will when they write one or edit an existing one. It's important to be sensitive to the preferences of someone who is contemplating giving to your charity and to tailor your stewardship based on these preferences. If they are willing to be open with you, it can be extremely useful to meet with them to discuss their involvement with your charity. Are they interested in specific projects? For example, when I worked for the British Red Cross as a Community Legacy Manager for Scotland, many of our supporters were interested in our international work. As this became apparent, I was able to calibrate my communications with them to suit their interest. Sharing updates from international projects that were ongoing in countries supporters had an affiliation with, and offering one-to-one calls with project workers in those areas, proved extremely fruitful in how loyal to the cause a supporter would feel and increased the likelihood that they would decide to pledge a gift.

Case study: One-to-one stewardship

At the British Red Cross, I worked with one pledger in Northern Ireland who was very specific about her wishes for her legacy. She contacted me out of the blue one day and asked how she could go about supporting the charity, but she was concerned she would be neglecting her local community by supporting a worldwide charity. I suggested we meet for lunch and I could share with her all the good work we did locally. We met at a local café and spent over an hour discussing the various projects ongoing in and around Belfast. We spoke several more times over a few months before she let me know she had included a legacy specific for emergency response in Northern Ireland. I was also able to arrange for her and her daughter to visit some of our volunteers who carry out this work, so she would know more about the impact she would be making. It could have been viewed as an expensive trip, but it proved worth the stewardship and she remained on my stewardship programme. It also meant her daughter knew what her mother's ongoing legacy would be.

Intenders

While many charities do differentiate between considerers and intenders, these two groups can be difficult to distinguish because it is hard to ascertain the moment when a supporter moves from considering a pledge to intending to pledge. For example, imagine Mrs Smith asks your charity about legacy giving (at this point she is considered an enquirer) and then she reads your charity's booklet on legacy giving and likes the sound of it (she becomes a considerer). When she thinks about leaving a gift to the charity, discusses it with her family and decides, 'Yes, I'd like to leave a charitable legacy', then she is an intender. It is clear, then, why it is difficult for a charity to know exactly when this transition – this point of deciding – takes place.

Pledgers

A pledger is someone who has included a gift to your charity in their will. This is the stage of the legacy journey to which you would ideally like all people who consider leaving a gift to your charity to reach. From there, it is about ensuring your charity remains in their will and, if possible, increasing their legacy. Leaving a gift in a will is such a private thing and sharing this can be easier for some people to do than for others. Having said that, in my experience, it is always at events and talks that supporters share their intentions.

When a pledge is made

At the point of the pledge being made, the key thing is obviously to thank your supporter. I like to find out whether they have a specific reason for choosing to support the charity. This will often lead to a more open-ended conversation and enable you to build up your relationship (or build upon an existing relationship). It is then easier to establish the necessary details which you as a fundraiser will need, such as contact details and preferences for contact. It is important to record as much information as possible from your conversations on your database, being mindful of how personal information is stored and who is privy to it. (Note that I personally do not attempt to find out what someone's pledge amount is unless they are open to sharing it. The direction the conversation takes will make this clear.)

This is the moment when you can establish whether there are particular areas of your charity's work which your supporter is interested in. For example, in my role as Regional Legacy Manager for Scotland at Cancer Research UK, I often find that supporters are interested in specific cancers, such as pancreatic cancer. I am then able to make sure that I keep them updated on progress in this area of research.

Recognising the pledge

How you choose to recognise a supporter's pledge will often depend on their preferences. While some people may like to see their name in an annual report, others wish to keep their pledge a private matter, and they may not even have discussed it with their family.

In a 2011 seminar, the Bible Society chose to recognise its pledgers in a lovely way. All pledgers were asked to choose their favourite Bible verse and, if they wished, also send in a photo. The reception of the charity's head office had a rolling digital photo frame on display which showed each pledger's chosen verse and photo.

At the British Red Cross, my colleagues and I developed a coffee-table-style photo book which would be sent to supporters who had pledged a legacy. Each book could be individually dedicated to each pledger and they were filled with pictures of the charity's work from around the world. There was no direct mention in the book of it being a thank you for a legacy pledge. We deliberately did this to ensure the privacy of each donor. It could be displayed with pride but with no awkward questions asked.

You can have a suite of thank you options, from cards to plaques to trees. However you choose to recognise a pledge, though, you must bear in mind that things like buildings, plaques, trees and books are all subject to being moved, lost or changed. A supporter's family may wish to be able to visit their loved one's name on a plaque in ten years' time, and, if your charity has moved office and not kept the plaque, the relationship could be severely damaged.

Why keeping in touch is key to good stewardship

There can be a temptation to leave a supporter alone once your charity has been included in their will, from fear that any contact could jeopardise the donation. However, if you consider the donor development pyramid (which represents the journey of the donor, where major donors are at the top of the pyramid),[2] a legacy is the ultimate donation and often the greatest gift that someone can ever give. Therefore, they should be treated like a high-value donor. You wouldn't consider ignoring a high-value donor.

Personal involvement

In an ideal world, you would meet with every legacy supporter in person. A one-to-one meeting is the easiest way to establish a relationship, to learn what motivates and inspires the supporter, and to earn their long-term trust. However, you should always consider your charity's lone-worker policy. If you are meeting in person, try to hold the meeting somewhere in public, or, if it is in the supporter's home, take a colleague with you. (See also 'Ensuring your own safety' on page 155.)

Depending on the area you cover, though, it might not be possible to meet with every pledger or they may not wish to meet. In this case, a telephone call will be best for enabling a full conversation.

Case study: The private pledger

I once had an experience with a pledger who had enquired about legacy giving and attended an event. However, she was a very private lady. I picked up on this at the event during our conversation and asked her whether she would like me to keep her updated following the event. We spoke a couple of times following the event before she politely expressed that she had drawn up her will and included the charity. However, she did not want any further specific legacy engagement from the charity as she now wished to forget about it and not 'tempt fate' by continuing to think about it. I followed her wishes by marking on the database that she wished for no further legacy contact.

Communications, newsletters and annual reports

The easiest way to keep in touch with your legacy supporters is to make use of your charity's existing communications. If you can persuade your senior management team of the value of legacies to charities, then the ideal is to include a legacy message in every communication. For example, at Cancer Research UK, we are fortunate to receive over a third of our donations from legacies. Therefore, over a third of our research is funded by gifts in wills. This carries an incredibly powerful message. Finding your charity's legacy unique selling point will be key.

Your charity will likely have regular newsletters. By having a good working relationship with all of the teams in your charity, you can remain up to date with ongoing work and seek opportunities to include a legacy article or update your supporters on progress – for example, an interview with a pledger or a case study showcasing an item funded by a legacy. When referring to a legacy, if you hope to use a legator's name, it is, of course, necessary to check with the executors whether the family is happy for you to share this information publicly.

Your annual report can be a great way of publicly thanking your legators. It is also a memento which can be sent out to legacy supporters regularly. In my experience, the baby boomer generation is even more concerned than earlier generations with how charities manage their money, so this is an easy and fitting way to keep them informed and reassured.

Getting to know your supporters is vital when managing which communications you send them. You will undoubtedly have a group of supporters you get to know better than others, to the point where you can send them birthday cards and get-well-soon cards. If your charity's purpose allows, then an annual communication all legacy supporters should receive is a Christmas card. I've been fortunate to work for charities where the direct marketing team could fulfil most of the work involved in this effort, which enabled me to spend time personalising cards to pledgers. However, it may be that the size of your charity does not allow this, in which case prioritising your pledgers, followed by your intenders, may be your best option.

Events

Legacy events are an increasingly popular way to steward supporters. They are the best way for supporters to get to know the various facets of a charity in person and even to visit a project or building. This is something you can also offer to a pledger's loved ones as a thank you for the legacy.

It is important to choose carefully who will be at your event representing your charity. While your project workers are excellent at their jobs, it does not mean they will automatically be good at talking to strangers and eloquently describing your charity's work. Public speaking and talking easily with strangers are not traits possessed by everyone. It is also fundamental to make sure your event does not appear extravagant. Supporters will love your event, but they do not want to see their money spent on caviar and smoked salmon. It is much better to put on a quality event with a simpler spread.

People give to people and an event is the perfect opportunity to grow the loyalty your supporters feel by justifying their trust in your charity. Greeting them warmly from the start and ensuring they are enjoying themselves and feel able to question you is essential. I often find at events that people are more relaxed and open to chatting with me after they have seen presentations about the charity's work.

It is crucial everyone invited to an event knows there will be a legacy side to the event. You do not want anyone to feel it has been sprung upon them. Never make a pushy ask, too; always aim for quite a gentle and respectful ask. Having explained all your charity has achieved thanks to your supporters and by showing how much of this has been thanks to gifts in wills, it is easier to then explain how important it is that everyone has an up-to-date will and how it is possible to include a charity in it. Whether they choose to include your charity is their own personal choice but your event will hopefully have shown that your charity does vital work and can be trusted with their donations.

Case study: Events as stewardship

It can be hard to track what prompted an enquirer to contact you, but, when I was at the British Red Cross, one supporter I stewarded got in touch via the charity's website. Initially he wondered whether we offered a free will service, but thankfully he was not deterred that we did not. He and I conversed by email initially, but, when later he needed more in-depth information, I spoke with him by phone. This enabled a more natural conversation and I could find out that he wished his legacy to be spent in the north of Scotland; I was able to advise on appropriate wording for this. When I held an event near him, I contacted him to see whether he would like to meet for a cup of tea or whether he would like to attend the event, which was at a local historic house. This was fortuitous, as during the tour of the house after the event, I spent time chatting further with him and his wife – not specifically about the charity or its work but about the venue. A few months after the event, he wrote to advise me he was drawing up his will that week and would be including a gift to the charity, and he mentioned that his decision had been made thanks to the friendliness of everyone at the charity on the day of the event. He had expected a pushy legacy ask and had been delighted to get to know the charity's staff in person. He had full confidence that we would respect his wishes and spend his legacy wisely. His wife also went on to include the charity in her will because of her experience at the event.

Other issues
Low-value and high-value gifts

The difficulty with any stewardship programme is knowing how much time to devote to each supporter. It can be tempting to devote all your time to those who you know are leaving large donations in their wills.

However, for those who have left smaller gifts, their legacy could be a fortune to them.

My way of managing this has been to have a rolling programme and calendar which each new enquirer, intender and pledger can be added into. It has various levels of contact within it:

• At the first level, you could automatically be reminded to send out newsletters, annual reviews and Christmas cards to your full rota of supporters.

• At the next level, supporters are likely to know more about you and (for example) which projects they are most interested in. You can send them specialist reports from projects workers in the field on top of the communications sent to all supporters.

• At the third level, you are likely to be in contact with supporters fairly frequently. Often your pledgers who are leaving higher-value gifts will want in-depth financial information, but you will have the opportunity to tailor your communications to them, as you will have fewer of this type of supporter.

Regular phone calls and handwritten letters are easy things to do. Speaking with your colleagues in finance, project work and senior management is important. They will need to know about the information these supporters require and why it is important to nurture their requests. People who have chosen to donate significant amounts to your charity have the potential to be stewarded towards donating larger amounts if it is within their means. Other pledgers may also be stewarded from leaving a specific amount to a percentage, which is often higher.

Case study: Seize every opportunity to steward

The British Red Cross is fortunate to have HRH the Prince of Wales as its president and the Queen as its patron. Upon the 150th anniversary of the charity, the Prince and Her Majesty held a garden party for volunteers and staff at Buckingham Palace. This was a perfect stewardship opportunity and, after inviting five of my pledgers who had included highly significant gifts to our charity in their wills, two were able to accept and I escorted them to the garden party. They were treated to a day in London in their finery, and they met devoted volunteers and members of staff as well as experiencing the glory of a royal garden party. It was a great way for me to spend quality time with them and to get to know them even better. I was also able to maintain this relationship afterwards by sharing photos and memories from the day. One of these pledgers even went on to increase her pledge to the charity as a result.

Changes of staff

It's a fact of life that there will be changes of staff within your charity. The important thing is not to let this affect a supporter's relationship with the charity. There should be contingency plans in place to ensure there is no dip in stewardship during a changeover period or a time of absence.

Your relationship database is your lifesaver here. Every conversation with a supporter should be recorded on it, being mindful of sensitive data. Another team member should be able to access your supporter's record and see a note of every instance of contact the charity has had with them. Keeping track of emails, letters and phone calls is the only way you can ensure a smooth continuation of the relationship.

Ideally, if you know you will be leaving, you can let your supporters know and introduce them to your replacement. You will also be able to leave a note of who your supporters are and what level of contact each one needs.

Guarding against impossible conditions

It is understandable that a supporter may want to restrict their legacy to a certain project or a certain area. For example, in my experience, Scots are sometimes very keen that their money is spent in Scotland. However, it may be that a chosen project is no longer running when the legacy is received. It is up to you to ensure your charity deals sensitively with a supporter's wishes, and you can either discuss the wording of a legacy for a particular purpose with your supporter or advise them to ask their will writer to contact you to discuss the wording directly. For example, I once had a supporter who wished to have his legacy spent on respite care in his home town. Through careful relationship management, I could explain that this was not a service currently offered by the charity. Instead he restricted his legacy to his hometown with a proviso that, should there be emergency care operating under the charity in that location upon his passing, it would be spent on that.

Such measures as this will help to ensure your charity can actually use the legacy when it is received, and you can also ask your pledger to specify that, if their desired specific purpose cannot be adhered to, their legacy may be used for your charity's general purposes. You can also drop into the conversation that legacies destined for general funds have just as much impact for your charity's cause as legacies for specific projects.

Undue influence

It can happen that a legacy is challenged on the grounds of undue influence. Keeping records of any meetings or contact you have with your supporters should ensure against that. You should never accompany a supporter into a meeting with their solicitor. Their choice of legacy should come from them and not be guided by anyone within the charity. If you are meeting with them, making sure the meeting is in a public place, or with another person present, is a good idea.

Lifetime gifts

You may have a supporter who wishes to give now, rather than later. Being able to give what's known as a lifetime gift enables a supporter to see what is achieved through their support and to be thanked in person. This can be a great way to develop your recognition programme as you will know what kind of acknowledgement a supporter is comfortable with. These donations normally sit within a legacy fundraiser's remit as the stewardship aspect is important, as the supporter may go on to gift more to your charity.

Conclusion

The decision to remember a charity in a will is not taken lightly. The word 'legacy' has such important connotations in all meanings of the word. By leaving a legacy to charity it is often someone's way of expressing their hopes for the future. Whether they choose to remember animals, children, the planet or medical research, it is an expression of their desire to see a better future for those their chosen charity champions. They therefore want to trust that their legacy will be in safe hands. This is why good stewardship is so important. It is your role to communicate why your charity is responsible and a good choice.

Communication is the name of the game. It is your role to learn about your supporter. What motivates them and what is their passion? How do these motivations and passions link to your charity? You can then utilise this to tailor your communications about your charity's achievements and future goals. Ensuring the communication is on the supporters' terms and not driven by your own goals will earn their trust and help your relationship to grow. Whether they wish to hear from you often or just once a year, if you keep your communications interesting, fresh and inspiring then you will not lose their loyalty.

Notes

1   *Legacy Trends 2017 Update: Discovering potential through data* [PDF], London, Smee & Ford, 2017, p. 3.
2   Frank Barry, Lawrence Henze, David Lamb and Katherine Swank, *Cultivating Lifelong Donors: Stewardship and the Fundraising Pyramid*, Blackbaud, www.blackbaud.com/files/resources/downloads/Book_CultivatingLifelongDonors.pdf, accessed 11 December 2017.

CHAPTER SIXTEEN

Giving in memory of others

Kate Jenkinson

Introduction

Giving in memory pairs naturally with legacy giving and, as such, the subject finds a natural place in this book. Many of the same sensitivities apply to both fundraising types, such as dealing with bereaved individuals. Legacy fundraisers are, therefore, the logical people to be seeking gifts in memory – not forgetting that the in-memory supporters they engage may also become legacy givers too.

What is in-memory giving?

In-memory giving is any type of charitable giving or fundraising that commemorates the life of someone who is special to the person giving. Sources of in-memory income are wide-ranging and include gifts from funeral collections, one-off or regular donations, the purchase of commemorative items (such as plaques and benches), fundraising events and tribute funds (charitable funds set up in memory of a loved one). In reality, any contact with a charity can be motivated by remembrance, whether it's volunteering in a shop or simply dropping a few coins into a collecting tin.

Since the mid-2000s, in-memory fundraising has become something of a rising star, benefitting from a significant focusing of energy across the sector. More and more, charities are coming to understand the importance of remembrance as a motivation for many of their supporters. While this may be particularly true for health charities, hospices and others offering people practical, end-of-life support, the opportunity is not exclusively theirs. 'Loved-in-life' organisations – including animal, religious and development charities – are also becoming alert to the potential. Of course, any cause can be loved in life. If the deceased had a lifelong interest in lifeboats, was a keen conservationist or simply loved children, an associated charity can be the natural choice for their next of kin when they are considering making a donation in their loved one's memory.

One reason in-memory fundraising has come a little late to the table is its tendency to get sidelined as the poor relation of legacies. While many charities rely on legacies to fund large sections of their work, the exact contribution made by in-memory income is hard to pin down. In-memory motivations have not always been revealed by the donor, or systematically captured by the charity, making the case for investment in this area an uphill struggle.

Yet the rewards can be great. According to research commissioned by Legacy Foresight, 35% of the UK adult population have given at least once to charity in someone's name over the past year. Legacy Foresight estimates that total voluntary income for the sector is around £410 million annually in the UK; that's around 5.5% of total voluntary income.[1] With so many donations still unattributed and so much income still hidden, however, this figure may well be just the tip of the iceberg.

Another fundamental barrier is the fear of communicating with people who are recently bereaved. While charities are more in their comfort zone discussing gifts in wills with supporters for whom death is still a distant or abstract prospect, talking about donations when grief is very raw can be a far more loaded proposition. When is the right time to raise the opportunity? What types of offer are the most welcome or the most appropriate? Where should boundaries be drawn when speaking to people in a heightened emotional state?

The combined impact of these factors has meant that, when the opportunity arises to talk to people about supporting a charity in a way that has associations with death, legacies have tended to win the day.

What does in-memory fundraising have to do with legacies?

For the donor, the act of giving in memory of a loved one can be an entry point to a profound relationship, often with long-term value for the charity. Emotional currency runs high at the point of bereavement and can be enduring. If the donor is properly stewarded and nurtured, ideal conditions for legacy consideration can be created further down the line.

Legacy Foresight research, based on data from 13 large charities, suggested that 'warm' in-memory donors (those with a previous transactional relationship with the charity) were twice as likely to be legacy pledgers or prospects than those who had no previous transactional relationship with the charity. Their legacies were of higher value, too. Those known to have given an in-memory gift left pecuniary legacies worth 38% more, and residual legacies worth 24% more, than other donors.[2] Both findings confirm the imperative for charities to identify gifts with an in-memory motivation and acknowledge them as such: a hidden in-memory donor could well be a hidden legacy prospect.

The key benefits of in-memory fundraising

Perhaps more than any other form of fundraising, in-memory giving can provide benefits not only for the charity but also for the donor. At Legacy

Foresight, my colleagues and I have observed that the benefits for the charity include:

• As well as the quick financial wins, in-memory fundraising offers charities an engaging new route to market. Tribute fundraising in particular can be primarily about the person who has died, with the cause itself quite secondary. It can attract people who may previously have had little or no interest in your cause, including younger supporters from a variety of backgrounds.

• There is no 'typical' experience either of the end of life or of grief. Tribute fundraising, with its values of choice and flexibility, acknowledges this, making it an ideal fit for the autonomy-driven baby boomer generation.

• In-memory stewardship offers unlimited points of contact for your charity to suggest other opportunities, including event participation, volunteering and merchandise sales.

And the benefits for the donor include:

• There is now a wide understanding and acceptance of the power of fundraising to mobilise and draw families together at a very difficult time and of the therapeutic benefits of doing good in memory of a loved one.

• In-memory giving can provide a point of focus and diversion – a channel for expending both positive and negative energy. It can aid the grieving process by recalling wonderful things about the person who has died.

• These benefits are particularly pertinent when there is a prevailing sense that a life has been cut short, or when death is associated with violence or injustice. In these cases, the natural human impulse to make some good come out of bad can be even more particularly acute.

For a charity whose raison d'être is looking after people in need, in-memory fundraising provides an excellent opportunity to extend its core duty of support.

The changing culture of grief and remembrance

The way we choose to mark the death of our loved ones is rapidly evolving. Since the late nineteenth century, these changes have been driven by the dramatic rise of cremations in place of burial[3] and by our dwindling interest in organised religion.[4] Most of us no longer have a physical point of connection to the person we've lost. In the face of this 'graveyard gap' – this lack of a memorial that we can visit to grieve – we constantly seek out intangible or symbolic substitutes that will satisfy our need to pay tribute.

We are reclaiming remembrance, which is far less prescriptive than it once was. An 'anything goes' culture has led to a proliferation of commercial products and services, driven by the US market. We can now create a scrapbook or a patchwork quilt in someone's memory, or make lasting jewellery, a coral reef or even fireworks out of their ashes. So far, the charity sector has kept well clear of these territories. But there is a clear opportunity for charities to feed the public appetite for capturing the essence of a loved one in ways that are highly relevant, personalised and individualistic.

By extension, it appears that our taboos around death and remembrance are breaking down. We are more comfortable than we have ever been talking about dying and its aftermath. Many of us are taking to social media sites such as Facebook to share – at least with friends and family – the grief that might once, beyond the funeral, have been privately expressed or internalised. Charities such as the NSPCC find that, when they post supporters' in-memory case studies, their organic social communities are highly responsive to other people's stories of loss and quick to offer their virtual support.[5] This 'comfort of strangers' syndrome is likely to grow, as long as our consumption of social media continues.

The public response to high-profile and celebrity deaths has created a new movement: we now witness whole tsunamis of public grief, played out on traditional and social media. Icons have been created, both from national treasures such as David Bowie and from those, such as the MP Jo Cox and the fusilier Lee Rigby, who were tragically cut down in their prime. As well as giving generously to associated causes, our response to these highly public incidents has revealed a trace of narcissism. We've felt compelled to broadcast to the world what that individual's death has meant to us personally.

High-profile deaths also make us think about own mortality and what we'll leave behind. Greater numbers of us than ever before are planning our own deaths, making wills and thinking about our assets, both financial and symbolic. On the practical side, we're increasingly using consumer channels (such as the product comparison site Moneysavingexpert.com) to put our affairs in order.

More bizarrely, a growing number of companies are beginning to offer products and services offering us digital immortality. We can keep our Facebook accounts running after we die, securely store our digital assets for eternity, even commission an intelligent avatar of ourselves that will interact with future events in the ways we might have done. With the speed of technological change, it is not difficult to imagine a time when physical death – rather than marking the end – is simply one point in the journey.

Planning an in-memory fundraising strategy

The dynamic, shifting culture discussed in the above highlighted text means you can be creative and imaginative in your strategy planning. However, perhaps more so than for any other area of fundraising, this is a territory that you must get right. A supporter might be open, even cavalier on social media, but make no mistake about it: they will have certain expectations of you as the charity that is benefitting from the death of their loved one.

Particularly if your organisation offers end-of-life support, the people who come forward to support you in memory of a loved one will expect exceptional stewardship in return. The real enemy of donor care is inadequate planning. With in-memory giving, this can damage not just the potential lifetime value of a donor but also the reputation and soul of your charity.

Key questions to consider before planning your in-memory strategy
What sort of charity are you?

Ask yourself, what makes you special? Why would someone be likely to associate your organisation, over and above any other, with the person they've lost? If you are a health or cause-of-death charity, you probably already have a source of in-memory donations coming through your service users and other stakeholder channels. For hospices in particular, there is a strong link between service use and the impulse to say thank you when a loved one dies.

On the other hand, your proposition will be different if you are a loved-in-life charity with no connection through your services to the deceased's family. If the reason you've been chosen is less about thanking and more about inspiring thoughts of the donor's loved one in happier times, the decision may have been more personal and heart-warming. Your in-memory offer might need to be the more celebratory for this.

What do you know about people who already support your charity in memory of a loved one?

If your charity provides services to the elderly, or has a database predominantly containing the details of elderly people, you may need a strategy more designed for an older cohort than, say, an infant bereavement charity whose main prospects are young parents. Age profile will help to shape your offer, too. An elderly spouse remembering someone who has lived a long and happy life is a very different proposition from a young mother remembering a baby taken from her via premature death.

It is always better to use real insight rather than assumption about what motivates people to support your charity in memory. For example, if you are a cancer charity engaged in both emotional support and medical research, people might donate in a loved one's name because they are grateful that you've been there for them. On the other hand, they may want their gift to help you find a cure, so other families don't have to go through what they have. First-hand qualitative research among in-memory supporters can help you to understand what makes you special in donors' eyes.

Approximately what proportion of your total income comes from in-memory giving?

Estimating the proportion of your total income that comes from in-memory giving will help you to define your objectives and drive your strategy. For example, do you believe that in-memory giving makes up the core of your charity's income and requires urgent focus? Is it a growing area of importance that you would like to expand at a gradual rate? Or are you starting from scratch, so needing to develop and test brand-new in-memory offers?

What size of organisation are you?

What does the size of your organisation say about the investment and resources you will be able to commit, particularly in terms of staff numbers? In-memory stewardship can be resource-heavy and emotionally demanding. There is little point investing in, say, a tribute fund programme if no one will be available to respond to contacts from tribute fund holders.

Does your charity have any wider organisational objectives that could be linked to an in-memory programme?

Perhaps you already offer a counselling or advice service? Free will-making? Spiritual guidance? Could you make in-memory giving an integral part of your overall offer of support? The animal charity Blue Cross has found that its Pet Bereavement Support Service integrates very neatly with its Pet Memorials product, generating a share of in-memory fundraising leads. Users of this service may go on to become donors and perhaps pledge a legacy to the Blue Cross after experiencing one, or both, of these products.[6]

Critical success factors of an ideal, integrated programme

It is not just people's responses to bereavement that are complex and diverse. In-memory fundraising itself is highly involved and requires careful forethought. There are several factors that need to be in place to deliver a programme successfully and with confidence:

- **Vision and commitment:** Your organisation will need to be united, single-minded and ambitious about maximising income from your existing in-memory donors, attracting new recruits and enhancing your relationships with all stakeholders. Taking a new approach to donors – rather than simply repackaging existing activity – might involve a change of mindset at your charity.

- **A senior champion:** Without senior buy-in, without someone who 'gets it' and who is excited by the potential, an in-memory programme can struggle to get off the ground. A single person at senior manager level taking overall responsibility for in-memory income is a basic requirement. For tribute funds in particular to realise their full potential, this income stream needs to be a part of the overall fundraising strategy and have the level of planning and resources that is applied to traditional income streams.

- **Regional reach, bolstered by central control:** The issue of the ownership of in-memory giving – where the programme sits, who drives it and who manages it on a day-to-day basis – can be contentious. Large network-based charities with deep roots in the community find that their in-memory and tribute income is driven by local fundraising and know that it is important to maintain and maximise community connections and keep giving people the chance to donate locally. For many charities, the role of other powerful stakeholders, including committees and medical professionals, must also be considered. But driving strategy, maintaining momentum and policing consistency are best achieved centrally.

- **Organisational buy-in:** For an in-memory programme to be really successful, all parts of the organisation need to understand how it not only raises significant sums of money but also provides a valued support service to bereaved people. It is essential – especially in organisations where service delivery brings the organisation close to the deceased – that frontline staff in particular are confident that the programme is appropriate and sensitive. For tribute funds, there are also issues to address related to income flow between different fundraising teams.

- **Dedicated resources:** This really is crucial and often most clearly makes the difference between success and failure. Charities succeed best when they have staff dedicated to in-memory and tribute funds. An example from my experience is the Motor Neurone Disease Association, which, in the very early days of its programme, seconded a member of staff to phone and support tribute fund holders – a simple role that proved to be the catalyst for its programme and a major factor in its success.

- **Appropriate systems:** The running of tribute funds requires simple but efficient database procedures, ensuring donations are allocated to the right funds and internal fundraising teams receive soft credits[7] to help motivate fundraisers to work collaboratively with colleagues within their team and in other departments. Poor systems can kill a programme before it starts. Digital platforms are now allowing for even more powerful tribute fundraising, significantly increasing donor involvement and fund performance.

• **Ongoing support, training and motivation:** It is essential that everyone involved in promoting in-memory and tribute fundraising is equipped with the tools, confidence and enthusiasm required to play their part effectively. This is especially true of organisations with high staff turnover and those operating regional networks dependent on a cascade system of communications. The organisation Cruse provides highly tailored courses aimed at charity staff who come into day-to-day contact with recently bereaved people.[8] These courses explore the challenges particular to the organisation and to the job roles of the staff involved.

First priorities

Getting right back to basics, your first considerations for your in-memory programme could be as follows.

Stick to the principles

• In-memory fundraising is about offering people freedom, flexibility and choice, not trying to shoehorn them into a prescribed model of behaviour.

• For the donor, this is all about the deceased – not about you. At the start of the relationship, you may be little more than the outlet they've chosen for channelling their grief.

Define your offer of support

• What does your complete package of services to bereaved people look like, incorporating in-memory giving? How can you link your fundraising and support services to prepare for an increased volume of contact from bereaved donors?

• If applicable, how can your medical professionals be persuaded to advocate the programme?

• What additional insight can be gained from research among your current in-memory supporters?

Put your house in order

• What key operational measures still need to be taken to give you the infrastructure and fail-safe processes necessary to support a programme that will be widely promoted?

Ownership and momentum

• How will the programme sit within your organisation and what is the likelihood of having dedicated staff? Who will have overall responsibility for the income line and ensure measurable return on investment? Who will train fundraisers, support staff and volunteers? If relevant, how will support resources be allocated across central office and the regions?

One single organisation

• How will you attribute accountability for in-memory income across all fundraising teams, your service teams and support staff? How will you avoid a culture where teams work in silos – seeing in-memory fundraising as the sole remit of the in-memory team rather than a motivation for giving that permeates all areas of fundraising? How will you give trustees, committees and other stakeholders – as powerful and potentially crucial advocates of in-memory fundraising – a sense of ownership without encouraging competition?

Getting the offer right: What will work best for your charity?

As part of your strategy, you might want to consider developing a new in-memory product. An in-memory product is anything your charity can offer someone – as part of a transaction – to satisfy their need or desire to remember a loved one. This 'anything' can be a physical item, a real or virtual experience, or a service that you offer. It acknowledges that the person has given, or done, something to support you in their loved one's name, and could become the beating heart of your programme.

There are a few main categories of product currently in use by charities, some – but not all – may be suitable for your organisation. In choosing a type of product, consider what you need it to do. Do you want a product that will encourage initial in-memory gifts? Recognise someone for their support? Encourage them to donate again, or donate more? Or keep somebody giving over time, building a long-term relationship with you? Your programme should ensure that people who are not immediately motivated by your in-memory product(s) are not excluded. They might be open to alternative offers, or simply need more time before they are ready to engage further.

You should also be prepared to test various approaches to establish how much hand-holding your supporters need. There is no point signposting people to JustGiving if the idea of autonomous fundraising horrifies them. Likewise, a simple phone call acknowledging their donation before your thank you letter arrives might be appreciated more than anything else.

There are various types of in-memory products in wide circulation. The following sections explore some of the options.

Funeral collections via pew envelopes

These are small printed envelopes that can be left on seats at a funeral service as a means of collecting donations. They allow friends and family to donate by either cash or cheque, incorporating Gift Aid. A discreet alternative to the traditional collection plate, they are usually still administered by the minister or funeral director. Families like them as they can be personalised, and they remove the administrative headache of organising a collection at a time of high stress. Many charities offer pew envelopes, and as such they have come to be regarded as the base-level offer to bereaved families.

Online and offline books of remembrance

Books of remembrance are used to record the names of everyone who has been honoured with an in-memory donation. Traditionally a tangible book kept at a single central office location, they are now more commonly a virtual equivalent, accessible to all. Like pew envelopes, books of remembrance are low maintenance for the charity in terms of cost and administration.

In-memory appeals

Some, though relatively few, charities target their known in-memory donors with tailored direct-mail appeals, usually at a time of year considered special for remembrance, such as Christmas, Mother's Day or Father's Day. Mailings can include inspiring engagement devices such as a personalised star to hang on a Christmas tree with a special tribute, or a packet of forget-me-not seeds. Response rates and average gifts can be particularly high when in-memory donors are targeted in this way. Contrary to what intuition might suggest, they have also been found to generate little or no negative reaction.

Commemorative items

Commemorative items – such as plaques, benches and engraved leaves on a tree of remembrance – are favoured by individuals who want their donations to buy something special or permanent, but shy away from the longer-term commitment of a tribute fund. Commemorative items are usually contingent on the charity having a physical display space, such as a wall, pathway or garden. Being able to visit a commemorative item dedicated to a loved one can be a great source of comfort to supporters; however, there are serious logistical considerations for charities around maintenance and upkeep. This, combined with the fact that many charities are spread over diverse locations, means that charities are increasingly evolving virtual offers, such as lighting a candle online or buying a virtual brick. Commemorative schemes such as Guide Dogs' Name a Puppy and the Woodland Trust's Dedicate a Tree have an inspiring extra dimension – the sense that the loved one's spirit is still thriving, embodied in a living being.

Fundraising events

Some charities offer events targeted exclusively at an in-memory audience, such as the hospice movement's Light up a Life event. Others – such as Alzheimer's Society Memory Walk – were conceived for people with a range of different motivations but have been warmly embraced by supporters remembering a loved one. A key benefit of mass-participation events is the strong vein of camaraderie: participants derive great therapeutic benefit from a celebratory atmosphere, like-minded company and the chance to share stories of loved ones.

Research from Legacy Foresight suggests that fundraising events are the largest segment in value terms, accounting for 45% of known in-memory income and estimates that 10% of the UK population have taken part in an event in memory at some point.[9] With the market quite saturated, devising new events is costly and high risk. However, ensuring that your existing events recognise, acknowledge and act upon the motivations of your in-memory supporters can be a quick win for your charity.

Tribute funds and online memorials

For those who feel they want to carry on fundraising in their loved one's name, tribute funds are ideal. They are particularly good for galvanising friends and family and concentrating the energies of young and active family members. They directly give donors something they want: a wealth of opportunities to pay tribute in ways fitting and appropriate to the individual who has died. Some charities provide their own tribute fund platforms, while many donors now use JustGiving, MuchLoved and other third parties. Their platforms allow families to post a wealth of collateral about their loved one – stories, pictures, memories and even favourite music tracks – while fundraising efficiently among their own social networks.

Tribute funds are not a new idea, but, while awareness and usage are growing, research suggests that their average donation values may be declining. Gifts made via tribute funds now account for around 7% of all in-memory donations.

Working with funeral directors

Funeral collections represent the biggest category of in-memory donations in volume terms, accounting for around 38% of all gifts. Charities have long regarded funeral directors as the gatekeepers of in-memory income, given their unique role in guiding next of kin through their options for the funeral service – including whether to have a charity collection in lieu of flowers, and their choice of beneficiary.

In my experience, funeral directors thrive on recognition and appreciation but feel this is rarely forthcoming from charities. It is extremely difficult for any charity to establish a profitable relationship with funeral directors and for it to be kept front of mind without sustained, personal face-to-face contact. Some charities have found that nurturing key funeral directors (for example, through a network of branch secretaries) pays greater dividends than attempting to push generic marketing materials through their branches.

Funeral directors like to be treated as important facilitators of the process rather than as faceless intermediaries. Courteous and prompt thanks by the charity is essential, but often neglected.

Funeral directors' working practices are evolving rapidly. Over the past three years, a number of alternative online collection platforms have been set up by groups of funeral directors. For the funeral directors, these systems can reduce the cost of collecting, administering and accounting for funeral gifts; for the deceased's family, they have the advantage of reaching more far-flung contacts who cannot attend the funeral. There is also the ability to reclaim Gift Aid on the entire collection.

Bringing it all together
Common pitfalls

Even with sound forward planning and the best of intentions, there are a few particularly challenging hurdles that a charity must overcome for its programme to fly rather than falter. Some common pitfalls and red flags for in-memory fundraising are as follows:

• **Misplaced fear of communicating:** Many charities are finding that, far from being reluctant to talk about their bereavement and about donating, in-memory prospects are actually glad to start the conversation. Fear of approaching people in this situation can be all in the mind of the fundraiser rather than the donor.

• **Importance of the first thank you:** Your thank you communication for the in-memory donor's first gift is all-important. It can allay any doubts the family might have about choosing you as its charity and is your first (and sometimes only) opportunity to surprise and delight. Don't forget that an abrupt, cold, impersonal or – worse still – overdue thank you reflects both on your charity and on the donor's sense of how their loved one is valued.

• **Neglect of the second gift:** Often charities struggle to re-engage with donors after they've given an in-memory donation for the first time. Donors will be more likely to give again if their initial experience is positive and leaves them feeling valued by your organisation.

• **Failure to keep it donor led:** Legacy Foresight's consumer research has suggested that, as a sector, charities over-rely on financial asks to their bereaved audience, neglecting other non-financial opportunities that might interest them, such as volunteering. In-memory donors want to feel that they are seen by charities as more than simply 'cash machines'.[10]

• **Careless stewardship:** Getting small details wrong in your communications – such as mis-spelling the name of the deceased – can be particularly upsetting for the donor in this context. This is a strong argument for the proper resourcing of in-memory fulfilment.

Quick wins

If developing an in-memory strategy is a medium-term objective for your charity, you might first consider a few basic actions to help you start driving up your prospect base:

• **Raise awareness of in-memory giving as an appropriate and valued way of supporting your charity** first among staff, volunteers and committees and then among your donors, support service users and the public. Promotional materials should be available at every point of contact with donors and the public.

• **Think about your digital in-memory presence** by starting to plan out a dynamic landing page on your website. This should explain to visitors exactly how they can remember someone and stress the special value you place on gifts of this kind. In-memory testimonials could be featured regularly on your website and in supporter newsletters and publications, using engaging donor stories.

• **Stories can be sourced** from scanning the in-memory sections of national and local newspapers for collections being made in support of your charity. Families often welcome the chance to see a small feature about their loved one and to gain recognition of the wonderful work you are able to do, thanks to gifts made in their memory. Local press can be used to publicise the gifts received.

• **Your own listings of acknowledgements** (such as in newsletters or annual reports) can be used to recognise people who have been remembered with a gift. Wherever possible, a representative from your charity should attend commemoration services at which you are benefitting from a collection.

• **'Flushing out' in-memory donors** is an important part of recognising their motivation for supporting you and will also provide indicators of their characteristics. A simple tick box (requiring a yes or no answer) can be used on all appeals ('Are you donating in memory of someone?') and for all events ('Are you taking part in memory of someone?').

Conclusion

A smart, considered and integrated programme of in-memory and tribute fundraising could make a major contribution to your growth and consolidate your offer of support to donors and service users with recent experience of bereavement. Acknowledging and accommodating people's desire to fundraise in memory of a loved one should be central to most charities' overarching fundraising strategy.

Notes

1　Figures provided directly by Legacy Foresight, January 2014.
2　In-Memory Insight benchmarking analysis, Legacy Foresight, 2011.
3　'National Cremation Statistics 1960–2014' [web page], The Cremation Society of Great Britain, 2015, www.srgw.info/CremSoc4/Stats/National/2014/StatsNat.html, accessed 11 December 2017.
4　For example, see Peter Brierley, *UK Church Statistics No 2 2010–2020*, Tonbridge, ADBC Publishers, 2014.
5　From research by Legacy Foresight in 2016 (available to the In-Memory Insight Learning Circle members).
6　In-Memory Insight charity case study research, Legacy Foresight, 2016 (available to Legacy Foresight and In-Memory Insight Consortium members).

7   Soft credits are a way of ensuring that donations income can be allocated against more than one fundraising department's targets for reporting purposes to ensure that shared effort and accountability are recognised, without actually double counting the income. For example, if an events team has worked with a tribute fund donor on an in-memory event, but the in-memory team takes the income for all 'in-memory' activity, the events team might receive a soft credit to show their contribution. This arrangement can provide managers with a useful, informal performance management tool, as well as a clearer sense of the real return on investment and added value of different fundraising activities.

8   For information on Cruse's loss and bereavement courses, see www.cruse.org.uk/node/1267.

9   Populus research for In-Memory Insight, Legacy Foresight, 2016 (available to In-Memory Insight Consortium members).

10   Legacy Foresight's 2015 consumer research into in-memory products.

CHAPTER SEVENTEEN

The law concerning succession to property on death

Rod Smith, Paul Sutton, Sarah Bolt and Daniel Harris

Introduction

This chapter provides a concise guide to the law of England and Wales relating to all aspects of the passing of property on death, whether by will or intestacy – the situation where someone dies without a will (a death 'intestate'). We include a detailed section on the types of gift that can be made by will (including charitable gifts), the circumstances in which they can fail (and what the consequences of failure are), and how estates are currently taxed.

This chapter states the rules at the time of writing and is a brief summary of the law in this area. The applicable rules (particularly regarding tax) must be checked at the relevant time. Readers working in charities based in Scotland and Northern Ireland should refer to the laws of succession applicable in their jurisdictions, which may differ in important respects from what is covered in this chapter.

Wills and codicils

A will is a written statement, completed with the required formalities, setting out intentions about what is to happen on or after death. Typically, a person writing a will (a 'testator') will deal with the appointment of executors (the people who will deal with assets and liabilities after the testator's death), the appointment of guardians for any infant children (i.e. minors – under the age of 18), and who will receive their property (the estate).

A codicil is a document that adds to or changes the provisions of a will. There can sometimes be many codicils supplementing a will.

The key elements of wills and codicils

The essential characteristics of wills (with or without codicils) are as follows:

• They must be in writing.

• They must be made by a person aged 18 or over.

• They must be made by a person of sound mind, memory and understanding. The testator should have a clear understanding of what is in their estate, whom they want to benefit and for whom they could make provision. They should also have a clear intention that the will should operate after their death.

• They must not be made as a result of undue influence – otherwise they may be challenged.

• The testator must know and approve of the contents of the will – i.e. they must understand its provisions and their effect.

• The will and codicil must be signed by the testator; alternatively, they may be signed on the testator's behalf in the presence and at the direction of the testator. It must be clear that the testator intended to give effect to the document by signing it.

• The signature of the testator must be made or acknowledged in the presence of at least two witnesses who are present together at the same time. Two independent adults should be asked to act as witnesses. It is crucial that no beneficiary or the spouse or civil partner of any beneficiary acts as a witness, since that would prevent them receiving benefits under the document. Where a will leaves a legacy to a charity, therefore, it is best that a trustee or employee of the charity should not act as a witness. Each witness must additionally sign the document in the presence of the testator. Ideally, the document should contain a statement (an attestation clause) confirming that these requirements have been met.

• Strictly speaking, a will does not need to be dated. However, it is good practice to insert the date when the testator signs it.

The effect of wills and codicils

A will or a codicil is only a statement of intention. Until the testator dies, the document may be revoked or altered at any time. It takes effect – or 'speaks' – from the date of death.

A person can use a will to dispose of any land and buildings (real property) and any cash, investments or other possessions (personal property) that they own. Wills do not, however, deal with all types of property. They cannot generally deal with property in joint names (for example, a house or a bank account) or property held in a trust. The legal rule is that property in joint names normally passes automatically (unless special arrangements have been made) to the surviving co-owner or co-owners on the death of one co-owner. There may also be restrictions on the extent to which a will can deal with foreign property. The law of the country in which the property is situated may mean that it is not possible for it to be disposed of under a will. For example, a surviving spouse or children may have automatic rights to it under the law of the country where the property is situated. (See chapter 19 for international legal considerations.)

There is no requirement that a will or codicil be registered, or that it be stored in any particular way. The prudent thing is to make sure that the document is kept in a safe place, and that the testator's family and executors know that it exists and where it is kept.

It is important to note the general rule that a will and any codicils will be revoked automatically by law if the person who made them subsequently marries or enters into a civil partnership. If a person divorces or their civil partnership is dissolved, their former spouse or civil partner is treated as having died before them and does not then receive any benefit under their will or take on the role of executor if they are appointed to that role in the will. In all other respects after a divorce, the will remains valid.

Intestacy

Intestacy is what happens when a person dies without leaving a valid will setting out how they want their property dealt with after their death. An intestacy can be either total or partial. Total intestacy occurs when there is no will at all or no valid will. Partial intestacy occurs where the will does not deal with all of the person's property.

Who may benefit from the estate?

On an intestacy, the family of the person who has died becomes entitled to the person's assets in the order set down in the Administration of Estates Act 1925. The intestacy rules provide that the estate will pass in accordance with table 17.1. The main point to note about these rules is that the surviving spouse or civil partner is *not* automatically entitled to all the assets. This is a common but mistaken assumption.

TABLE 17.1 RIGHTS ON INTESTACY IN CASE OF DEATHS ON OR AFTER 1 OCTOBER 2014

Relatives surviving[1]	Distribution of estate where spouse or civil partner survives[2]	Distribution of estate where no spouse or civil partner survives
1. Issue (i.e. a person's direct-bloodline descendants, including children, grandchildren and great-grandchildren)	Spouse or civil partner takes: a. the personal chattels; b. statutory legacy of £250,000 net, free of inheritance tax and costs, plus simple interest from death at Bank of England base rate; c. half of the remainder of the estate absolutely. The issue take the other half of the remainder of the estate absolutely 'on the statutory trusts' (i.e. following the statute, the remainder of the estate is held for them until they reach 18. If they are 18 or over they inherit straight away). If the residuary estate is worth less than £250,000, the spouse or civil partner receives everything and the issue receives nothing.	All to the issue on the statutory trusts.

2. Parents	All to the surviving spouse or civil partner absolutely.	All to the parents (in equal shares if both survive).
3. Brothers and/or sisters 'of the whole blood' (the legal term for when people have both parents in common), including the issue of any brothers or sisters who predeceased the intestate	All to the surviving spouse or civil partner absolutely.	All to the brothers and sisters and issue of predeceased brothers and sisters of the whole blood on the statutory trusts.
4. Brothers and/or sisters 'of the half blood' (the legal term for when people have one parent in common), including the issue of any such brothers or sisters who predeceased the intestate	All to the surviving spouse or civil partner absolutely.	All to the brothers and sisters of the half blood and issue of the predeceased brothers and sisters of the half blood on the statutory trusts.
5. Grandparents	All to the surviving spouse or civil partner absolutely.	All to the grandparents (if more than one, in equal shares).
6. Uncles and/or aunts of the whole blood (including the issue of any such uncles or aunts who predeceased the intestate)	All to the surviving spouse or civil partner absolutely.	All to the uncles and aunts and issue of predeceased uncle and aunts of the whole blood on the statutory trusts.
7. Uncles and/or aunts of the half blood (including the issue of any such uncles or aunts who predeceased the intestate)	All to the surviving spouse or civil partner absolutely.	All to the uncles and aunts and issue of predeceased uncles and aunts of the half blood on the statutory trusts.

8. Relatives not in any of the above classes who attain an absolute vested interest; i.e. a relative who is entitled without there being any condition attached	All to the surviving spouse or civil partner absolutely.	All to the Crown.

Under the Inheritance (Provision for Family and Dependants) Act 1975 (as amended by the Inheritance and Trustees' Power Act 2014), certain specified classes of people may apply to the courts (i.e. either the High Court or the county courts) for provision from the person's estate if they can show that the provisions of the will, or the intestacy rules, do not make 'reasonable financial provision' for them.

On a partial intestacy, beneficiaries must bring into account any benefits they receive under the will in determining the application of the intestacy provisions.

Who can apply?

The people who can apply under the 1975 Act are:

• a surviving spouse (even if judicially separated) or civil partner;

• a former spouse who has not remarried or a civil partner who has not entered into a subsequent civil partnership;

• a person who, during the whole of the two-year period before the death of the deceased, lived in the same home as the deceased or the spouse or civil partner of the deceased;

• a child of the deceased; this would include adopted children and children whose parents were not married (defined as 'illegitimate' in the statute);

• any person treated as a child of the family – i.e. a person for whom the deceased acted as a parent;

• any other person who immediately before the death was being maintained, either wholly or partly, by the deceased.

Changes made to the Inheritance (Provision for Family and Dependants) Act 1975 by the Inheritance and Trustees' Power Act 2014 only apply to deaths on or after 1 October 2014.

What orders can be made?

Where an application is made under the 1975 Act, the court has to decide whether the will or the intestacy rules make 'reasonable financial provision' for the applicant. If not, the court then has to make an objective decision about the provision to be made.

In making this decision, the court has to consider a number of issues specified in the 1975 Act, including the financial resources and financial needs of the applicant both now and in the foreseeable future, the obligations and responsibilities that the deceased had towards the applicant (and any other beneficiaries), and the size and nature of the deceased's estate. Where the applicant is the deceased's spouse or civil partner, the court has to have regard to what the likely award would have been upon divorce (in the case of marriage) or annulment (in the case of civil partnerships).

In the cases of spouses and civil partners, 'reasonable financial provision' means such provision as is reasonable for a spouse or civil partner to receive, irrespective of whether such provision is required for their maintenance. In the case of all other claimants, 'reasonable financial provision' means such provision as it is reasonable for the applicant to receive for their maintenance.

The court can, among other things, order periodical payments, lump-sum payments, and transfers and settlements of property. A court order can relate to any property in the person's estate, including any property that might be left to charity under a person's will. Thus, an order under the 1975 Act can override a charitable legacy.

Case study: *Ilott* v. *The Blue Cross and others*

In the landmark case of *Ilott* v. *The Blue Cross and others* [2017] UKSC 17 (formerly known as *Ilott* v. *Mitson*), Mrs Ilott had been long estranged from her mother, Mrs Jackson, who died in 2004 leaving all of her estate to three charities. Mrs Ilott subsequently brought a claim against her mother's estate under the Inheritance (Provision for Family and Dependants) Act 1975 (the 1975 Act). Mrs Ilott was awarded £50,000 at first instance and the Court of Appeal increased this to a lump sum of £143,000 (which would have enabled her to purchase her house at the time under the right-to-buy scheme) and an option to also receive a further £20,000 in one or more instalments; so structured to avoid the loss of her means-tested benefits.

The three charities appealed against the Court of Appeal decision. In allowing the appeal, the Supreme Court restored to the charities the initial £50,000 award to Mrs Ilott made in the first instance. The outcome of this decision is good news for charities,

---

many of which depend heavily on testamentary gifts for their funding.

The crux of the Supreme Court decision was that the Court of Appeal had no proper basis for interfering with the first instance decision. The judgment provides a helpful clarification of the position in relation to claims for reasonable financial provision made by adult children of the deceased under the 1975 Act. Specifically, it upheld the fundamental principle of testamentary freedom; and it confirmed that such awards should be limited to maintenance rather than providing legacies.

Specifically, the UK Supreme court found:

• testamentary freedom should not be lightly disregarded;

• 'maintenance' should be limited to the ordinary cost of living;

• maintenance can be paid as a lump sum;

• if maintenance extends to the provision of real property, then a life interest is more appropriate than an outright gift;

• behaviour of the parties and estrangement are legitimate considerations;

• gifts to charities should be respected.

Executors and administrators, or personal representatives

The generic term for the person entrusted with the task of winding up a deceased person's estate is a 'personal representative'. They are the person who, as executor or administrator, steps into the shoes of the deceased and has full legal authority to deal with the estate.

Confirmation of this legal authority is given by a document called a 'grant of representation'. This is a formal document issued and sealed by the Probate Registry. Where there is a will, the document will usually be called a 'grant of probate'. Where there is an intestacy, the document will usually be called 'letters of administration'. Usually, no grant of representation is necessary where the estate is a 'small' estate, defined as below £5,000 in value.

Identifying the personal representative

It is normal practice for a will to contain an appointment of one or more persons to act as 'executors'. Typically, a person may appoint their spouse, civil partner, children, close family friends or relations, or perhaps a professional adviser or bank.

On a total intestacy, the Administration of Estates Act 1925 sets out rules for deciding who is entitled to be the personal representative; in this situation they are called the 'administrator'. The order of entitlement is as follows:

- surviving spouse or civil partner;

- children;

- grandchildren;

- parents;

- brothers and sisters;

- nephews and nieces;

- grandparents;

- uncles and aunts;

- cousins;

- the Crown or creditors.

On a partial intestacy – where a will does not deal with all of a person's property – the executors will technically act as 'administrators' in relation to the assets subject to the intestacy, and will deal with them in accordance with the intestacy rules described in table 17.1.

A will may sometimes have no valid or effective appointment of executors in it – for example, if the executors named have died before the testator or refuse to act. In that case, the beneficiaries of the residue of the estate, or of particular legacies, can apply to act as personal representatives and would be described as 'administrators with will'. In the absence of any such person, the Crown or creditors can act.

The role of the personal representative

The overriding duty of the personal representative is to wind up and administer the estate according to law and in accordance with the will or the intestacy provisions. Although technically not trustees, personal representatives share many of the duties of trustees. They are obliged to act as a 'prudent man of business'[3] and to take appropriate advice on what should be done. They must act in the best interests of the estate and the beneficiaries, and be prepared to account for all their actions and omissions and for what they have done with the assets in the estate. The Trustee Act 2000 contains a framework of further powers and obligations for trustees.

The administration of an estate generally falls into three phases.

1. The information-gathering stage

In the first phase the personal representative will identify all the assets and liabilities in the estate, organise any necessary date-of-death valuations and identify the beneficiaries of the estate.

As part of this first phase, it is necessary to complete information for HM Revenue & Customs (HMRC). The personal representative must consider whether they need to complete a full inheritance tax account (HMRC form IHT400).

A full inheritance tax account will not need to be completed in all cases. HMRC does not require a full account of the estate (and a basic IHT205 can be completed instead) if the deceased died domiciled in the UK (had their permanent home in the UK) and there is no tax to pay, either because it is under the inheritance tax threshold (which is a tax threshold made up of the available nil rate bands) or because the gross value of the estate is not more than £1 million and all or part of it is exempt from tax, passing either to a surviving spouse or to charity. As stated, in this instance, a short-form return of estate information (IHT205) can instead be completed, and this is submitted directly to the Probate Registry with the probate application.

Where a full inheritance tax account (IHT400) is required the account is sent to HMRC with payment of any inheritance tax due. The applicant also prepares a summary sheet for HMRC (HMRC form IHT421), which they will then receipt on payment of the tax and return to the applicant. The receipted IHT421 is then submitted to the probate registry with the application for probate.

2. Applications

Applications made in person

The personal representative completes forms obtained from the Probate Registry and submits them with the original will and codicils (if any), death certificate and application fee to the Probate Registry. The Probate Registry then invites the personal representative to attend an appointment at the Probate Registry for an interview and to swear an oath, or alternatively prepares an oath which the Probate Registry sends to the applicant and which is sworn before an independent solicitor. A grant is issued and posted to the personal representative.

Applications made through a solicitor

The personal representative swears or affirms an oath (also in this context called an 'affidavit') prepared by the solicitor in front of an independent solicitor or commissioner for oaths. The solicitor then sends the oath, the original will and codicil(s) (if any), and the IHT205 or receipted summary sheet (IHT421), together with an application fee to the Probate Registry. The draft Finance Act 2016 planned that from May 2017 probate fees would be calculated pro-rata (see table 17.2) and apply to all estates valued at £50,000 and over. For example, an estate of £300,000–£500,000 would pay £1,000 and estates of £2 million or more would pay as much as £20,000.

The government put this provision on hold for the 2017 general election but, as the Ministry of Justice believes the projected income would have been £300 million, it may well be reintroduced.

TABLE 17.2 PROBATE FEES

Value of estate (before inheritance tax)	Proposed Fee
Up to £50,000 or exempt from requiring a grant of probate	£0
£50,000 to £300,000	£300
£300,000 to £500,000	£1,000
£500,000 to £1 million	£4,000
£1 million to £1.6 million	£8,000
£1.6 million to £2 million	£12,000
Above £2 million	£20,000

The grant is then issued by the Probate Registry and sent to the solicitor.

3. Winding up the estate

Once the grant of representation has been issued, the personal representative will have the legal authority to deal with the deceased's assets. The personal representative will be able to close bank accounts and sell assets, including the deceased's house. The personal representative will pay from the deceased's estate all outstanding liabilities and expenses, settle any legacies and pay what is left of the estate to the residuary beneficiaries.

The personal representative may often prepare final estate accounts for the beneficiaries to show what has happened.

Legacies and gifts

Unlike in many continental countries, where there are often legal requirements that limit a testator's ability to dispose of their estate as they choose, the basic principle under English and Welsh law is that people are free to dispose of their property under their will to whomever they would like to benefit. However, it is fair to say that this principle has to some extent been diluted by the Inheritance (Provision for Family and Dependants) Act 1975 (discussed on page 217).

Gifts of assets via wills and codicils fall into two main types:

• **Legacies of particular assets (such as land, buildings or personal possessions) or cash sums:** Gifts of land and buildings are also called 'devises'. Gifts of particular personal possessions are often called 'specific legacies', and gifts of cash are called 'pecuniary legacies'.

• **Legacies of all or part of the residue of a person's estate (a 'residuary legacy' or a 'residuary devise'):** The beneficiary (called a 'residuary legatee' or a 'residuary devisee') may be given a particular share or percentage of the residue. It will be up to the personal representative to decide how legacies of the residue will be paid. They may sell all the assets in the estate and pay out the net cash proceeds. Alternatively, they may transfer particular assets in the estate (for example, stocks and shares) to satisfy a legacy. The technical term for this transfer of assets is an 'appropriation' of assets.

Conditional and reversionary gifts

Gifts in a will may be made 'conditional': that is, they will take effect only if a particular condition is satisfied. For example, a child may have to reach the age of 18 or 25 before being able to inherit.

Gifts may also be 'reversionary': in this case, the gift will take effect subject to a prior interest. For example, under their will a person may leave their assets to be held on trust to pay the income to their spouse for the rest of the spouse's life, with the assets being inherited by their children or a charity on the spouse's death. The gift to the children or charity is reversionary.

It is crucial that the conditions attaching to a gift, or the terms setting out when it will take effect, are carefully and effectively drafted.

Charitable legacies

A legacy to a charity must be clearly drafted. The particular charitable body or purpose should be clearly identified, and it should be checked, when the legacy is drafted, that the body or purpose is truly 'charitable' under English and Welsh law. Registration with the Charity Commission is not necessary in order for an organisation to be a charity, but registration is conclusive evidence that a body or purpose is charitable.

If the intention is that the charity should use the gift for a particular purpose or campaign, then this should be carefully and clearly expressed. If the gift is intended for the general benefit of the charity, rather than being restricted to a particular purpose or campaign it should be stated that the gift is for the 'general purposes' or 'general charitable purposes' of the charity.

Failure of legacies and gifts

Legacies may fail in a number of circumstances, including the following:

• The beneficiary died before the testator.

• The legacy was subject to a condition (for example, that the beneficiary reaches a particular age) that is not satisfied.

• The legacy may be essentially invalid, particularly in the context of a cross-border gift. See chapter 19.

• The asset subject to the legacy was no longer owned by the testator at their death.

• The beneficiary or their spouse or civil partner acted as a witness to the will.

• The beneficiary may disclaim (i.e. refuse) the gift.

• The will may have been wrongly witnessed or fail to meet the required formalities.

• The will may be successfully challenged as invalid.

• The courts may make an order overriding the legacy.

If a legacy of a particular asset fails, the result may be that the asset will form part of the deceased's residuary estate. If the gift that has failed is a gift of residue, the intestacy rules will apply if the will does not provide for what happens if a gift of residue fails. Wills should ideally be drafted to cover as many eventualities as is reasonable.

Failure of charitable legacies

A gift to a charity may fail in a number of circumstances, in addition to those set out above. For example:

• The charity identified in the will has ceased to exist or never existed.

• The objects of the charity or the charitable purpose specified in the will cannot be carried out.

• The charity cannot be identified from the will.

• The charity has merged with another charity or has converted to a different legal structure and charity number (for example, an incorporation).

Legacies to charities that have ceased to exist following a merger take effect as gifts to the merged charity if the merger has been registered with the Charity Commission under provisions introduced by the Charities Act 2006. However, if the legacy carries a precondition (for example, that the old charity exists at the time of the testator's death), this cannot happen and instead the legacy may fail. At the time of writing, the Law Commission is proposing changes to this position. For the time being, however, all charities that have completed any such restructuring exercises should therefore consider registering their merger if they have not done so. There is no time limit on registration and so such changes can be registered retrospectively, going back many years.

Even if there is a potential failure, an application may be made to a court to save the gift if certain conditions are satisfied. The Charity Commission also has power to determine such issues, including whether a particular failed legacy can be applied to other similar charitable purposes. The Charity Commission has a concurrent jurisdiction with the court in this respect. Finally, the Attorney General and the Solicitor General have the power to determine the recipient of a charitable gift where there is no trust involved and the gift is an unconditional gift, but no particular objects or trustees have been selected by a testator. This is under what is known as the Royal Sign Manual.

If the application is to a court, first the court will need to be satisfied that the testator had a 'general charitable intention': in other words, a clear purpose to benefit charity, even if their gift to a particular named charity fails. If this overriding intention can be identified, the court will seek to give effect to it. This is called the 'cy-pres' rule.

Second, the court will need to be satisfied that it can find another way of carrying out the testator's general charitable intention in a way which is as close as possible to that specified by the testator (for example, to pay it to another charity whose objects are very similar to those of the charity that has ceased to exist). On the other hand, if a legacy is expressly for a special purpose that the charity has already carried out, or for a special appeal that has ended, then it may be difficult for a court to find general charitable intention and make a cy-pres order, and the gift may fail.

It is entirely up to the court to consider whether a cy-pres application may be made. The court will look at all the circumstances – including the actual terms of the will – to see whether the testator had a general charitable intention. A legacy expressed for the 'general charitable purposes' of a charity may assist a court in finding general charitable intention.

In view of the cy-pres rule and its limitations, it is critical to ensure that legacies to charities are correctly drafted. The expense, complexity and uncertainty of an application to the court invoking the cy-pres rule must be considered. It may be preferable to avoid a legacy limited to a specific purpose or appeal, unless the will says that the legacy will pass for the general charitable purposes of the charity if the purpose or appeal cannot be carried out at the date of death. From the point of view of the charity, it is ideal if a legacy is expressed to be for the general purposes of the charity with a non-binding wish as to the specific way in which the charity should use it. An application to the Charity Commission to determine a cy-pres question has the advantage of being cheaper, and should also take significantly less time, than an application to a court.

Taxation of estates

The following summary should be treated with caution. Tax rules generally change each year in the Budget. It is essential that the tax treatment of any specific situation is checked carefully at the time.

Pre-death tax

The personal representative will be responsible for ensuring that the pre-death tax affairs of the deceased are finalised. They should ensure that tax returns up to the date of death are filed with HMRC, where required, and that all income and capital gains tax is paid, and all necessary claims for repayment are made.

Income tax after death

The personal representative will be responsible for paying income tax during the period of administration of the estate. They will have to account for any income arising to the residuary beneficiaries, who will generally be taxable on the income in their own right.

Capital gains tax after death

For capital gains tax purposes, all assets in a person's estate will be revalued as at the date of their death. All pre-death gains will be wiped out, and the executors and the beneficiaries inheriting the assets will use the value of those assets at the date of death as the value for calculating any future gains.

Any capital gains arising in the estate during the course of administration – for example, on the sale of shares or a house – will be payable by the personal representative at a tax rate of 28% for residential property and 20% for non-residential property. The personal representative will be entitled to a tax-free allowance (£11,700 as at 6 April 2018) for the tax year in which death occurred and two subsequent tax years. After this no allowance is available.

If all or part of an estate passes to charity, the personal representative can take advantage of the charity's exemption from capital gains tax by appropriating a particular asset or share of an asset to a charity before it is sold. The personal representative then holds an asset as a 'bare trustee' for the charity when selling it, i.e. the personal representative holds the legal title, so the asset is registered in their name, but the equitable title – the value – belongs to the charity, which gives instructions as to how the assets should be managed. The personal representative can then claim the charity's exemption.

Inheritance tax

For inheritance tax purposes, a person is treated as making a taxable transfer of all their assets at the date of their death. The value of certain gifts made by the deceased during the seven years before death – for example, gifts to other individuals – will also be taken into account on their death and made subject to inheritance tax.

The current rules provide for two rates of tax. The rate of tax applying to the value of a person's assets up to £325,000 (from 6 April 2009) is 0%. This is known as the 'nil rate band'. The rate applying to assets over that figure is 40%.

There are various exemptions that may place assets outside the scope of inheritance tax altogether. Gifts between spouses and civil partners are exempt, so, if a person leaves all their assets to their spouse on their death, all those assets will be exempt from inheritance tax. Similarly, any gifts to a UK charity are exempt from inheritance tax. This is also the case for gifts to EU charities that would qualify as UK charities – at least until Brexit (see chapter 19 for more details).

Since October 2007, spouses and civil partners have had the benefit of the 'transferable nil rate band'. This means that any unused portion of the nil rate band on the death of the first spouse or partner can now be claimed and transferred to the estate of the survivor, meaning that up to two full nil rate bands are available to offset against the value of the estate. Crucially, it is the value of the nil rate band in force at the time of the survivor's death that is transferable to the survivor's estate. Further, since 6 April 2002, the estate may qualify to pay inheritance tax at the reduced rate of 36% if the testator leaves at least 10% of the net estate to charity.

Lastly, since 6 April 2017, there has been an additional 'residence nil rate band' for an estate if the testator leaves a home to their children or other direct descendants. The additional rate begins at £100,000 and will increase each tax year by £25,000, reaching £175,000 in the tax year 2020–2021. Any unused residence nil rate band can also be transferred to a surviving spouse or partner. Unsurprisingly, there are conditions which need to be met and these will need thorough investigation.

Inheritance tax and gifts to charity

Where a charity benefits from a person's estate, the charity should be entitled to reclaim from HMRC income tax on any income arising during the course of the administration of the estate that is treated as belonging to the charity. In order to do this, a charity should be provided with an HMRC form confirming net income due to the charity from the estate (form R185).

For inheritance tax purposes, as explained above, all gifts to charities are exempt. A difficulty can arise, however, where part of a person's estate passes to charity and is exempt from inheritance tax, but part of it is not. The general rule under the Inheritance Tax Act 1984 is that any inheritance tax must be borne by the non-exempt gift.

For example, a person leaves £500,000 to be divided equally between a charity and her daughter. Assuming that the nil rate band has been used up by lifetime gifts, so that the £500,000 is subject to a 40% rate of inheritance tax, then the position is that the total inheritance tax bill is £100,000. This is because the gift to the charity is exempt, so the total inheritance tax payable is 40% of the half (£250,000) passing to the daughter. The application of the rules in the 1984 Act described above requires the £100,000 to be deducted from the daughter's share. Thus the daughter will receive £150,000 and the charity £250,000.

The testator may be astonished at this result. The intention may have been, in the example above, that the £100,000 should be taken out of the estate, leaving the remainder (£400,000) to be divided equally between the daughter and the charity. The testator may be equally astonished to find that the 1984 Act expressly prevents the terms of a will overriding this rule. This question was subject to a case in 1995 – known as *Re Benham* – where the charity involved was the RNLI.[4] The court decided that, if a testator intends to achieve equality between their residuary beneficiaries –

for example, if the testator described above intended that her daughter and the charity should benefit equally – then, if the will is properly drafted, the court must ignore the rules of the 1984 Act and give effect to those intentions.

The way that this would be done in the example described above would be to 'gross up' the gift to the daughter to allow for the tax that the 1984 Act says the gift must bear. In the figures mentioned above, the daughter would notionally be allocated £312,500 of the residue. Deducting 40% from that figure would leave £187,500, which would be the amount received both by the charity and by the daughter, with £125,000 paid in tax. As a result, HMRC and the daughter would benefit, and the charity's entitlement would be reduced.

The more recent case of *Re Ratcliffe* in 1999[5] did not follow the judgment in *Re Benham* but applied the rules set out in the 1984 Act. The judge suggested that *Re Benham* had not laid down any principles and, therefore, he was not bound to follow it.

The case *of Re Benham* is, however, still of concern to charities. While the decision was not followed in *Re Ratcliffe*, and has been seriously questioned by legal commentators, it has not been overruled. Pending further legislation, it is essential that wills containing gifts to charities and other non-exempt beneficiaries are drafted with extreme care, and that testators are advised carefully in relation to how exactly they would like the residue divided up.

Charities should carefully examine estate accounts to check that inheritance tax has been allocated correctly between them and non-exempt beneficiaries.

Notes

1   Note that if the circumstances in one row of the table are fulfilled, the calculation stops and no further people (in the rows below) are eligible. For example, if grandparents survive but brothers and sisters also survive, the calculation stops at line 3 (the grandparents would not receive any part of the estate).

2   Civil partners are only entitled in the case of a death on or after 5 December 2005.

3   Acting as a 'prudent man of business' (first articulated in *Speight* v. *Gaunt* [1883] UKHL 1) is a commonly used statement in case law regarding the duty of care of trustees. It means that a trustee must use the same care and skill when administering a trust as they would in their own business dealings.

4   *Lockhart* v. *Harker (Re Benham's Will Trusts)* [1995] STC 210.

5   *Holmes* v. *McMullan (Re Ratcliffe)* [1999] STC 262.

CHAPTER EIGHTEEN

Potential legal pitfalls

Paul Sutton and Sarah Bolt

Introduction

It is essential for you as a fundraiser, especially when working on a one-to-one basis with supporters, to be aware of certain legal pitfalls which may, at worst, cause legacies to charities to fail for want of care and attention. This chapter identifies some of these pitfalls – those encountered both during the lifetime of the supporter and upon their death. The chapter should also be useful as an outline for financial staff tasked with receiving legacies on behalf of charities.

Lifetime legacy giving

Charities need to encourage their supporters to make gifts to them following their deaths through their wills, an activity which probably represents the single most significant opportunity any individual has to make a charitable gift. When approached by individuals who wish to make a significant lifetime gift, you should encourage these supporters to think very carefully before making particularly substantial gifts to a charity during their lifetimes. They may need the money in old age to live off. You should remind supporters that your charity will be unable to return the money at a later date if requested to do so. Equally, you need to be very mindful of the reputational risks in this area and the need to avoid putting undue pressure on your supporters.

You will therefore need, as part of your basic fundraising materials, to be able to guide supporters as to how to make gifts in their wills, explaining the various types of gift and helping supporters to understand how much of a difference legacy income makes to your charity.

Canvassing and undue influence on donors

Anyone can leave money to a charity in a will. A number of charities offer schemes to pay the cost of preparing a will. The Charity Commission stresses that:

> no-one connected with your charity should help to prepare a will that contains a donation for your charity. This includes acting as a witness to the will. This helps to reduce any risk of a legal challenge.[1]

There can be circumstances in which the benefits outweigh the potential disadvantages of a charity's staff becoming involved directly with drafting wills (and there has been one case in which the Charity Commission exonerated a charity whose staff prepared wills for supporters). However, in general, charities are recommended to avoid such arrangements and, instead, to encourage their supporters to engage their own solicitor or professional will writer to provide them with this service.

Free will campaigns

There are many examples of free will-writing campaigns that have been very successful in enabling large numbers of wills to be written, with some evidence of resulting legacies being made to charities. One of the best-known examples is Will Aid, which describes itself as 'a special partnership between the legal profession and nine UK charities'. Each November, participating solicitors waive their fee to draw up a basic will and instead ask their clients to consider making a donation to the Will Aid charities. Since being founded in 1988, Will Aid has enabled legal firms to raise over £19 million for nine of the UK's favourite charities.[2] At the same time, the campaign has encouraged and helped thousands of people to write their will.

There remains a degree of scepticism over the extent to which involvement in such campaigns is genuinely an effective way of generating legacies, and you should weigh up very carefully the pros and cons of being involved.

Conflicts of interest

Charities or their employees acting as executors of supporters' wills

It will often be the case that charities, if they develop close links with their supporters, will be asked whether either they or their employees could act as executors of their supporters' wills. There is no hard-and-fast rule here, although we would counsel great caution before accepting. Inevitably, such an appointment can lead to potential conflicts of interest because the nature of an executor's appointment involves an overriding duty towards the estate of the deceased supporter, the deceased's creditors and any other beneficiaries under the will, which may not necessarily coincide with the charity's wishes.

There may be a few cases where a charity is aware that a supporter has no family or close friends whom they would trust to act as executors, and where the charity has sufficient knowledge of the supporter's circumstances to feel confident that taking on such an appointment should not be problematic. In such a situation, it might cause offence and not be in the charity's interests to decline such an appointment. If your charity finds itself in this position, we would strongly recommend that you ensure that your supporter sees an independent solicitor (*not* the charity's solicitor), so that preparation and completion of the will can be dealt with in a transparently independent way.

The legal options when charities act as executors

If your charity is appointed as an executor, it will need to consider the precise nature of its involvement. The first possibility is for your charity itself to act in its corporate capacity as executor. This can only be done where your charity is structured as some form of company, in which case it is possible (provided that its constitution allows it to act as a trustee) for it to obtain what is known as 'trust corporation status'. Many large charities that have significant legacy income have obtained trust corporation status, which can be achieved by obtaining a certificate either from the Lord Chancellor (through the Ministry of Justice) to obtain general authority to act or, for specific cases only, from the Charity Commission. One of the main benefits of trust corporation status is that it enables a charity to accept executor appointments and administer estates either alone or jointly with any persons appointed in the will.

The second possibility is for a named individual or individuals (usually senior employees of your charity) to act as executors or administrators on behalf of your charity. This can most easily be achieved by trustees completing a resolution to authorise the holders of specific *positions* within the charity to perform such appointments on behalf of the charity; this avoids difficulty where a named individual takes up such an appointment but then moves on to another job.

In either case, you should obtain legal advice to ensure that the probate formalities are properly dealt with.

Legacies to fundraisers

While executor appointments can create difficulties, still greater care needs to be exercised if a supporter wishes to leave a legacy to someone working within your charity. Again, the cardinal rule, if an employee becomes aware of such a proposal in a supporter's lifetime, is to ensure that the supporter receives the benefit of independent legal advice on any such proposed gift. If your charity receives high levels of legacies and works closely with your supporter base to encourage such legacies, we consider that it would be sensible to develop written policies and codes of conduct to help your staff deal with such situations. Such policies could indicate, for example, that employees will be required to indicate to any such supporter that they are not allowed to accept any gifts whatsoever from supporters (or anything other than purely token gifts). However, this is a very difficult area, and it is probable that such gifts will generally come to light only after a supporter's death – again, a written policy could indicate how any such gifts would be dealt with. These may be situations where trustees, or even the Charity Commission, may need to become involved to establish whether such gifts may be retained by the individuals, altered into gifts to the charity or simply disclaimed.

Remember that the reputation of your charity is of paramount importance in all these areas of potential conflicts of interest, and that the perception of a conflict can be just as damaging as the reality. If in doubt, take legal advice.

Legacy administration: Executors and administrators

The executors appointed under a will may not be able to (or may choose not to) act for a number of reasons, some of which are given below:

• We have already noted that charity employees acting as executors in wills may create a conflict of interest between the estate and the charity. They can choose to renounce probate (step down from the role) provided that they have not begun to administer the estate.

• They may renounce probate for other reasons, perhaps because they are out of the country or simply do not want to.

• The person appointed may not be old enough. Executors may be appointed when they are under 18 but must have reached 18 by the time they act.

• They may be mentally or physically incapable of acting.

• They may have died before the testator (i.e. the person making the will).

• The courts may decide that a person should not be appointed executor or may allow the executor to retire from the office of executor.

A will does not fail for want of an executor. Instead the court appoints an administrator to administer the estate. The court will grant what are known as 'letters of administration with will annexed', as opposed to a 'grant of probate' (which is the name of the grant issued by the court to the executors). When courts are determining who may be granted letters of administration with will annexed, the order of priority includes 'any residuary legatee or devisee of a will'.[3] ('devisee' is the technical term for someone who is left a gift of real property under a will).

Charities can be named as executors in wills, and they are entitled to apply for a grant if there is no executor able to act and the charity is named as a residuary beneficiary or legatee of the estate. Figure 18.1 describes how a grant can be obtained on behalf of a charity in these circumstances.

FIGURE 18.1 HOW TO OBTAIN A GRANT ON BEHALF OF A CHARITY

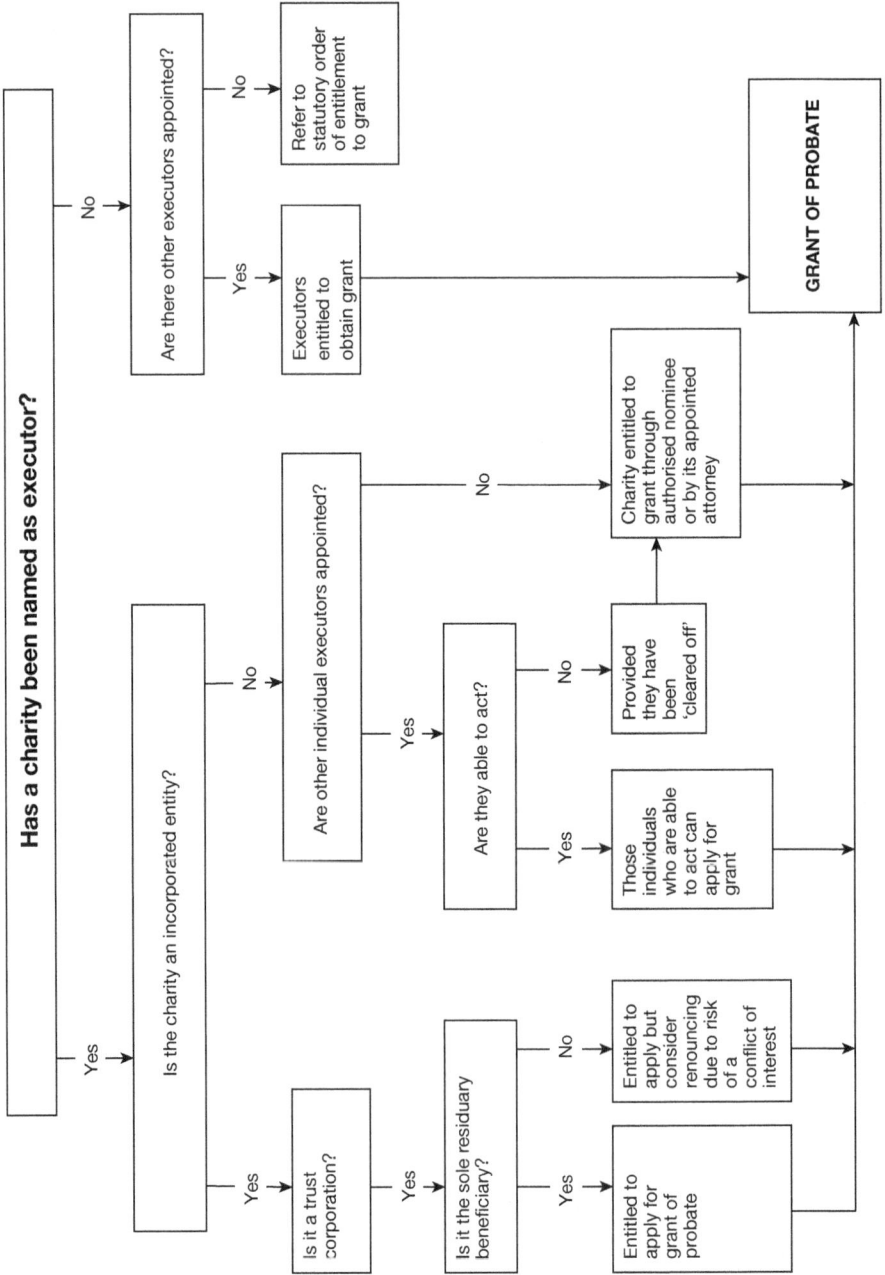

Some common pitfalls and problems with charitable legacies

The following are common problems that charities may encounter as part of the administration of estates under which they have been left legacies.

The will wrongly refers to a charity

If the charity has changed its name since the testator made their will, it should provide the personal representatives (the people entrusted with the task of winding up a deceased person's estate) with details of the change of name. If the charity has changed its legal status since the will was written, it should also provide the personal representatives with the appropriate documentation. It is good practice to advise supporters to include the charity's registered charity number when the will is drafted in order to avoid any problems in identifying the charity. If charities merge and the merger has been registered with the Charity Commission in accordance with the Charities Act 2011, the gift will automatically fall to the successor charity.

The legacy is made to a local branch or committee of the charity

A number of charities have local branches or committees. It is important to clarify whether the local branch or committee of a charity is recognised as a separate entity which is capable of receiving legacies (some local branches and committees cannot receive legacies under the terms of their constitution) and whether the testator intended for their gift to be left to the charity generally or to the specific branch or committee.

The legacy is for a specific project

Where a gift is left to a charity, it is generally applied to where it is needed within the charity. The majority of legacies are left without specific instructions as to how they should be used. It may be that a testator wishes to give a legacy for a specific piece of research or a campaign, such as building a school and/or funding a lifeboat. If a testator wishes to benefit a particular project or purpose, it would be beneficial to consider whether to express this as a wish so that the gift can be applied to an alternative project in the event that the gift cannot be used for the desired purpose or project, or the purpose or project comes to an end.

The will leaves a legacy for a charitable purpose but does not name a particular organisation

We have already seen in chapter 17 ('Failure of legacies and gifts', page 224) the circumstances when personal representatives can make applications to the Charity Commission and the court when charitable legacies fail. When no particular charity is identified in a will but a charitable purpose is identified (for example, a legacy to 'cancer research' when no charity with that name actually exists), the personal representatives can apply to use the 'Royal Sign Manual' procedure. Under this procedure, the personal representatives apply to the Attorney General for a direction. They do this by writing to the Treasury Solicitor with a copy of the will and any evidence as to which charity the testator might have intended to benefit. If your charity is the subject of such an application, it is particularly important to check your donor database to see whether the testator was one of your supporters. This might just indicate that they intended to benefit your charity and not others with similar objects. The Attorney General will look at the evidence and issue a signed direction as to which charity should benefit, taking into account the testator's perceived intentions.

A legacy given to a charity is subject to conditions that conflict with the charity's objects

Where a charity's objects mean the condition on a legacy cannot be complied with, it is first worth checking whether the legacy is in fact subject to a binding condition or whether what the testator specified is simply a non-binding expression of wishes. If it is a binding condition, the charity may have to consider disclaiming its legacy if its acceptance would mean that it would have to act contrary to its objects.

A similar point arises if the charity considers that being associated with the source of the gift may be damaging. In such a situation, it may be prudent to take legal advice and/or consult the Charity Commission before deciding whether it is appropriate for your charity to disclaim the gift.

There is an unreasonable or unexplained delay with the payment of legacies

The personal representatives should endeavour to keep all beneficiaries up to date with the administration of the estate as matters progress. You are entitled to ask for updates if there are any unexplained periods of delay. There are no general time limits as to when legacies, of whatever nature, should be paid. However, pecuniary (i.e. cash) legacies should be paid out within one year of the testator's death (known as the 'executor's year'). After this date, late-payment interest is applied at a rate equivalent to the basic rate for funds held in court (set at 0.1% a year at the time of writing).[4]

An item specifically gifted under a will was disposed of by the testator during their lifetime

A specific legacy will 'adeem' (i.e. fail to take effect) if it is not in the testator's ownership at the time of their death. In these circumstances, the beneficiary receives nothing, will not be compensated and is not entitled to the proceeds, if any, that resulted from the sale of the property.

The assets of the estate are insufficient to pay the debts and liabilities due on the testator's death

Legacies will 'abate' (i.e. reduce) in accordance with the statutory order contained in section 34(3) of the Administration of Estates Act 1925 unless the wording of the will specifies otherwise. The following list (contained in Part II) of the first schedule of the Administration of Estates Act 1925, provides a hierarchical order for the abatement (reduction) of assets where an estate is insolvent. The statutory order is as follows:

1. Property of the deceased undisposed of by will, subject to retention of a fund sufficient to meet the pecuniary legacies.

2. Property of the deceased not specifically devised or bequeathed but included in a residuary gift, subject to retention of a fund sufficient to meet the pecuniary legacies.

3. Property of the deceased specifically appropriated or devised or bequeathed for the payment of debts.

4. Property of the deceased charged with, or devised for or bequeathed, subject to a charge for the payment of debts.

5. The fund, if any, retained to meet pecuniary legacies.

6. Property specifically devised or bequeathed, rateably according to value.

7. Property appointed by will under a general power, including the statutory power to dispose of entailed interests, rateably according to value.

A charity is not notified that it has been left a legacy in a will

It is generally the personal representatives' responsibility, at an early stage of the administration process, to advise a charity of its entitlement under the will. Your charity can sign up to a notification service provided by Smee & Ford (www.smeeandford.com). This will notify you of your charity's entitlement if you are named in wills that are proved at the Probate Registry. However, not all wills need to be proved at the Probate Registry,

and there is an obvious risk that some less-than-honest personal representatives acting fraudulently who do not need to apply for a grant may
decide not to pass legacies to charitable beneficiaries.

If you discover that you have been left a legacy, in the first instance
you should write to the personal representatives and request that your
legacy is paid in accordance with the terms of the will. You may also feel
it appropriate to ask why your legacy has not been paid sooner. If the
personal representatives have distributed the estate and are unable to pay
the legacy, they have breached their duty to administer the estate in accordance with the terms of the will, and they are personally liable to pay the
legacy from their own resources.

A charity has been left a legacy in a will but a subsequent will has been discovered in which the charity does not benefit

There is very little that can be done in these circumstances since the later
will, if drafted and executed correctly, should have revoked the previous
will. This is always a hazard of estate administration and it is particularly
important to make sure the personal representatives are administering the
correct will; full enquiries should be made as to the potential whereabouts
of other wills. A central wills register might help in reducing this
uncertainty.

A charity is left a foreign asset in a will

Foreign assets may be left to UK charities either in foreign or UK wills.
Whether a UK will disposes of a particular foreign asset depends on the
scope of the will (whether it is expressly restricted in scope to just, for
example, England and Wales) and whether the English will is both
'formally' and 'essentially' valid in the foreign jurisdiction. These rules are
explained in more detail in chapter 19, but their effect can mean that gifts
fail. For example, if your charity has been named in a UK will to inherit a
deceased supporter's assets in Saudi Arabia, the Saudi authorities may not
accept a UK will as valid, if it does not comply with Saudi Sharia principles. Instead, the entitlement to the assets may be determined by Saudi
Sharia law. For more information, see chapter 19.

Assets of the estate have been sold without the residuary beneficiaries being consulted

The personal representatives have a duty in general to consult with the
residuary beneficiaries as to whether they would like a particular asset that
comprises the estate appropriated to them, in satisfaction or part-satisfac-
tion of their entitlement, or whether they would like the asset to be sold.

Assets or parts of assets can be appropriated to charitable beneficiaries before they are disposed of by the personal representatives, to mitigate capital gains tax in the event that the asset sells for more than its value at the time of death. The personal representatives are under a duty not to waste the assets of an estate, and a charity that is a residuary beneficiary could consider bringing a claim against the personal representatives if it can be shown, for instance, that such a sale was not in the best interests of the charity or that capital gains tax was incurred unnecessarily and that unnecessary loss was suffered.

If, however, the asset needs to be sold in order to meet the liabilities of the estate, then the beneficiaries are not generally given the option to have it appropriated. Such assets may then need to be sold in the course of the administration (and capital gains tax may be unavoidably incurred).

Assets have been sold without advice being sought before the sale is agreed

As a general rule, charities are required to seek the permission of the Charity Commission before selling land unless they can comply with the requirements set out in section 117 of the Charities Act 2011. Personal representatives who are disposing of land on behalf of charitable beneficiaries may be required to follow the requirements contained in the Charities Act 2011.[5] However, whether or not the requirements of the Charities Act strictly apply, we consider it to be good practice for personal representatives to instruct an independent qualified surveyor to prepare a report on the disposal of the land on behalf of charitable beneficiaries and make recommendations as to its valuation and the appropriate method of disposal. Doing this should avoid any possible need to obtain consent for the sale of the land from the Charity Commission.

The personal representatives should also generally seek professional advice before selling stocks and shares or other assets, such as valuable antiques and other collectables. Advice on the sale of stocks or shares, for example, should come from a stockbroker, who will be able to indicate whether it is better to sell a particular holding or retain it in the hope that its value increases. It is also prudent to seek advice from a suitably qualified specialist when disposing of antiques, collections and other high-value personal possessions.

Interpreting estate accounts

When the administration of the estate nears an end, residuary beneficiaries should be provided with a set of estate accounts that detail the assets received, the income receipts and the liabilities settled, so that they can see how the estate has been distributed. If your charity is a residuary beneficiary, it is important for you to check through these accounts to ensure that the estate has been administered correctly and to give your agreement to them before accepting your final entitlement from the estate. The following are pointers which your charity can use when receiving estate accounts:

• Did assets sell for more or less than their date-of-death value and are there any apparent reasons for this?

• Do the liabilities and administration expenses appear reasonable?

• Are the professional costs in line with estimates given, or do you require further information?

• Have all cash legacies been paid and taxes settled in full?

• Could capital gains tax have been avoided or reduced by assets being appropriated to charities that are exempt from capital gains tax?

• Has your entitlement been calculated correctly in accordance with the terms of the will?

• Has inheritance tax been calculated correctly and deducted from the right beneficiaries where the residue is shared between exempt and non-exempt beneficiaries?

• Are any expenses claimed by the personal representatives reasonable? Strictly, non-professional personal representatives are not entitled to profit from the estate and can only claim reasonable out-of-pocket expenses. Anything more must have been agreed with the residuary beneficiaries.

• Has money been held on deposit earning interest before being distributed?

• Have you received tax deduction certificate(s) to enable you to reclaim the income tax paid by the personal representatives?

Claims against estates: When can a will be challenged?

Chapter 17 considered the key elements of a valid will (see 'Wills and codicils', page 212). Non-compliance with the formalities of execution required under the Wills Act 1837 and/or the Wills Act 1963 will render a will formally invalid (see chapter 19 for details on what constitutes formal validity). Even if the will is properly executed, its formal validity may be challenged in the courts if the circumstances surrounding its making warrant such a challenge. There are five main legal grounds (explored further below) upon which the courts can pronounce against a will's validity:

• lack of testamentary capacity;

• undue influence;

- fraud;

- want of knowledge and approval; or

- mistake.

Testamentary capacity

A testator must have the necessary mental capacity to make a will. The legal test of capacity was laid down in the well-known case of *Banks* v. *Goodfellow* (1870) LR 5 QB 549. The case concerned a testator who suffered from the delusion that a long-dead grocer, together with evil spirits, were pursuing him. However, the delusion did not prevent him from managing his own affairs and the court held that it did not prevent him from making a valid will in favour of his niece (although in a number of cases the courts have held wills to be valid even though the letter of the Wills Act 1837 has not been adhered to).

The case laid down the principle that a testator must understand:

- the nature of the act – i.e. that they are completing a document that will govern the disposition of their estate on their death;

- the effect of the will – they must understand its terms, although not necessarily its precise legal effect;

- the extent of the property which they are disposing of, although they need not know its precise value;

- the nature of the moral claims on their estate – i.e. which other people deserve to be supported by them.

There is a presumption of capacity unless it is established that the testator lacked capacity. However, if credible evidence is presented to rebut the presumption, then the onus is on the propounder (i.e. the person attempting to establish the will's validity) to prove that testamentary capacity in fact existed. The presumption of capacity is now enshrined in the Mental Capacity Act 2005, but the Act has not changed the test for capacity.

The courts also encourage solicitors preparing wills to follow the 'golden rule', where they are making a will for an old or infirm testator, that the firm ought to get the will witnessed and approved by a medical practitioner. While it is not a legal requirement (a will cannot be deemed invalid simply because the golden rule was not followed), it is a prudent step to take to try and avoid a legal challenge.

The *Banks* v. *Goodfellow* test was applied by Mr Justice Henderson in *Kostic* v. *Chaplin and others* [2007] EWHC 2298, the facts of which were strikingly similar to *Banks* v. *Goodfellow*. However, in the *Kostic* case, the judge found that the delusion from which the testator suffered had impaired his ability to assess the moral claims on his estate. The judge therefore pronounced against the validity of a will in which Mr Kostic had left his entire £8.2 million estate to the Conservative Party with no provision for his former wife or his son, both of whom he was convinced were involved in an international conspiracy against him. However, at the time of writing, the Law Commission has produced a consultation document which, amongst other things, suggests that the test for capacity should be brought into line with the Mental Capacity Act 2005. The consultation is considering proposals to change the test for capacity to make a will to take into account the modern understanding of conditions like dementia and to provide statutory guidance for doctors and other professionals conducting an assessment of whether a person has the required mental capacity to make a will.

Undue influence

Undue influence means, in a word, *coercion* by a third party over the testator such as to deprive them of their own free will. There is no presumption of undue influence in relation to wills. It carries with it a heavy burden of proof for the person attacking the will: the person would need to provide evidence that the testator had been forced to change their will. If someone were to *persuade* the testator to change their will, yet at the same time the testator makes the decision to do so freely, this would not be considered to be coercion.[6]

A successful and good example of undue influence was provided by the case of *Killick* v. *Pountney and another* (2000) WTLR 41. The testator was 86 when he made his will and unmarried but very close to his brother's family. He lodged with a landlord and became very attached to his home. At age 85 he went into hospital and instructed his solicitor to prepare a new will under which his estate went to the landlord's son. After his death, it was discovered that the landlord had extracted large sums from the testator and had threatened not to allow him back into his lodgings if he saw his family.

Fraud

Undue influence needs to be distinguished from the complete fabrication of a will. A good example of fraud is set out in the case of *Henderson* v. *Davies* [2017]. The testator died in 2013 at the age of 76. He left a pecuniary legacy of £25,000 to his young wife, with the remainder of his £600,000 estate passing to his only daughter and a close friend. The testator's wife claimed she had found a more recent will hidden inside a discarded bag of Dorito crisps in the attic of their home in which she would inherit £550,000 of his estate. The challenge was dismissed by the

Court on fraud, with the most obvious error to be that the forged document referred to it being 'her' last will rather than 'his' and the story concocted by the wife was 'ridiculous'.

Want of knowledge and approval

The testator must know and approve (effectively understand) the contents of any will executed (i.e. they must appreciate and endorse its provisions). It used to be thought that, if the will had been read out or explained to a testator with mental capacity and then duly executed by them, this was conclusive evidence of knowledge and approval, but this is now considered only to raise a presumption of knowledge and approval.

Where a will is made in circumstances which 'excite the suspicion of the court'[7] (for example, where a person who arranged for a testator to make a will is a beneficiary under it), burden of proof rests with the person seeking to prove that the testator 'knew and approved' of its content. Mental capacity and want of knowledge and approval are separate and different requirements.

Mistake

'Mistake' arises where the testator did not know and approve of particular words or clauses in a will. If the court is satisfied that a will is so expressed that it fails to carry out the testator's intentions, because of a clerical error or of a failure to understand their instructions, it may order that the mistake in the will be rectified so as to carry out the testator's intentions.

Effect of a successful legal challenge

When a will has been successfully challenged in the courts, it is set aside. The court will normally grant probate of any validly made earlier will. If there is no such will, then the rules of intestacy take effect (see 'Intestacy', page 214).

Proprietary estoppel

Proprietary estoppel is a key (and increasingly common) way that challenges are made against wills. 'Estoppel' means 'stop', or to stop a person doing an 'unconscionable act'. Estoppel claims are sometimes brought against an estate when the deceased raised an expectation in the claimant that they would acquire an interest in the deceased's buildings and land (hereafter just 'land') after their death. An example of this can be seen in the following scenario:

> Where the owner of land (A) in some way leads or allows the claimant (B) to
> believe that they have or can expect some kind of right or interest over A's

land, and B relies upon that assurance to their detriment, but A then refuses B the anticipated right or interest in circumstances that make that refusal unconscionable, an 'equity' arises in B's favour. This gives B the right to go to the courts to seek relief.

So there are three essential elements to estoppel:

- a clear *representation* that B can expect to acquire an interest;
- *detrimental reliance* upon that representation by B;
- a refusal by A to adhere to their promise which is *unconscionable*.

In such cases, the courts may give effect to the promise made to the claimant by the deceased, for example by ordering a transfer of the land promised to the claimant or by awarding them the proceeds of sale, but the courts have wide discretion as to what relief they can grant.

Notes

1   'Raising Funds through Wills and Charitable Legacies' [web page], Charity Commission, www.gov.uk/guidance/wills-and-charitable-legacies, 2013, accessed 15 January 2018.
2   'Introducing Will Aid' [web page], Will Aid, 2017, www.willaid.org.uk/about, accessed 12 December 2017.
3   Rule 20 of the Non-Contentious Probate Rules 1987.
4   'Court Funds Office: Change to interest rate for basic accounts' [press release], Ministry of Justice, www.gov.uk/government/news/court-funds-office-change-to-interest-rate-for-basic-accounts, 26 May 2016.
5   For a detailed analysis of when the Charities Act provisions apply to legacy cases, see *ILM Factsheet: Approved factsheet on section 117 Charities Act 2011 – August 2012* [PDF], Henmans LLP, 2012, http://legacymanagement.org.uk/wp-content/uploads/Section-117-Charities-Act-2011.pdf, accessed 12 December 2017.
6   *Hubbard* v. *Scott* [2011] EWHC 2750 (Ch).
7   *Brennan* v. *Prior* [2015] [2015] All ER (D) 119 (Nov).

CHAPTER NINETEEN

International legal considerations

Daniel Harris

Introduction

Gifts to charities of foreign assets present particular challenges, both from a planning perspective and in terms of what happens after your supporter has died. To ensure a gift to charity is successful, the drafting solicitor, or the legacy professional dealing with a cross-border administration, must consider whether their supporter's will is 'formally' and 'essentially' valid. What constitutes the difference between formal and essential validity will be outlined in the following sections.

Formal validity

A supporter's will is formally valid in the case that a particular jurisdiction's legal formalities have been observed correctly. Formal validity concerns the 'form' of the will, which for English and Welsh *domestic* wills is governed by section 9 of the Wills Act 1837, the main constituents of which are paraphrased in chapter 17 under the heading 'The key elements of wills and codicils' (see page 213).

The formal validity of *overseas* wills in England and Wales is governed by section 1 of the Wills Act 1963, which validates foreign wills if they comply with:

> the internal law in force in the territory where it was executed, or in the territory where, at the time of its execution or of the testator's death, he was domiciled or had his habitual residence, or in a state of which, at either of those times, he was a national.

Section 2 further validates foreign wills from jurisdictions in which the deceased owned immovable property (i.e. buildings and land) – but only the parts of the will respecting the foreign property.

Unsurprisingly, formal validity requirements differ across the globe. In some jurisdictions, wills are formally valid merely if they are in the handwriting of the testator (i.e. the person making the will); sometimes no date or signature are required. In other jurisdictions, for a will to be formally valid, it must be an 'authentic' will, drafted and executed by a notary or other authorised legal professional – sometimes with compulsory registration.

In England and Wales, however, it follows that a basic, handwritten, undated and unsigned foreign will gifting assets to a charity can potentially be formally valid.

Recognition of English and Welsh wills overseas

It is not just England and Wales that has provisions to recognise foreign wills. Indeed, the Wills Act 1963 mimics the 1961 Hague Convention on Testamentary Dispositions, which provides rules for the formal validity of wills in a cross-border context and has been adopted by 33 (mainly European) countries.

Moreover, those EU countries who are signatories of the Hague Convention are bound by similar provisions, courtesy of section 27 of EU Succession Regulation 650/2012, and there are other unilateral and bilateral provisions for the recognition of the formal validity of wills between jurisdictions, as well as mechanisms such as the 1973 Convention Providing a Uniform Law on the Form of an International Will (also known as the Washington Convention) for the creation of a formal standard for 'international wills'. Charities must consider all of these when evaluating the formal validity of a supporter's will.

Essential validity

Essential validity concerns whether or not the terms of a will are valid. In other words, whether the testator's wishes can (under the laws of the jurisdiction in question) be carried out. For example, if a supporter attempts to give assets to a charity that they do not have the power to gift, then that part of the will (or in some jurisdictions the whole will) is said to be 'essentially invalid'. In a cross-border context, this could relate to assets governed by any of the following:

• **Forced heirship:** This is a system of rules that prevents an individual who has issue (i.e. direct-bloodline descendants, including children, grandchildren and great-grandchildren) leaving all of their estate to whomever they wish. In France, for example, a sole child is entitled to half of the deceased's estate, two children are entitled to two-thirds and three children or more are entitled to three-quarters. These gifts are all *per stirpes*, meaning if one of the children has died, their share goes to the deceased child's children equally, and if any of those children has died, that share in turn passes to their children equally, and so on. Importantly, forced-heirship rules override the provisions made in a will.

• **Protected spousal shares:** Some countries have systems where such shares (typically 25% of a deceased's estate) take precedence over provisions made in a will, entitling the spouse to this predetermined percentage of the deceased's estate.

• **Matrimonial property regimes:** These are marriage contracts which determine how spouses' property will be divided and transferred to another party on death and divorce. They can be entered into at the time of marriage and also after marriage. They are common globally, they can be mandatory and there are usually default provisions which can be varied. Again, they override wills.

• **Proprietary rights:** In England and Wales, a person who owns property as a joint tenant cannot give it away in their will. Similar structures exist overseas, such as assets held *en tontine* (which is roughly the same as when a joint owner of property under English/Welsh law dies and the property is transferred automatically to the surviving owner) in France.

• **Oral succession agreements:** Under certain circumstances in England and Wales it is possible to give property away orally (for example, military personnel who are in active service are permitted to do so) and there are formal structures in some jurisdictions overseas, such as in China and certain US states, where oral wills can be legally valid. Although the idea of oral wills may seem strange, we should remember that proprietary estoppel (see page 243) and *donatio mortis causa*, where a person makes qualifying gifts on their deathbed, are types of oral gift.

• **Other claims against the estate:** These include contractual or even 'moral' claims arising in jurisdictions where there are provisions similar to, for example, the Inheritance (Provision for Family and Dependants) Act 1975.

Private international law

Jurisdictions such as England and Wales practise a 'schismatic' system, meaning they distinguish between immovable property (buildings and land) and movable property (everything else). In practice this means that a deceased supporter's immovable assets transfer from one party to another under the laws of the jurisdiction in which the property is situated (*lex situs*), while their movable property passes under the laws of their domicile (*lex domicilii*).

Jurisdictions such as France (and in fact all states that are bound by EU Regulation 650/2012), however, apply a 'unitarian' approach, which makes no distinction between these types of property.

Connecting factors

'Connecting factors' link each of us as individuals to a system of private law. The connecting factors that apply to a particular jurisdiction can be found in that jurisdiction's private international law rules. England and Wales use the connecting factors of domicile and *situs* (where the property is situated) to connect movable and immovable property respectively, while unitarian systems use just one connecting factor for both movables and immovables.

In the case of France, this jurisdiction does not use the connecting factors of *situs* or domicile, but rather the connecting factor of 'habitual residence'. In practice, this means that if a supporter leaves assets in France, but is habitually resident in Switzerland, then all of their French assets (regardless of whether they are movable or immovable) will pass under the succession laws of Switzerland.

Other examples of single connecting factors include:

- habitual residence;

- nationality;

- religion;

- domicile;

- *situs*.

To determine which law applies to which assets, the private international law of the applicable jurisdictions must be determined and then the rules must be applied in conjunction with *renvoi*.

Renvoi

A full explanation of *renvoi* is beyond the scope of this chapter, but put simply it is an element of private international law which determines whether the laws of England and Wales or of a foreign jurisdiction apply to the devolution (i.e. who gets what) of a supporters' assets – remembering that devolution under the rules of other countries doesn't necessarily mean the supporter's gift to charity will fail.

Tax in a cross-border context

When dealing with cross-border matters, charities must remember:

- Succession and taxation matters are governed by different rules.

- Not all jurisdictions afford a tax-free (or reduced) status to charities.

• Some jurisdictions do not grant the same tax advantages to UK charities that they give to local charities.

• It is often possible to avoid at the planning stage many of the post-death complications.

Brexit

Succession

Because the UK opted out of the EU Succession Regulation 650/2012 (Brussels IV), the UK is already treated as a state outside the EU, so, when the UK leaves the EU, from a succession perspective there will be no change to the way the regulation is applied.

Taxation

From a taxation perspective, there is cause to be less optimistic. Currently, principles laid down in the case of *Hein Persche* v. *Finanzamt Lüdenscheid* (C-318/07) [2009] ECR I-00359 ensure that each EU state is obliged to apply the same tax concessions it applies to its own charities, provided the foreign charity would qualify as a charity in the taxing state. In response, a number of jurisdictions have changed the qualification requirements for a domestic charity to make them more difficult for a foreign (in this case, UK) charity to attain.

In any event, this protection only extends to member states and so by implication tax may become payable after Brexit on gifts to UK charities of assets in EU states.

Conclusion

The complexity of estate administration increases exponentially when foreign assets are involved and although it is possible (as has been done in this chapter) to summarise the overarching rules, it is not possible to provide a template that covers all eventualities in all jurisdictions. Each international and cross-border matter requires charities not only to consider each of the individual matters detailed above but also to understand how they affect and interrelate with each other. For example, changes to succession under the rules of one jurisdiction can have adverse taxation consequences in another jurisdiction.

Above all, it is important to be aware that it cannot be assumed that UK succession and taxation legal principles will be the same, or even similar, overseas, and particular caution should be exercised where the names of the principles are the same. *Domicile* in France, for example, is not the same as domicile in the UK and even other common-law countries such as Canada and the USA have subtly different domicile tests. Likewise, the rules relating to capital gains tax in the UK are not the same as those in Spain or the USA, even though the terminology may be similar.

Despite the potential pitfalls, many of the succession and taxation problems that arise in cross-border matters can be mitigated at the planning stage. Importantly, it is not enough to direct a supporter to a 'foreign' lawyer for advice on the devolution (who gets what) of foreign property, instead specialist advice must be sought. This is because overseas, as in the UK, even very experienced trusts and estates lawyers are usually ill-equipped to deal with cross-border matters, because when it comes to overseas jurisdictions (and particularly the interrelationship of overseas private international law with the private international law rules of England and Wales), non-specialist lawyers don't know what they don't know.

CHAPTER TWENTY

Legacy administration systems

Eifron Hopper

Introduction

This chapter gives a simple overview of what legacy administration is about, before going on to talk about why legacy administration systems are important and how to choose one. Legacy administration is often misunderstood by both charity staff and managers. On the one hand, it is sometimes seen as just 'banking and thanking', where all that is needed is to send out a few standard letters and make sure the cheques are paid in on time. Those who view legacy administration in this way often take the view that anyone can do it and end up tacking it on to other administrative functions.

On the other hand, some people see legacy administration as something of a dark art, practised by mysterious people who, if they are seen in daylight at all, are to be found quoting Latin phrases, such as *bona vacantia* and *donatio mortis causa*, as if everyone should know what they mean.

Of course, neither is true. Legacy administration is a specialist discipline that demands particular skills and experience. When undertaken properly, legacy administration can maximise the value of a gift left in a will through proactive engagement, provide invaluable information on which to base forecasts and plan future campaigns, and enhance the public reputation of your charity.

For more information about how to conduct legacy administration, visit the Institute of Legacy Management's website (www.legacymanagement. org.uk), which also has details of excellent training courses for both new and experienced legacy administrators.

What happens in legacy administration?

From a charity's perspective, the purpose of legacy administration is:

1. to ensure that the gifts that it has been left in supporters' wills are received in full and on time;

2. to preserve the good name of the charity in all the necessary dealings with solicitors, banks, executors, the deceased's family and the general public.

To achieve the first of these, the person handling the administration will need a good grasp of the law relating to wills, probate and succession, as well as considerable understanding of the vagaries of income tax, capital gains tax and inheritance tax as they relate to the administration of estates. To achieve the second, your charity and its representatives should seek to behave decently and honourably in all your dealings and have at least one eye on what the (largely anti-charity) press would make of what you are doing.

It is not possible to overstress the importance of keeping on good terms with executors. That means not just expressing gratitude for the legacy but also not badgering them unduly for information and being polite and professional in all your correspondence with them. Many years ago, as a trainee solicitor, I was told that each letter I wrote should be written in such a way that I would be happy for it to be read out in court by a High Court judge. While this is still true, nowadays you should add 'in such a way that you wouldn't be ashamed if it appeared in the press or on social media'.

Uncontested cases

The legacy administration process usually begins with a notification that someone has died and left your charity a gift in their will. This may come from the solicitor or other person responsible for administering the estate, or it may come from legacy specialists Smee & Ford (www.smeeand-ford.com). For a fee, Smee & Ford will search the Probate Registry records and give you advance notification that your charity has been mentioned in the will of someone who has recently died, along with other valuable information such as the address of the donor, the name of the executors and details of the other charities mentioned in the will.

Once your charity has received this notification, you will want to open a file and record as much relevant information as you can, including:

- name (including former names) and address(es) of the deceased;

- age at death;

- gender;

- dates of last will, grant of probate and notification;

- name(s) and address(es) of executor(s);

- name of next of kin;

- size of the estate;

- size and type of gift;

- other charities mentioned in the will.

If you have heard nothing more after some time has elapsed (normally several months), you should usually contact the executors or their solicitors and, in the case of a residuary gift (a share of the estate), ask for a copy of the will and details of the assets making up the estate. In the case of a pecuniary gift (a fixed amount of money), you should ask to see a copy of the relevant clause in the will. In both cases, it is wise to express your charity's gratitude for the gift and to ask for this to be passed on to any remaining family.

The relevant provisions of the will (such as any gifts that have to be honoured before your charity gets its share, or the existence of 'life interests' – i.e. provisions in the will that mean your charity will not receive its share until another beneficiary has died) need to be noted, as will the details of the assets so that the estate accounts can be properly checked at the end of the administration.

Many cases then proceed relatively smoothly (with perhaps just a few questions over such matters as the sale price to be asked for a house or the appropriation of shares to beneficiaries) until the administration nears its end and the executors or solicitors send out a set of estate accounts for checking and approval. At this stage, you should check, among other matters, that:

• the assets in the estate have been sold for the best price reasonably obtainable and none of the assets has been left unaccounted for;

• all the debts of the deceased and the estate have been met;

• the gifts left in the will have been, or are about to be, paid to the correct beneficiaries and no gifts have been made that are not authorised by the will;

• income tax, capital gains tax and inheritance tax have all been paid at the proper rates and due regard has been taken of the circumstances in which charities are exempt from these taxes;

• solicitors and other professionals involved in the administration of the estate have not overcharged for their services.

If all of these matters are in order, and the estate accounts are approved, the charity can usually expect to receive a transfer of funds (or a cheque) anywhere between 9 and 18 months after the death of the donor.

Contested cases

These simpler cases notwithstanding, a great deal of a legacy administrator's time will be taken up by files in which there are complications. There may be disgruntled family members who dispute the will or make some other claim against the estate, or the executors may have made an unauthorised payment to a neighbour who was not named in the will. It may be that inheritance tax has not been appropriated correctly, or there may even be suspicion of fraud.

There are several firms (most of them to be found on the Institute of Legacy Management's website) that have developed particular expertise in acting for charities in these matters, and it is well worth thinking about instructing one of them if the need arises. In practice, there are often several charities involved in any one case, so the costs and the expertise can be shared.

In all these situations, your charity will be all the better served for having an effective legacy administration system and competent legacy administrators to operate it.

Why have a legacy administration system?

There are three main reasons (explored further in the sections that follow) for investing in some sort of legacy administration system:

1. to facilitate the proper management of the relationship between your charity and the solicitor or executor, so that your charity receives the gift that it is entitled to and retains its reputation;

2. to provide the data that your charity needs to be able to forecast its legacy income;

3. to provide information and insights that will inform and assist legacy marketing campaigns.

Proper management

Proper legacy administration cannot be assumed to happen automatically, so keeping complete and proper records, ensuring things happen on time and being able (gently but firmly) to protect your charity's interests are vital aspects of your job as a legacy administrator.

The question of reputation is something that has grown in importance for legacy administrators – especially as some sections of the media (and, sadly, some members of the legal profession) seem intent on portraying charities in the worst possible light. On the wall in my office I have a reminder to be 'wise as serpents and gentle as doves', which I take to mean that we should behave decently, politely and with absolute integrity, but be no one's pushover. In practical terms, this means that legacy administrators who feel they have to take a firm stand must have the full facts at their disposal and be circumspect in their tone of voice.

As a legacy administrator, you may know that you have a duty to gather in everything to which your charity is entitled; you may even feel that a particular solicitor or executor is 'trying it on'. However, the fact remains that, in matters of reputation, perception is everything. If you are involved in a matter that begins to get contentious, it is wise to consider the public relations implications of your actions and to speak to colleagues in the public relations department. Most of the solicitors who act for charities on a regular basis are able to provide support in this area.

Providing data

Forecasting legacy income is notoriously difficult; however, because legacies often form a large proportion of a charity's income, it is something that most charities should try to do. The question of forecasting is dealt with in more detail in chapter 8. However, any forecasting system will depend upon, and only be as good as, the records kept by the legacy administration team concerning:

• the number and type of notifications;

• the average value of gifts received;

• what gifts are in the pipeline (i.e. notification has been received but payment has not);

• the time taken to complete the administration of the estate;

• the asset mix in the estate (what proportions are in cash, shares, or land and buildings);

• historical trends in all of the above.

Providing information and insights

During the course of an administration, your charity will gather a wide range of information about the donor and their situation which can be analysed to provide vital intelligence for legacy marketing campaigns. Some examples follow:

• Even simple facts such as age and address will help marketers (sometimes with the use of other analytical tools) to build up a profile of your charity's typical legacy donor and show them where to look for more of the same.

• Knowing which other charities are mentioned in the will can help to inform decisions about joint or reciprocal marketing campaigns. For example, when I was at the Children's Society in the 1990s, my colleagues and I realised that (unsurprisingly) we often shared legacies with the local parish church. This led to a number of joint promotion initiatives and helped us to target our advertising to various church-based audiences. The same principle would apply to, say, an animal charity that notices that it often shares legacies with a particular conservation charity, with the result that they might consider working together.

• You may uncover, sometimes quite by accident, the reason why a legator chose to support your charity, which can be very useful information that shapes the content of, and decides the target groups for, legacy campaigns.

• Legacy marketers can benefit hugely from knowing the trends in the type and size of gift that people are leaving so that they know how to frame their messages to other potential legators.

• Stories about interesting or unusual legacies and the people who leave them are very useful for giving colour to legacy campaigns and materials. They are not something that would necessarily be the subject of analysis, since they vary so much, but it is legacy administrators who come across those stories, so any legacy administration system should contain a way of recording and passing on these vital bits of information.

What sort of legacy administration system should you have?

The legacy administration system you use should be appropriate for the size of your charity and the number of legacies that you receive. Larger charities may have whole teams of specialist staff, supported by software programmes, handling hundreds or even thousands of legacy cases a year. Other smaller charities may only receive a few legacies, which are administered by someone for whom legacy administration is only part of their job.

Wherever your charity sits on this spectrum, it is important, if legacy income is to be maximised and your charity's reputation protected, that your legacy administration team knows what it is doing (or knows where to find help if it does not) and has a proper system in place to ensure that records are kept and nothing is missed.

Many charities (even the larger ones) still use systems that are, in part at least, paper-based. There is nothing intrinsically wrong with that, but software-based systems enable information to be stored, retrieved, analysed and reported upon much more quickly and efficiently.

What to look for in a legacy administration software system
Bolt-on or stand-alone?

Ideally, any legacy administration software system you use should be one that is designed specifically for that purpose. Partial solutions may be found by adapting databases and spreadsheets, but they will remain only partial solutions.

Some more general database systems may have legacy administration functionality as part of what they offer, but it is wise to ensure that this is fully integrated and not something that has been tacked on as an after-thought. If it has, your needs as a legacy administrator may not have been given due consideration, with the result that the system is hard to use and your legacy administration is not as effective as it should be.

One of the main reasons often given for having a legacy administra-tion system that is a module on a general fundraising database is that it enables legacy information and fundraising information to be shared for the purpose of developing donors and maximising their value to the char-ity. This is, indeed, a very important consideration, but is it more important than having an effective, usable legacy administration system?

In fact, the two are not mutually exclusive, so whether you go for a system that is an add-on or one that stands alone, you should try to ensure that it is both fit for purpose and compatible with your fundraising database.

Ease of use

As with all software systems, a legacy administration system should be clear and easy to use. It should make it easy for you to find the legator record you are looking for and you should be able to pull up reports using a variety of criteria – for example, files where there are residuary legacies only or legators who lived in particular parts of the country. When you open a legator record:

• the information about the legator and their gift should be displayed in a logical manner and should be easy and quick to reach;

• you should be able to store comprehensive biographical data about the legator;

• you should also be able to store details such as the date of the last will and any codicils, as well as important dates during the administration, including the notification date, the date of the executor's first letter and the dates when you received a copy of the will, the list of assets and liabilities, and the tax deduction certificates.

Detailed records

Recording details about legacies is important. You should be able to main-tain and update the value of the legacy as you receive information from the executor (and/or Smee & Ford). It is important (not least for forecasting purposes) that you have up-to-date values for all of your current legacy files.

A legacy administration system should be able to quickly provide you with reports that calculate your overall legacy pipeline (legacies that you have been notified of but not yet paid). Similarly, other reports should provide automatic information for accrual and SORP (Statement of Recommended Practice) reporting, calculated in a similar manner.

For legacies with a residuary element, you need to be able to record your charity's share. For those with a life interest element, you need to be able to record information about the life tenants and trustees.

Multiple contacts

A considerable part of a legacy administrator's work is concerned with liaising with other people and agencies. Your legacy system should enable you to record the details of all contacts associated with each legacy, including contacts with people such as executors and contacts at other charities.

Standard letters

At a minimum, your system should allow you to use a set of standard letters (which you can maintain and update) from which you can quickly create correspondence. The system used to create your letters should automatically enter all data associated with the legator and other contact details, such as the name and address of the correspondent and the name and related details of the legator.

Reviews

In order to record and plan the progress of each legacy, your system will require a sophisticated system of reviews. This should enable you to see quickly what legacies are coming up for review, and for what reasons, and also allow you to look back at what reviews have been completed.

Conclusion

It will take time and money – neither of which are easy to come by – to introduce or update your legacy administration system, but it will be worth it. A good system saves time and money by:

• allowing you to load Smee & Ford data straight onto your system;

• enabling you to produce letters quickly and easily;

• providing a comprehensive reviewing system that ensures that matters are dealt with and deadlines are met;

• providing quick and accurate reporting.

The best systems, such as FirstClass, also enable you to calculate, record and report upon the value you have added to the estate through proactive legacy administration. This fact alone should help you to demonstrate that this much-misunderstood discipline can play a vital part in maximising your charity's income.

CHAPTER TWENTY-ONE

Making a will and choosing an executor

Sebastian Wilberforce

Introduction

This final chapter underscores the importance of having a professionally written will and describes the options available when choosing an executor, i.e. someone to give effect to the contents of a will. As a legacy fundraiser, having knowledge of this process, and the potential pitfalls of doing it badly, is crucial for helping inform the people you have legacy conversations with – some of whom may be entirely unfamiliar with the process. As highlighted in chapter 14, this lack of familiarity and understanding is one of the major barriers that hinder people from getting their will made, and therefore from including a gift to your charity.

This chapter also covers the benefits and potential drawbacks of your charity being appointed as an executor.

Making a will

An important point is that wills should be professionally written. Home-made wills are a fruitful source of family disputes and even, in some cases, litigation. Having a will professionally drawn up does not guarantee a problem-free administration, but it does minimise the risk of something going wrong.

It is a false economy to save a solicitor's fee for writing a will by writing it oneself. It is very easy to use ambiguous or unclear language or to miss out important provisions; the cost of rectifying mistakes could be many times the cost of using a solicitor in the first place. It is important to remember that a will affects all of a person's estate whatever the value, be it thousands or millions. In proportion, therefore, the solicitor's fee is worth paying to ensure that the right people benefit in the right way.

Choosing executors

Care is needed when choosing executors: they may have control of substantial funds and – although they ultimately have to account for their actions in distributing the estate – they will, for a time, have almost absolute discretion in what happens to those funds. The office of executor is also a burden, and the responsibilities can be onerous.

The welfare of the beneficiaries chosen by the will maker might depend entirely upon the good sense or otherwise of an executor's actions, so the person making the will should be diligent in their choice of executor. That choice is between one or more of the following:

• a private individual, usually a family member or friend;

• a professional person, such as a solicitor or accountant;

• a trust corporation, such as a clearing bank, some charities or the Public Trustee.

Individuals as executors

Given the amount of work that may be involved, if the will maker wants to appoint a private individual, they should discuss this potential appointment with the person concerned before naming them as executor. The individual they choose needs to be businesslike, trustworthy and someone whose appointment will not cause conflict with other family members or the beneficiaries.

It is generally sensible to appoint two individuals as executors, in case one is unable or unwilling to act (for example, through ill health). In addition, at least one individual should be younger than the person making the will, in case the other appointee dies first (but remember that no one can act as an executor until the age of 18 years).

Private individuals who have been named as executors in a will can appoint a professional (such as a solicitor) to act on their behalf. Or, if an individual wants to do the work personally, there are useful publications available, some of which are listed in the appendix. The Principal or District Probate Registries will generally help with the completion of the necessary forms, and HM Revenue & Customs will give advice. Most major charities' legacy administrators will also give advice. A private individual should be under no illusion, however, about the amount of work involved and the possible complexity of even what may seem to be a straightforward estate.

The transfer of certain assets, such as land, may require two trustees if a trust is set up in a will, although a sole executor will be sufficient to ensure that the asset is validly transferred where no trust exists.

Professional executors

If the will maker wants to appoint a professional executor, they should discuss doing so with the person or firm they have in mind. They should consider the cost, the firm's or the person's experience (different from expertise) and the person's (or people within the firm's) level of empathy with the beneficiaries of the will. Location is also important: the will maker must take account of where a surviving spouse lives, for example, and try to ensure that the administration can be handled locally (note that banks tend to have central administrations).

If the will maker doesn't already have a solicitor, it is worth their contacting several. A particular solicitor can be asked to be an executor if, for example, the will maker likes their sympathetic but businesslike approach or thinks that they will handle beneficiaries well. It is important to consider the solicitor's age, however, and whether or not they are likely to still be in practice when the will needs to be administered. If the person making the will does not prefer any particular solicitor, they can appoint the partners of a law firm (whoever they are at the date of death), which will ensure that the administration work stays with that firm without the will maker having to name individual solicitors.

Appointing a professional executor to act in conjunction with a relative or friend has several advantages. While the professional deals with legal technicalities, the lay executor can perform the more sensitive tasks (arranging the funeral, clearing the house and so on), for which a solicitor or bank would charge. By appointing a private executor as well as a professional, it is also easier to keep control of both the costs and the speed at which the estate is administered.

Charities as executors

A charity can act as an executor only if it has trust corporation status (see 'The legal options when charities act as executors', page 232). Although there is nothing to prevent a particular charity employee from being named as an executor, this should not be encouraged. The employee may not have sufficient technical expertise or, indeed, may no longer be employed by the charity when the appointment takes effect.

As an executor, your charity can either administer estates in-house or, if necessary, appoint a local solicitor to act on its behalf (it generally makes sense to use a local solicitor given the need to deal with house clearance, local estate agents and so on). Either way, your charity would have a greater measure of control over costs than would normally be the case.

There is something to be said for charities providing an executorship service. A charity's ability to do so can be a key incentive in supporters leaving it a legacy. It also puts the charity in a position of power as far as speed and efficiency of administration are concerned, whether in-house or using an external agency.

Anyone considering appointing a charity should be encouraged to discuss doing so with the charity beforehand. Your charity should only accept such an appointment when the person making the will is considering leaving it a significant legacy. If the costs of administering the estate exceed the benefit received, the charity may lay itself open to censure for misuse of charitable funds. On the testator's death, like any other executor, your charity can always decline its appointment, provided that it has not 'intermeddled' in (i.e. begun to deal with) the estate.

A charge can be made against the estate to cover the cost of the administration. However, your charity should seek legal advice on this point before offering a full executorship service. The aim should be purely to cover costs. It is inadvisable for a charity to run such an operation on a profit-making basis, since that would be a non-charitable activity.

Regarding charitable companies, if a non-trust corporation is appointed as an executor, the appointment has no effect and the company may not obtain a grant of probate. However, the company can obtain a grant of letters of administration with will annexed (see 'Legacy administration: Executors and administrators', page 233) by nominating a person or appointing an attorney to obtain the grant. It is entitled to this grant only if any other executors named have died before the deceased or have relinquished their right to probate, as their right to a grant ranks higher in priority under rule 20 of the Non-Contentious Probate Rules 1987.

The Public Trustee

The Public Trustee was created by Act of Parliament in 1906 to provide an executor and trustee service on a non-profit-making basis to the general public. Appointment of the Public Trustee as executor is particularly worth considering when there is no other person available to act or where the natural choice, such as a surviving spouse, is too infirm for the role. Further information on the role, responsibilities and charges of the Public Trustee can be obtained from the government guidance 'Appoint the Public Trustee as executor of your estate', available at www.gov.uk/public-trustee-executor-will.

Conclusion

This book has brought together leading thinkers in the legacy fundraising sector, who have authored chapters in their speciality areas. As the book's editors, it has been our pleasure to work with such an insightful group.

Although the chapters are authored by a number of different experts, we have noted a number of key themes running through them. We bring those themes together here in our final reflections.

Understanding legacy supporters

The theme of insight runs through many of the chapters. A number of contributors stress the importance of a deep understanding of donors: their feelings, attitudes and behaviours towards will-making and legacy giving in general, and your cause in particular. They stress how legacy giving is a reflection of people's lives: their cares, values and passions; the people they have loved; and those who have cared for them. There is a particular focus, across the chapters, on using these understandings to fundraise in a supporter-centric, rather than organisation-centric, way.

Fundraising ethically

Linked to the theme of insight, several authors suggest that the more you know about supporters, the more you can create communications that are appropriate for them. The chapters also stress the importance of weaving an explicit consideration of ethics into your practice, making sure that your fundraising is compliant with legalities but also that it offers a fulfilling experience for supporters.

Crafting your fundraising practice

Drawing on your understanding of donors and your reflections on ethical practice, you can craft clear, effective messages about legacy giving that express the needs of your organisation but that are also tailored to meet the needs of your supporters. You can also ensure that your legacy fundraising activities – from solicitation through to the all-important stewardship of supporters – are designed to suit your donors.

Focusing on multiple stakeholders

A number of authors discuss the importance of focusing not just on existing or potential legacy donors but also on the various types of stakeholder in the legacy giving process, from senior management in a charity to fundraising colleagues to solicitors and other third parties. In order to make the most of legacy fundraising's potential, as our contributors stress, it would be wise to create this culture of legacy giving across your organisation.

Attention to process

As well as creating attractive fundraising propositions and programmes, it is vital to ensure that the processes you use to underpin your legacy fundraising are robust. It's not just *what* you do but the *way* you do it that matters. A number of our authors outline ways to ensure that legacy fundraising is underpinned by robust processes, including forecasting, using data effectively and ensuring that an effective administration system is in place.

Final thoughts

While the chapters in this book offer a range of helpful insights on specific topics, it is also important to consider how these topics interact as parts of a whole. Ensuring that you consider these overarching themes as you develop your legacy fundraising practice is likely to help ensure that you create a robust legacy programme – a programme that will help to raise funds to deliver your charity's vision while enabling your supporters to benefit a cause they care deeply about long into the future.

Claire Routley and Sebastian Wilberforce

Sources of further help

Finding and using a solicitor

Most firms do wills and probate work. The best means of finding a firm is through word of mouth. Alternatively, there are various directories (the Law Society's directory, for instance, at http://solicitors.lawsociety.org.uk, or the Society of Trust and Estate Practitioners at www.step.org). Don't forget the database of solicitors that your legacy administrator may have compiled.

The Solicitors Regulation Authority (www.sra.org.uk) provides information on how to make a complaint against a solicitor and how to challenge their fees. Solicitors who practise charity law can be found through the Charity Law Association (https://charitylawassociation.org. uk). You may also find the Institute of Legacy Management's list of corporate partners helpful: http://legacymanagement.org.uk/partners.

Legacy administration
The Institute of Legacy Management

The Institute of Legacy Management is the membership body for legacy professionals – those responsible for the successful and sensitive administration of donors' final gifts to charitable organisations. The institute was established in 1999 to provide individual legacy professionals with a network of support and dedicated training services. Today it represents and supports almost 600 individuals working in over 350 charities, not-for-profit organisations and associated professions. Its vision is to 'ensure every generous donor's final wishes achieve their greatest potential'.

To find out more about the Institute of Legacy Management – including its training and events programme, its Certificate in Charity Legacy Administration qualification and its Good Practice Guidance for legacy administration – visit www.legacymanagement.org.uk.

Legacy fundraising and marketing
The Institute of Fundraising

Legacy fundraisers are on the whole very happy to share their experience and knowledge. The Institute of Fundraising hosts a Legacy Marketing and In Memoriam fundraising special interest group, which is open to anyone with an interest in legacies or in-memory fundraising. The group runs an online discussion forum, shares appropriate resources and holds regular events in London and the north of England. For more information, visit www.institute-of-fundraising.org.uk/groups.

Remember a Charity

Remember a Charity is a consortium of charities working together to promote gifts in wills. In addition, members of Remember a Charity benefit from research, networking and training.

There are several will-making schemes involving charities. Will Aid is an annual scheme held each November on behalf of member charities. Solicitors donate their time for free during the month, and participants can make wills in exchange for a donation to the participating charities. Free Will Month is organised by Capacity Marketing on behalf of a number of charities which pay for a number of wills to be written in specific geographical areas.

A valuable resource for news, publication information and job vacancies is www.fundraising.co.uk.

SOFII

SOFII (the Showcase of Fundraising Inspiration and Inspiration: http://sofii.org) is a free, online, easily accessible archive of effective fundraising from around the world which gives fundraisers the knowledge and inspiration they need to raise more funds for their important causes. SOFII has a whole section of its website dedicated to advice and actual case studies about effective legacy fundraising: http://sofii.org/the-main-areas-of-fundraising/legacies-and-bequests.

Legacy Foresight

Legacy Foresight is Europe's foremost analyst of the legacy and in-memory giving sectors. It appraises the state of the markets, produces income forecasts and researches donor motivations. Since its first legacy project in 1994, it has worked with over 100 UK and continental charities on performance management and strategic development. See www.legacyforesight.co.uk.

Digital communications

See the following web pages for useful advice on digital communications: 'Writing for the web' (www.usability.gov/how-to-and-tools/methods/writing-for-the-web.html), 'How to fundraise using social media' (https://knowhownonprofit.org/how-to/how-to-fundraise-using-social-media) and

'7 tips that take your content from Flat to Fabulous' (www.crazyegg.com/blog/outstanding-website-content).

Data analysis

The Institute of Fundraising hosts the Insight in Fundraising special interest group, which aims to take a practical approach to furthering individuals' development in the world of data analysis and to increase understanding of the importance of analysis and its impact. See www.institute-of-fundraising.org.uk/groups/sig-insight-in-fundraising and www.insightsig.org for more information.

For training in data insight and analytics, including tips for analysts in the sector, see http://adroitthinking.com/training-mentoring/tips-n-tricks.

Training sources

For all information on the legacy fundraising training that the Directory of Social Change (DSC) provides, visit www.dsc.org.uk/category/fundraising/legacies. DSC's annual Fundraising Fair regularly has sessions on legacy fundraising (see www.fundraisingfair.org.uk).

The Institute of Legacy Management provides training in legacy administration. See http://legacymanagement.org.uk/education/courses.

The Institute of Fundraising provides legacy fundraising training (see www.institute-of-fundraising.org.uk/events-and-training/training/short-courses/legacy) and runs legacy sessions at the annual National Convention (www.fundraisingconvention.uk).

Smee & Ford provides a number of training webinars on its website: https://smeeandford.com/webinar/index.

Legacy Voice, a legacy consultancy, provides legacy administration support to UK charities including an outsourced service, temporary cover for legacy officers and training: http://legacyvoice.co.uk.

Publications

From time to time, the journal *Philanthropy Matters* has useful articles on legacy fundraising; see https://philanthropy.iupui.edu/news-events/philanthropy-matters. The journal is published by the School of Philanthropy at Indiana University. Likewise, the *Journal of Nonprofit & Public Sector Marketing* (published by Taylor & Francis) and the *International Journal of Nonprofit and Voluntary Sector Marketing* (published by John Wiley & Sons) periodically have articles of value. It is worth signing up for the email newsletters from Howard Lake's www.fundraising.co.uk since they regularly contain legacy news of value, as do the magazines *Fundraising* (published by Civil Society: www.civilsociety.co.uk/

fundraising.html) and *Third Sector* (www.thirdsector.co.uk). See also Legacy Foresight's legacy bulletins, available at www.legacyforesight.co. uk/documents.

You can find out more about ongoing research into legacy giving through the University of Plymouth Hartsook Centre for Sustainable Philanthropy (www.plymouth.ac.uk/schools/plymouth-business-school/centre-for-sustainable-philanthropy) and Texas Tech University (http://www. encouragegenerosity.com).

How to Love Your Donors (to Death) by Stephen Pidgeon shows you how to look after your minor donors properly. The author mines his extensive knowledge from 30 years of fundraising campaigns to offer examples of bad practice that will make you cringe but also case studies of good fundraising that will have you leaping from your chair to get started. Look out for his 'practical tips' and trademark 'Stephen's rants'. See www. dsc.org.uk/lov.

Charity Commission guidance

The Charity Commission provides guidance on how to legally and ethically raise money through legacies in its guidance *Raising Funds through Wills and Charitable Legacies* (www.gov.uk/guidance/wills-and-charitable-legacies).

Fundraising Regulator

The Code of Fundraising Practice now sits with the Fundraising Regulator (www.fundraisingregulator.org.uk). The specific section of the code that relates to legacy fundraising is available at www.fundraisingregulator.org. uk/18–0-legacies.

The Fundraising Series

For a full list of titles in the DSC's Fundraising Series, go to www.dsc.org. uk/publication/fundraising-series.

Other sources

On will making, administering an estate and what to do when someone dies, *Which?* offers some helpful guidance on its website and in its publications *Wills and Probate* and *What to Do When Someone Dies*. See www. which.co.uk.

There are also some useful government web pages, including 'What to do after someone dies' (www.gov.uk/after-a-death) and 'Appoint the Public Trustee as executor of your estate' (www.gov.uk/public-trustee-executor-will).

Useful addresses
Charity Commission

Charity Commission Direct
PO Box 211
Bootle
L20 7YX

Tel: 03000 66 9197 (technical support helpline; the Charity Commission only accepts calls to this number if the query cannot be resolved using online forms or guidance, so check the website before calling)

www.charitycommission.gov.uk

Directory of Social Change

352 Holloway Road
London
N7 6PA

Tel: 0207 697 4200

www.dsc.org.uk

HM Revenue & Customs (HMRC) Charities

Charities, Savings and International 2
HM Revenue and Customs
BX9 1BU

Tel: 0300 123 1073

www.gov.uk/charities-and-tax

Institute of Fundraising

Charter House
13–15 Carteret Street
London
SW1H 9DJ

Tel: 020 7840 1000

www.institute-of-fundraising.org.uk

Institute of Fundraising Scotland

Hayweight House
4th Floor, 23 Lauriston Street
Edinburgh
EH3 9DQ

Tel: 0131 474 6152

www.institute-of-fundraising.org.uk/groups/national-scotland

Institute of Fundraising Wales/Cymru

1st Floor
21 Cathedral Road
Cardiff
CF11 9HA

Tel: 0292 034 0062

www.institute-of-fundraising.org.uk/groups/national-cymruwales

Office of the Public Guardian

PO Box 16185
Birmingham
B2 2WH

Tel: 0300 456 0300

www.gov.uk/government/organisations/office-of-the-public-guardian

Smee & Ford Ltd

6–14 Underwood St
London
N1 7JQ

Tel: 020 7549 8646

www.smeeandford.com

Suzy Lamplugh Trust

National Centre for Personal Safety
218 Strand
London
WC2R 1AT

Tel: 020 7091 0014

www.suzylamplugh.org

Index